Craving for
Ecstasy
How Our Passions Become Addictions
and What We Can Do About Them

excitement to achieve feeling of well-being P. XIV

Relaxation   excitement   Fantasy
adventuring P.V   Shock em   amuse em
Feed em

Styles of coping P.18   arousal   Fantasy
Satiation

Depressants   Stimulants   Hallucinogens
Heroin   Amphetamine   LSD mushroom
Binge on food   Cocaine   Right Hemisphere peyote
                         Crazy gambling   thinks
                         risk taking   Dreamlike thoughts
                                                 rapidly shifting imagery
                                                 artistic

Enkephalins + endorphins P.30

Carnes "Sexual addiction"
Liebowitz "The Chemistry of Love" P.47
Freud "Three Essays on the Theory of Sexuality"

About the Authors

HARVEY MILKMAN is professor of psychology at Metropolitan State College of Denver. He is founder and director of the Center for Interdisciplinary Studies and project director and principal investigator for Project Self Discovery. In 1985–86 he was recipient of a Fulbright-Hays Lectureship award at the National University of Malaysia. He has studied addictive behaviors in Africa, India, and southeast Asia. He has been a consultant and featured speaker in Iceland, Turkey, Yugoslavia, Germany, Peru, Australia, The Netherlands, and Brazil. He is coauthor with Stanley Sunderwirth of *Pathways to Pleasure: The Consciousness and Chemistry of Optimal Living* (Lexington Books, 1993) and coauthor with Kenneth Wanberg of *Strategies for Self-Improvement and Change: A Cognitive-Behavioral Approach for Treatment of the Substance Abusing Offender* (Sage, 1998).

STANLEY SUNDERWIRTH is professor of chemistry at Indiana University Purdue University-Columbus. He has received five Fulbright Awards, four to Uruguay and one to India. In addition, he has held two NSF/AID consultantships to India and was invited in 1979 by the Instituto National de Docencia of Uruguay to present a three-week seminar. He has also given scientific presentations in Japan, Costa Rica, Iceland, and Peru. He recently represented the U. S. by giving several presentations at the Iberoamerican Congress on Medicine and Science Applied to Sports in Bogota, Colombia. He is coauthor with Harvey Milkman of *Pathways to Pleasure.*

Craving for
Ecstasy

*How Our Passions Become Addictions
and What We Can Do About Them*

by

HARVEY B. MILKMAN
STANLEY G. SUNDERWIRTH

Jossey-Bass Publishers • San Francisco

Published by Jossey-Bass
A Wiley Imprint
989 Market Street, San Francisco, CA 94103-1741   www.josseybass.com

Jossey-Bass books and products are available through most bookstores. To
contact Jossey-Bass directly call our Customer Care Department within the U.S.
at (800) 956-7739, outside the U.S. at (317) 572-3986 or fax (317) 572-4002.

Jossey-Bass also publishes its books in a variety of electronic formats. Some
content that appears in print may not be available in electronic books.

Library of Congress Cataloging-in-Publication Data

Milkman, Harvey B.
  Craving for ecstacy : how our passions become addictions and what
we can do about them / Harvey B. Milkman, Stanley G. Sunderwirth.
    p.   cm.
  Originally published: Lexington, Mass. : Lexington Books, 1987.
  Includes bibliographical references (p.   ) and index.
  ISBN 0-7879-4132-8 (pbk.)
  1. Compulsive behavior.   2. Substance abuse.   I. Sunderwirth,
Stanley G.   II. Title.
RC533.M55   1998
616.86—dc21   98-21171

Printed in the United States of America

PB Printing   15

To Meredith
—H.B.M.

To my family
—S.G.S.

All this the world well knows; yet none knows well
To shun the heaven that leads men to this hell.

— William Shakespeare

Contents

Preface and
Acknowledgments

Craving for Ecstasy was first published in 1987. In the decade that followed, we remain awed by the enormity of compulsive pleasure seeking. This new edition of the book includes an updated discussion of the chemistry of craving. There is now a unified model for explaining the biochemical link between such diverse pleasures as sex, eating, drug use, and gambling. Although there are a few more addictive manifestations, such as internet pornography, rave parties, and Tamagotchi computer pets, the underlying biological, psychological, and social principles for addictive processes remain the same. This book continues to provide a comprehensive explanation for the compelling urge to feel wonderful.

We spend much of our lives in relentless pursuit of fleeting moments of exalted delight. But the consequences of compulsive pleasure seeking—whether through activities or use of substances—are often devastating. Preventive education is our best ally in the struggle to reduce massive suffering at the hands of immediate gratification.

Learning the basic principles of compulsion and loss of control may itself be a pleasurable experience. Through vivid case examples, artistic renderings, and straightforward discussion, we have endeavored to merge the impersonal worlds of biological and social science with the pulsating emotions of real human beings. Whenever possible, we have discussed effective treatment approaches as they were applied in actual clinical practice.

The drawings for this book were done by Ibrahim Mohammed Said in Kuala Lumpur, Malaysia. Ibrahim worked in collaboration with Harvey Milkman who was participating as a visiting Fulbright-Hays lecturer (1985–1986) at the National University of Malaysia.

Ibrahim spoke very little English and had never been to the Western world, yet the biological, psychological, and social concepts that he so skillfully illustrated were well within his conceptual scope. We are indebted to Ibrahim, not only for enlivening our prose with stimulating visual images, but for adding credence to our suspicion that craving for ecstasy is indeed a universal phenomenon.

Finally, we are grateful to the untold number of people who have been vital characters in our reflections about behavior in excess. As we look back on both of our lives and the impulses that we couldn't or wouldn't control, we breathe a sigh of thanks to the friends, relatives, and teachers who kept us from the road to oblivion—which was always right around the bend.

Harvey Milkman
Stanley Sunderwirth
1998

Introduction

A RE criminals, cocaine users, sky divers, police, and lovers motivated by a similar adrenaline rush? Are comparable needs being met through alcoholism, overeating, and membership in a spiritually oriented group? The term *addiction* was once reserved for dependence on drugs. Today it is applied to a range of compulsive behaviors as disparate as spending too much time on the internet and eating too much chocolate. In fact, there are essential biological, psychological, and social common denominators between drug use and other habitual behaviors. Whether your pleasure is meditation or mescaline, cocaine or cults, you are addicted if you cannot control when you start or stop an activity.

In this book we examine the age-old search for pleasure from a new perspective. We transcend the inconclusive debate that surrounds substance abuse and focus instead on more basic issues of human compulsion and loss of control. The drive to feel good is inadequately explained as a function of a weakness of character, chemical imbalance, or spiritual defect. At a time when overindulgence is epidemic, the public naturally relies on explanations and remedies that have succeeded in the past. Runaholism, workaholism, and sexaholism have emerged as lay diagnostic terms, closely paralleled by treatment programs fashioned after traditional approaches to alcoholism. However, the knee-jerk antidotes of "stop the disturbing behavior, go to meetings, get a sponsor, ask for help" can be of little value in reducing the alarmingly high incidence of problem dependencies.

Drug abuse statistics are astounding. In 1994 the number of annual deaths attributed to alcohol and tobacco were 100,000 and 419,000 respectively. Barry McCaffrey, the nation's drug czar, says the drug problem costs America $18 million and 55 deaths every day. U. S. citizens spend between $25 billion and $30 billion a year on illegal substances. Roughly 1.5 million Americans smoke marijuana compulsively, while 20 million are occasional users. According to the 1995 National Household Survey, the number of teens who smoked pot nearly doubled between 1992 and 1994, with one in every eight eighth-graders having tried the drug. Nearly 2 million Americans are thought to be addicted to cocaine, with about one-third of young Americans having tried the drug by the age of twenty-eight. One hundred million Americans use alcohol, and 10 to 13 million are considered alcoholic. Forty-six million Americans—26 percent of the adult population—smoke cigarettes, with an addiction rate of about 90 percent. A sizable proportion suffers dual addiction to tobacco and alcohol. The business community has become so alarmed at the indiscriminate use of mind-altering substances, particularly in the executive sector, that more than one-quarter of all Fortune 500 companies screen their employees for illicit drug use.

On the international level, a drug war is now being waged between the developed and developing nations. Through the permeable membrane of international police, legislative censure, and social condemnation, high-tech pharmaceuticals are being smuggled into Third World nations. The U. S. government spends an estimated $14.6 billion each year to fight the drug war and control illicit drug traffic coming into the country. However, only 5 to 10 percent of all illegal drugs entering the United States are intercepted. Law enforcement cannot manage the enormous international challenge of drug trafficking, experimentation, and addiction. Preventive education, guided by humanitarian concern, is our most valuable resource as we endeavor to turn the tide of wanton self-destruction.

Scientifically, we have reached a turning point in our perennial battle with passion and pleasure. Sound principles from psychology and sociology can now be integrated with rapidly emerging discoveries in brain science. Science is a fine tool, but it is a poor master. Addiction researchers and theorists characteristically rely on technical jargon and obscure discourse to communicate their findings to an elite group of professionals. The average person remains bewildered and awed by the multitude of lives that become subjugated to a moment of ecstasy and years of suffering.

These pages were written for the nonprofessional who seeks a mature understanding of what is now known about compulsive pleasure seeking. What are the origins and symptoms of addiction? How are drug abuse and alcoholism related to other forms of problem dependency, social deviance, and mental illness? What methods of treatment and prevention might have a reasonable probability of success?

Adults can no longer defer society's responsibilities for prevention to school personnel or law-enforcement officials. Part of the solution requires a concerted effort to provide early education at home and in the classroom about the dangers associated with drugs. We must be careful, however, not to arouse a child's curiosity and sense of challenge in regard to drugs. A young person may choose to experiment with the very substance that he or she discovers through a well-intended school presentation on the dangers of drug abuse. Furthermore, children may unearth other means of thrill seeking—such as alcohol, automobile racing, and pornography—not covered by narrowly defined prevention devices.

In this book we have taken a commonalities approach to addiction, avoiding undue emphasis on the use of illicit substances and sidestepping the nonproductive, inconclusive, and grueling debate on the relative dangers of drugs versus alcohol. Our approach not only improves the reader's understanding of compulsive pleasure seeking, but helps to bridge a widening communication gap between parents and children.

The stage was set for a deeper understanding of euphoria when, in 1974, John Hughes and Hans Kosterlitz discovered morphine-like compounds that exist naturally in the human brain. The discovery that the central nervous system can produce its own narcotics has evolved into a reexamination of the fundamental causes of human behavior. In the past decade alone, thousands of scientific treatises have explored relationships between thoughts, feelings, behavior, and brain chemistry. The "soul's frail dwelling place" is not only an enormous switchboard housing trillions of interconnected pathways; it is a giant pharmaceutical factory that manufactures powerful, mind-altering chemicals.

A deeper understanding of the role of pleasure in addictive behavior has recently emerged. It has been shown that the key to pleasurable experiences resides in a major reward center of the brain known as the nucleus accumbens. In order to experience feelings of well-being, this area must be activated by an adequate supply of dopamine, a neurotransmitter often referred to as the "feel-good chemical." It appears that many drugs as divergent as cocaine, heroin, morphine, nicotine, and marijuana— as well as certain behaviors including sex, gambling, or crime— have the ability to activate the reward center by increasing the flow of dopamine. In fact, a considerable proportion of human pleasure—such as hugging a grandchild, kissing a lover, listening to music, and of course, taking drugs—may be thought of as a burst of dopamine in the nucleus accumbens. The addiction that may result from pleasure seeking through drugs or activities is not to the drug (morphine, cocaine, etc.) or to the activity (risk-taking, sex, etc.) but to the euphoria brought about by the rush of dopamine into the reward center. Repeated activation of the nucleus accumbens, whether by drugs or pleasurable behavior, raises the possibility of countermeasures by the brain to down-regulate this activation to the point where the individual becomes dependent on the drug or behavior to avoid dysphoria. Clearly, the brain is more complex than this simple model, but the latest research attributes an enormous role to dopamine and its interaction in the nucleus accumbens to account for pleasure and its accompanying addictive potential.

The close relationship between mood and brain chemistry is illustrated by Ronald Reagan's reactions following extensive bowel surgery. As a standard clinical procedure, the patient was given morphine to reduce the trauma of his surgical ordeal. Only an hour and a half after leaving the operating room, the president quipped: "Why don't I give a press conference right now?" When asked whether he would like to rest before resuming his job, he replied: "No, gimme a pen . . . I feel fit as a fiddle."

Mr. Reagan's exalted mood was most probably related to the combined effects of morphine and endorphin, both of which increase dopamine in the brain's reward center, the nucleus accumbens. His doctors understood that euphoria would soon give way to postoperative discomfort, and no one seemed even remotely concerned that the president might become dependent on morphine—one of the most addictive substances known. Actually, there was no need to worry. Those who develop a "taste" for heroin or morphine are usually people who deal with stress passively, through physical withdrawal and emotional isolation. These protective maneuvers seem very much at odds with Reagan's characteristic extraversion and apparent self-confidence. In light of present knowledge of brain chemistry, we would say that Mr. Reagan normally had an abundant supply of dopamine in this reward center and had no need to further supplement dopminergic neurotransmission once the pain had subsided.

From a psychological perspective, voluntary courtship of any drug or activity depends on how well it fits with one's usual style of coping. The drug of choice is actually a pharmacologic defense mechanism; it bolsters already established patterns for managing psychological threat. We repeatedly rely on three distinct types of experience to achieve feelings of well-being: relaxation, excitement, and fantasy.

These are the underpinnings of human compulsion. As they say in show business, "You've gotta feed 'em, shock 'em, or amuse 'em."

Those who become excessively reliant on relaxation may privately gorge themselves with food, overindulge in watching TV, or use depressant drugs. Addicts of this kind seek to reduce discomfort, which may originate from external events or internal conflict. They search compulsively for tranquility, often to maintain control over their own hostility. When the universe is calm, there is less likelihood of losing composure in an uncontrolled fit of rage. The chemical payoff for ritualized repose may be compared to the effect of a sedative drug. TV addicts, for example, are tranquilizing themselves with visual valium.

In sharp contrast, the compulsive thrill seeker maintains a posture of active confrontation toward a world perceived as hostile and threatening. "Arousal" types tend to compensate for deep-seated feelings of inferiority through repeated attempts to demonstrate physical prowess or intellectual ability. They are usually extroverts, given to boasting about their sexual conquests, artistic talent, or mental agility. They tend to conceal their insecurities behind an overinflated sense of self-worth. As expected, their invigorated facade may be temporarily contrived through stimulant drugs and unnerving behavior. The sky diver's adrenaline rush is remarkably similar to the short, exhilarating jolt from a line of cocaine. Excessive risk takers often mix danger with drugs.

Those compelled by fantasy enjoy activation of the right hemisphere of their cerebral cortex. They pursue mystical experiences and may become lost in occult practices that involve bizarre images and strange patterns of thought. They often have an adolescent preoccupation with the quest for cosmic unity or spiritual oneness. Fantasy addicts maintain a special reverence for subtle nuances in interpersonal communication and are prone to find special meaning in accidental occurrences. Marijuana and hallucinogens, such as LSD, ecstasy, psilocybin, and peyote, are highly prized vehicles for imaginative transport. It is not surprising that there appears to be a link between prolonged use of LSD and some forms of mental illness.

The particular agents that we select for relaxation, arousal, or fantasy escapes are cultivated through powerful social influences. The nuclear age, computer technology, and mass media provide the context in which outlets for rapidly reducing tension have evolved. Rave parties, lotteries, internet pornography, telephone escort services, and video arcades are just a few examples of widely available escapes from routine existence. Advertising plays on the human wish for an effortless means to make our dreams come true. Tobacco and alcohol propaganda provide the most blatant examples of this phenomenon. Viewers are presented with idealized situations in which success is attributed to the use of particular commodities. In effect, advertising makes an implied promise; by drinking such-and-such whisky or smoking X brand of cigarette, we will become more like the people we have always wanted to be.

The tightly woven fabric of culture and personality shapes the varied costumes in which we clothe our instincts. Early predilections toward addiction may be inherited or learned from those around us— an alcoholic parent, a promiscuous relative, or a neighbor who gambles. Preliminary patterns are then channeled by society into an array of potentially deviant careers. Equally disquieting life-styles may become organized around drink, money, sex, calories, or cards. The predictable voyage from routine pleasure seeking through biochemical craving and eventual loss of control may be allegorically represented as a journey to oblivion.

The notion of addiction as a life-threatening journey originates from a series of lectures presented by E. M. Jellinek at the Yale Summer School of Alcohol Studies in July 1951 and June 1952. Jellinek advanced the position that alcoholism is a progressive and potentially fatal disease, with identifiable signs and symptoms. Since this early formulation, the disease model of alcoholism has been embraced by Alcoholics Anonymous (AA), the National Council on Alcoholism, the National Institute on Alcohol Abuse and Alcoholism, and the American Medical Association. Recently the disease concept has been expanded to include overeating, gambling, promiscuity, and nearly all forms of addictive and compulsive behavior. The disease model has helped an otherwise miserable multitude enter treatment for their problem dependencies. When loss of control is attributed to biochemical irregularity rather than moral depravity, addicts can acknowledge problems that they previously denied. They are willing to admit to addiction as a disease, largely because the stigma of being mentally deranged or ethically blameworthy is no longer a part of problem recognition.

Yet the idea of addiction as illness has been criticized. It is said to diminish personal and social responsibility. Succinctly stated by the late Norman Zinberg of Harvard Medical School, "The disease model is good for treatment but bad for prevention." An adventurous teenager might very well rationalize that since he doesn't have an addictive disease, he can experiment with a variety of drugs and activities that others can't control. Furthermore, a theory that stresses biochemical causes for addictive disorders allows corporate entrepreneurs to lure us into harm's way by continuing to pollute our atmosphere with all sorts of seductive advertising.

It is hardly conceivable that anyone can escape the myriad of influences that draw us toward addiction. Therefore, a sizable proportion of our readership may have more than an academic interest in this book. Many will peruse the pages that follow with an eye for reconciling their own concerns with compulsion and loss of control. To be sure, nearly everyone has at least one friend, family member, or business associate who is currently struggling with a problem dependency.

Furthermore, the average reader is both inundated and confused by the aggressive marketing campaigns of purportedly upstanding institutions selling relief from this or that addictive behavior. When a person reaches the junction of seriously seeking help, he or she becomes especially vulnerable to charlatans—pseudospiritualists or crooked health practitioners—who specialize in extracting money from the wounded. Those who proclaim fantastic success rates in a short time with minimal suffering or effort are likely to be corrupt merchants of health. The vast majority of people who begin therapy for problem dependencies, whether alcoholism, overeating, drug abuse, or others, relapse within twelve months of their starting date. The longer they remain in treatment, however, the better are their chances for recovery.

From the abundance of treatment promises that are readily available, how then should one rationally select a legitimate program for obtaining help? We have developed a self-administered Counseling Interest Inventory, through which readers are guided to recognize the systems of psychotherapy that are most likely to match their beliefs about the nature of a helping relationship. Treatment effectiveness has been shown to increase dramatically when clients are comfortable with the values, assumptions, and treatment principles that guide the work of their therapists.

In the following chapters, we examine the interdisciplinary substratum of human compulsion and loss of control. Vivid case examples provide readers with a basic understanding of the multiple influences that promote problem dependencies. Throughout our study we have been impressed by the biochemical, psychological, and social similarities that underlie the avalanching need for more—more sex, more food, more anything. We have refrained from using technical jargon with the aim of communicating the most advanced theoretical, research, and treatment perspectives to nonprofessional readers.

1

Doorway to Excess

some to dance, some to make bonfires, each man to what sport
and revels his addiction leads him.
— *Othello*, Act 11, Scene 2

The Broad Scope of Addiction

In the drama of human excess, experience is the protagonist, and
drugs or activities are merely supporting actors. We are compelled
by repetitious urges to become energized, to relax, to imagine. These
three citadels of consciousness are the beacons of compulsive
behavior.

Recognition that the term *addiction* should transcend drug abuse
has emerged from the problem of categorizing so-called nonaddictive
and addictive drugs. By the late 1960s it became clear that some
people could become compulsively involved with marijuana and
LSD, substances that seemed to have a relatively low potential for
physical dependency. Meanwhile, it was quietly discovered that
some users could maintain relatively casual relationships with
opium derivatives such as heroin or codeine, customarily associated
with rapidly increased tolerance and severe discomfort upon
discontinuance.

Gradually addiction came to imply psychological need, over and
above the traditional constructs of physical demand and distress
upon withdrawal. Those who displayed alcohol-related behavior
problems—irrespective of whether they were physically dependent—were increasingly regarded as alcoholic. Certainly, alcoholism
has psychological and social characteristics far more subtle than the

seizures or hallucinations often associated with hospital-based recovery programs.

By the early 1970s the concept of addiction was further extended to include nonintoxicating substances, so that smoking and eating were widely accepted as addictive behaviors. Even some tobacco executives have admitted that nicotine is addictive. Compulsion, loss of control, and continuation despite harmful consequences became new criteria for the determination of addiction. Furthermore, the notion of a drug of choice suggested that some individuals would become harmfully involved with only some substances, depending on their specific needs. This implied that despite the inherent pleasure-inducing properties of certain drugs, only a proportion of those who experimented would slip into a pattern of compulsive use. Moreover, not only did people react differently to the same drug, but the same person might display entirely different patterns of use or abuse at various times of life. Some users might shift from cocaine abuse to heroin; or from marijuana and LSD to heavy consumption of alcohol and cocaine.

In the 1990s cigarette smoking and overeating (300,000 die each year due to obesity) have been universally acknowledged as major threats to physical well-being; yet millions of people attest to their inability to control these behaviors and regard themselves as addicts. Parallels have been drawn between traditionally held ideas about drug involvement and a host of pleasure-fueled activities far removed from the compulsive intake of food or drugs. It has become regular practice for people to describe themselves as "addicted" to seemingly harmless activities like aerobics or watching MTV. Media-construed syndromes such as "chocoholism," "workaholism," or "Dungeons and Drago-holism" have suddenly appeared, along with a plethora of biologically oriented explanations for these behaviors. Phenylethylamine, found in chocolate, is rumored to be the chemical of love, and endorphins, our internal opiates, are proposed as the special rewards for runners who push beyond the "wall." Television, magazines, and newspapers have all jumped on the bandwagon of a commonalities approach to habitual behaviors.

An impressive assembly of researchers, writers, and theoreticians have contributed the professional underpinning to media's obsession with addition. The addictive personality is described in various scientific reports as impulsive, rule breaking, nonconformist, and depressed. Youngsters who later develop compulsive problem behaviors often experience difficulty in school and in their family relationships. Auto accidents, fighting, truancy, delinquency, and vicious struggles with parents are common. Perhaps the entire spectrum of antisocial behavior patterns provides some relief to unfortunate juveniles who encounter familial inadequacy, poverty, bereavement, or geographic instability.

It is unnecessary to develop separate sets of principles to explain how drug use and other compulsive behaviors gain control over human life. Drugs, food, sex, gambling, and aggressive episodes all give prompt, salient, and short-lasting relief to the people who indulge in them. In addition to sharing pleasure-inducing properties, both substance use and other mood-altering activities tend to produce an initial state of euphoria, which is then followed by a negative emotional state; that is, a high followed by a low. This posteuphoric discomfort gives further impetus to repetition of the rewarding activity. The old "hair of the dog" remedy of drinking to relieve hangover symptoms is consistent with this idea.

Abraham Wikler has developed a two-stage model for the origins and progression of narcotics addiction, which is applicable to other compulsions as well. In the *acquisition* phase, the novice begins and continues a potentially compulsive activity because of pleasurable sensations brought about through the experience. The environment where the desired feeling occurs becomes associated with a "rush," or sense of well-being. The pleasure setting becomes a composite of cues that stimulate craving for the need-satisfying activity. The alcoholic, for example, who has previously enjoyed the euphoria brought on by drink cannot resist temptation when fate delivers him or her to the neighborhood bar or an old friends' New Year's Eve party. The human body eventually adapts to most novel stimulation by reducing the potency of its effect. The user or performer soon needs more of the mood-altering activity in order to experience similar alterations in feeling. The addicted climber must increasingly seek out more difficult cliffs, and the hooked sky diver compulsively finds more challenging and frightening drops.

In the *maintenance* stage of addiction, a person is no longer motivated by any sense of pleasure from the need-gratifying behavior. Rather, the repetitive activity now serves only to relieve the sense of despair and physical discomfort that is felt when the mood-altering action or substance is not present. The user can only "break even"

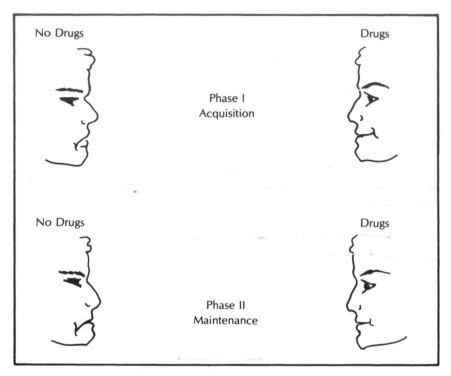

Figure 1–1. WIKLER'S TWO PHASES OF ADDICTION

by performing his or her tension-relieving activity. Without it, the addict suffers from a devastating combination of physical dependence and an even more complicated and stressful environment. The compulsive meditator, for example, increasingly seeks out quiescent relaxation to escape from stress that builds around increasing social isolation and decreased productivity at home and at work.

Loss of control and progressive deterioration of social, economic, or health functions have emerged as the familiar course of human compulsion. Treatment techniques for a variety of habitual problem behaviors have thus become increasingly modeled after widely publicized drug and alcohol intervention approaches. In juvenile crime prevention, for example, Scared Straight! is a technique that parallels the Synanon Game for drug addicts. High-risk juveniles are systematically exposed to severe baiting and verbal confrontation by a group of convicts at various phases of their rehabilitation. Gamblers Anonymous, Overeaters Anonymous, and Sexaholics Anonymous are contemporary treatment organizations that rely heavily on the twelve-step recovery process originally developed by Alcoholics Anonymous. For example, the sex addict who accepts treatment subscribes to a dictum only slightly modified from the first of the Alcoholics Anonymous Twelve Steps: "We admitted that we were powerless over lust {alcohol}—that our lives had become unmanageable." It is not surprising that similar treatments are effective for what appear to be different addictions as these divergent addictions are characterized by similar patterns of disruption and neurochemical processes.

The person who regards himself or herself as "sexaholic" acknowledges that he or she has lost control over sex and no longer has the power of choice. Sex has become an addiction, just as drinking is for the alcoholic who can no longer control his or her consumption. For the married sexaholic, sobriety means having sex only with the spouse. Any form of lust, including sex with oneself or with other partners, is considered progressively destructive. For the unmarried sexaholic, sexual sobriety involves freedom from lust and sex of any kind.

The contemporary emphasis on viewing each instance of human compulsion as a separate diagnostic entity has led to enormous conceptual redundancy and economic waste in our prevention and service-delivery systems. In many ways, the noun "sexaholic" could be replaced by any other human activity in which we are prone to excess. The essential Alcoholics Anonymous message for self-help remains the same: Stop the behavior! Go to meetings! Get a sponsor! Ask for help!

Biochemistry: The Gateway to Excess

Addiction is evident when one becomes progressively unable to control the beginning or end of a need-fulfilling activity. Yet below the surface of this descriptive formulation are more profound explanatory links. The seemingly unrelated ramblings about "newly discovered" addictions, which have been reported in countless media presentations, are actually connected by a biochemical thread. The 1974 discovery of enkephalins by John Hughes and Hans Kosterlitz set the stage for a higher level of conceptualization regarding human compulsion. Enkephalins and related compounds called endorphins are pain-killing molecules that are produced naturally in the brain. These potent, mood-altering chemicals bear striking structural similarity to opiates and appear to behave in similar ways. The realization that the brain can produce its own opiates has led to a reexamination of the biochemical mechanisms of human behavior. In the past decade thousands of scientific treatises have explored relationships between thoughts, feelings, behavior, and brain chemistry.

Advances in scientific understanding of the reward centers of the brain (see Chapter Three) have led to a significant departure from the increasingly archaic spiritual and moralistic definitions of addiction. It has become obvious that individuals can change their brain chemistry through immersion in salient mood-altering activities as well as through ingesting intoxicating substances. Imagine the rush (altered brain chemistry) of first leaping and then free-falling from an airplane at an altitude of 13,000 feet. Recognizing that danger seeking may involve a compulsive alteration in brain chemistry, we are inescapably led to redefine addiction.

Addiction: self-induced changes in neurotransmission that result in behavior problems. This new definition encompasses a multidisciplinary understanding of compulsive problem behaviors that involves the concepts of personal responsibility (the behaviors are self-induced); biochemical effects (the body's neurotransmission changes); and social reactions (society absorbs the costs of consequences of problem behaviors).

In the past advocates for mind-altering substances have rationalized drug use in terms of "mind expansion" or "spiritual discovery." Peyotism is currently practiced in the United States by several thousand members of the Native American Church. This group believes that ingestion of the hallucinogenic buds of the peyote plant will serve as an antidote for alcoholism and as a conduit to spiritual healing. Scientifically, these alterations of perceptual reality are the result of self-imposed changes in the delicate electrochemical balance of the brain. The schism between science and the heart is perhaps most evident when a "flower child" resists the notion that his or her cherished drug experiments are simply mucking up or crudely interfering with natural brain functions.

Compulsive problem behavior is solely the responsibility of the brain, which may be described as the most complex entity in the universe. Its fifty billion or so nerve cells, called neurons, communicate with each other through trillions of interconnections. This "talking" is referred to as neurotransmission, and its language is chemistry. More specifically, neurotransmission is the way in which signals or impulses are sent from one neuron to another. From a

Figure 1–2. SELF-INDUCED CHANGES IN
NEUROTRANSMISSION

purely biochemical standpoint, neurotransmission controls all emotion, perceptions, and bodily functions. In essence, this process is responsible for all thoughts and actions. If we should lose a hand or a foot, we are still recognized as the same person, but if our synaptic chemistry changes dramatically we seem to possess altogether different personalities. The often frightening hallucinations and bizarre

Axon

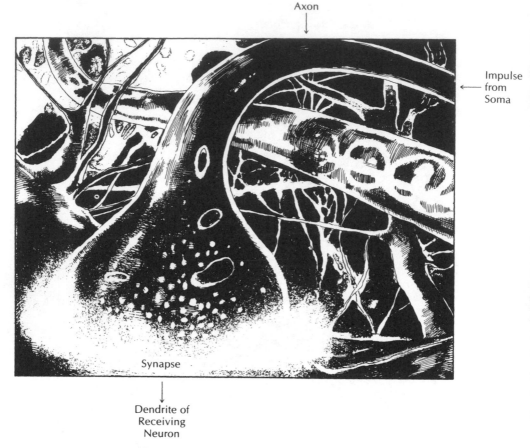

Impulse
← from
Soma

Synapse

Dendrite of
Receiving
Neuron

Figure 1–3. THE ELECTROCHEMICAL JOLT

Adapted from R. Restak, *The brain* (New York: Bantam Books, 1984), 36–37.

delusions of those with schizophrenia are poignant examples of this
phenomenon.

   The brain's neurons are composed of three basic parts: the soma
or cell body, the axon, which carries impulses away from the soma,
and the dendrites, which receive impulses from other neurons. The
soma acts as a small computer. It must decide from a "discussion"
with a multitude of surrounding neurons whether to "fire" and send
the impulse to the axon, or to remain dormant. Since this is the
soma's only decision, and it is made very quickly, we may think of
the soma as a "fast idiot." As with pregnancy, firing either occurs or
it does not, in accord with the "all or nothing" principle. There are

no weak or strong impulses; all impulses are of the same magnitude. The intensity of feeling is determined by the *frequency* of neuronal firing rather than by the strength of the electrochemical jolt.

One of the more interesting facts about the brain is that it is not hard-wired. That is, unlike the telephone system, the brain has no physical contacts among its trillions of interconnecting neurons. Each nerve cell is physically separated from the fifty billion other collaborating brain units by a small space called a synapse. When the soma fires, the impulse travels down the long fiber of the axon to the synapse separating the axon of one neuron from the dendrites of another. The impulse is carried across the synapse to the receiving neuron by small molecules that are released into the synapse. These molecules, known as neurotransmitters, move across the synapse and attach themselves to sites known as receptors, which are embedded in the membrane of the postsynaptic terminals of the dendrites. The receptors are tailor-made to receive only neurotransmitters that have a shape that complements that of the receptor. This relationship between neurotransmitter and receptor is very much like a lock and key. Just as only a key with the correct shape will work in a given lock, only those neurotransmitters with the right shape will activate the specific receptors designed for them.

If a sufficient number of receptors on the postsynaptic membrane become occupied by neurotransmitters, there is a change in the electrical balance of this membrane that results in a transfer of the impulse from the presynaptic neuron to the postsynaptic neuron. The impulse then travels to the soma of the postsynaptic neuron, where it is combined with inputs from many other synaptic junctions. The soma of the postsynaptic neuron must now make its own "decision" of whether to fire based upon the multitude of synaptic inputs.

Just as it is possible to put keys of slightly different shapes into a given lock, it is possible to introduce into the synapse molecules with shapes similar to neurotransmitters that will attach to the receptor sites. However, these pseudo-neurotransmitters (chemical prostitutes) do not change the electrical balance of the postsynaptic membrane, and in fact block the receptor sites from receiving neurotransmitters that transfer the nerve impulse. The blocking of the receptor sites with phony neurotransmitters is much like putting a Ford key in a Mercury ignition. The key will fit but will not turn the switch and in fact will prevent inserting the Mercury key that

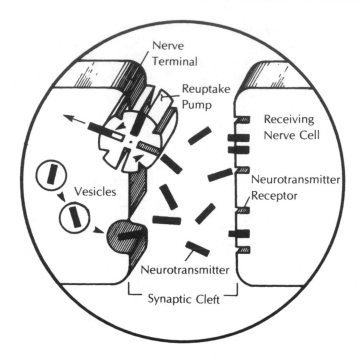

Figure 1–4. ORDINARY ACTION IN THE BRAIN

Typically, cells communicate with chemicals called neurotransmitters.
The supply of the transmitters is kept in balance by the ability of the
transmitting cell to reabsorb—scientifically called "reuptake"—some of the
chemical in the synaptic cleft.

Source: Reprinted from *Scientific American* by *The New York Times*, March 22, 1983.

would turn the motor on. Introduction of man-made chemicals that
block certain receptor sites is the basis for the chemical treatment of
schizophrenia. A drug (for example, Haldol) occupies receptor sites
on the postsynaptic membrane, normally occupied by the neurotransmitter dopamine. The electrical balance of the cell membrane
remains intact, and the impulse cannot be transferred to adjacent
cells. This reduces the overactive neurotransmission usually associated with schizophrenia.

   When an impulse has been transmitted to the postsynaptic neuron, the electrical balance of that neuron must be restored before it
can receive the next impulse. This balance is restored through the
release of neurotransmitters from the postsynaptic receptor sites. Re-

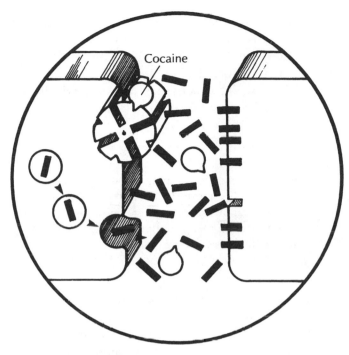

Figure 1-5. COCAINE IN THE BRAIN

Cocaine slips into the reuptake pump inhibiting its ability to balance the amount of neurotransmitter traveling between cells. This can result in an overstimulation of the receiving cell. Some have linked that interaction to euphoria.

Source: Scientific American. The New York Times, March 22, 1983.

leased neurotransmitters may be reabsorbed and safely stored in the synaptic vesicles of the presynaptic terminal, where they are protected from destruction and may be reused as needed. However, a number of interesting things can happen to the neurotransmitters before they reach the safe hiding place of the synaptic vesicle. If cocaine is ingested, this tends to prevent the neurotransmitters from being recycled into the presynaptic terminal, resulting in an excess of neurotransmitters in the synapse. Since more neurotransmitters are available for attachment to receptor sites, more receptor sites will be occupied, with a resultant increase in the rate of neurotransmission and thus the state of arousal. This, of course, is why the individual ingested cocaine in the first place.

The more rapid the neurotransmission in particular parts of the brain, the more intense is the feeling. Both substances (such as cocaine) and activities (such as skydiving) have the ability to alter neurotransmission and therefore change the way we feel about ourselves and the outside world. That activities can dramatically affect our mood is illustrated by a sensationalized example:

> You are sitting alone in your room feeling sorry for yourself because of the loss of a close relationship. All of a sudden, out of nowhere, there appears a full-grown, person-eating Bengal tiger obviously looking for her meal. Your depression instantly disappears in a rush of rapidly accelerating neurotransmission. You grasp a chair and thrust it menacingly toward the ferocious beast, while shrieking obscenities at the top of your lungs. You run as fast as your legs will carry you.

This highly arousing situation has obviously provoked powerful alterations in your brain chemistry. As if you had ingested a strong dose of cocaine or amphetamine, your neurotransmission is so fast that relaxation or sleep is out of the question and your depression is nowhere in sight. In a similar manner, activities can evoke sensations of relaxation that correspond to decreases in neurotransmission. The distress and agitation caused by a shouting match with your spouse can be diminished through an orgy of eating.

People may repeat certain behaviors to bring about alterations in neurotransmission consistent with their characteristic ways of dealing with stress. That is, the person who actively confronts fear or tension repeatedly seeks out risk-taking activities or stimulant drugs in order to increase neurotransmission. The person who is prone to passive withdrawal seeks out activities or drugs that lower neurotransmission.

In today's chemical society, people are more likely to reach for drugs than to engage in activities that alter neurotransmission. However, regardless of whether we choose activities or substances, the possibility of addiction always lurks in the convolutions of our brains, where all compulsion originates. Biochemically, addiction results from neuronal adaptation to repeated and salient attempts to alter "normal" levels of neurotransmission. For example, the person who seems to thrive on becoming energized attempts to raise neurotransmission above the "normal" or baseline level. Unfortunately, he or she is confronted with enzymatic and receptor changes in the brain that counter the desired rise in neurotransmission.

In the acquisition phase of an arousal addiction a person is able, almost at will, to alter his or her neurotransmission by engaging in activities or drug use. As has been said, however, "It is not nice to fool Mother Nature"; that is, it is not wise to synthetically alter the balance of the human brain. A corollary is: "You can't fool Mother Nature for very long." Repeated mind-altering episodes of the same intensity soon bring about changes in the amount of receptors and enzymes required for neurotransmitter-induced reactions to occur. These enzymatic changes result in the need for higher doses of activities or drugs for the person to reach the level of subjective arousal experienced at the beginning of the addictive process.

In the maintenance phase of addiction, brain chemistry is so altered that the addict compulsively attempts to maintain a level of neurotransmission that will reduce the imbalance and suffering induced by enzymatic changes. Enzymatic changes occur *slowly*, and the time required to attain dependency (reach the maintenance phase) varies from person to person. Also, brain enzyme levels that have been gradually altered do not immediately return to normal even though the activity responsible for the changes has ceased. For this reason, the stopping or reducing of compulsive stimulation is often followed by a subjective experience of depression, or "crash." This is because enzyme levels have slowly adapted to counter the repetitive elevation in neurotransmission, brought about through activities that are suddenly eliminated. The brain's altered and more slowly responding enzyme levels remain constant for the immediate future. Hence the maintenance-phase addict who goes "cold-turkey" suffers biochemical withdrawal—whether habituated to cocaine or rock climbing.

In a similar manner, activities that lower the brain's neurotransmission are countered by similar changes that hold neurotransmission at a normal level. In the end, Mother Nature wins again. The addict must choose between attempting to maintain an acceptable level of neurotransmission by increasing sedation—through drugs or activities—or "kick" the habit. Cessation introduces a dramatic state of agitated discomfort, because the substance or activity responsible for lowered neurotransmission has been removed, while the powerful enzymatic changes that battled to raise the level of neurotransmission remain present.

Pick Your Parents Carefully

A genetic component is known to exist in addictive behavior. Behavior geneticists have studied heritable factors in such diverse phenomena as schizophrenia, criminality, and cigarette smoking. These forms of behavior and virtually all other addictions that have been studied seem to be influenced by both genetic and environmental factors. Behavioral geneticist Gerald McClearn of Pennsylvania State University suggests that the enzyme produced by a given gene might influence hormones and neurotransmitters in a way that contributes to the development of a personality potentially more susceptible than most to external influences, such as peer group pressure. A genetic predisposition of this type may ultimately become an important determinant of how an individual lives his life. Yet identical twins, who possess exactly the same genetic make-up, do not always develop similar patterns of behavioral excess. We must look at individual differences in experience to understand more completely the origins and progression of addiction. It is not nature *or* nurture but nature *and* nurture that seem to influence many behavioral traits. As one man has said, "The frightening part about heredity and environment is that we parents provide both."

More than 140 research studies indicate an increased incidence of alcoholism in families where one or more members had been diagnosed as alcoholic. In general, these studies show that the children, male or female, of an alcoholic father or mother have two to four times the probability of becoming alcoholic than is the population norm. Relatively little has been done to study the role of genetic factors in other compulsive problem behaviors. The studies that have attempted such assessments of eating disorders and cigarette smoking find that although inheritance is a significant factor, human compulsion answers heavily to the social setting in which it may or may not occur.

The genetic basis of alcoholism has been traced to the deficiency of an enzyme (aldehyde dehydrogenase) necessary for the body's disposal of alcohol. The relationship between genetics and enzymatic susceptibility is as follows. Enzymes are the proteins in our body responsible for the breakdown or metabolism of drugs. They bring about a change (usually an increase) in the speed of bodily processes. Any aberration or alteration in those enzymes involved in the metabolism of alcohol or drugs is reflected in the way the body disposes of the drug. The enzyme's dysfunctional response to the addict's chosen drug is at the core of the concept of inherited addictive disease.

The relationship between enzymes and parentally transmitted genes is schematized below.

Parents → DNA → RNA → Enzymes

Enzymes are formed from a template of ribonucleic acid (RNA), which in turn is generated from a template of deoxyribonucleic acid (DNA). DNA is the genetic material that we inherit from our parents. If they should provide us with defective DNA, this would be reflected in faulty enzyme systems. For this reason, besides abstinence, a most effective way to avoid addiction is to "pick your parents carefully."

Patching Yourself from Without

Given that we may voluntarily alter our neurotransmission to achieve a desired feeling, why do only some of us become compulsively involved in this pursuit? After all, most people can have a drink or occasionally rage at the race track without going off the deep end. Most addictionologists—even those who disagree about other matters of causation and treatment—agree that low self-regard is a crucial factor in all forms of addiction. The chronic absence of good feelings about oneself provokes a dependence on mood-changing activity. Manifest or masked, feelings of low self-worth are basic to most dysfunctional life-styles.
One way of coping with disquieting factors is to immerse oneself in an activity that is incompatible with serious self-evaluation. The climber, clinging to a mountain face with only a rope, pitons, and a tenuous foothold, has few moments to spare on self-derogation. The risk taker may figuratively bridge the crevasse of his or her sense of inadequacy by temporary surrender to something outside the self. A 32-year-old male cocaine user reported a particularly vivid dream that illustrates this point: "I recall seeing my personality as a huge concave surface. It looked like a great ceramic bowl with irregularly spaced craters on an otherwise smooth surface. Somehow I could patch the holes with an ultrafine putty made of cocaine paste. The new shimmering surface appeared nearly unmarred."

The user's drug or activity of choice often depends on his or her style of coping with troubled feelings about the self. In a research study at Bellevue Psychiatric Hospital in New York, Harvey Milkman and William A. Frosch found a striking relationship between personality and drug of choice. Those who prefer heroin usually cope with stress through relaxation and isolation. In sharp contrast, amphetamine users are likely to confront a hostile or threatening environment with physical or intellectual activity. Clinical observations of people who use hallucinogens such as LSD confirm that they characteristically rely on imagery, daydreaming, and altered thought processes to reduce tension. The examples shown in table 1–1 illustrate differences between compulsive users of heroin, amphetamine, and LSD in their management of self-esteem.

The key that opens the doorway to excess for the preaddict is the good feeling that he or she learns to create, and repeatedly recreate, through self-determined activity. Unaccustomed to the wine of success, the novice experiences as a godsend any involvement that provides escape from the increasing sense of despair borne of repeated failures in the "straight world." He or she not only delights in a reprieve from tension but experiences elevated feelings of self-worth for having discovered the ability to produce a pleasurable sensation. In *The Road to H*, Isidor Chein and his collaborators describe the addict's infatuation with self-determined mood change.

> In [heroin] addicts with strong craving . . . it is in large measure a psychic consequence of achieving a state of relaxation and relief from tension or distress through one's own activities, not through a physician's recommendation or prescription, but through an esoteric, illegal and dangerous nostrum. We can observe an analogous phenomenon in people who win the Irish Sweepstakes; win on dice, cards, horses or numbers; or even in persons who park in no-parking zones without getting a traffic ticket. They feel important, worthwhile and interesting, they feel a sense of pride and accomplishment. Such an illusory achievement is an important psychic phenomenon, particularly important when it stands out by contrast with the remainder of a person's life.

Table 1–1
USE OF VARIOUS DRUGS TO REGULATE SELF-ESTEEM

Heroin	*Amphetamine*	*LSD*

How do you feel about yourself generally?

Lousy. I don't like myself.	I think I'm all right ya'know.	I feel like a voyager in an awesome adventure.

What about your looks, do you think you're good looking?

I don't like them and I don't know why.	I think they're all right. I'm satisfied. Yeah, I think I'm good looking.	Sometimes I feel like an alien, like I'm a gorgeous being from another planet.

How do you compare with others your age?

Right now I know I don't compare well. I can't control my desire for drugs. I can't do what I want to do . . . I can't be a man, I am not doing anything.	I don't think I'm as mature, serious, or business-minded as a 25-year-old should be. As a man I'm all right. I'm big and strong and I try to be kind. I love women and I dig kids.	I don't compare myself to others. I just think about how I'm dealing with my own Karma so I can improve my chances now and in a future life.

What do you believe that other people think of you?

That I'm a cop out; some people would say degenerate.	I think others like me a great deal. They really do not say it but I know they do. I make friends easily and people smile and they embrace me and make me feel like I'm not rejected.	They think I'm on a path of spiritual discovery. That I am in touch with some cosmic force that they would like to understand.

What kind of person would you like to be?

I'd just be average and get along, say middle class. I want to be able to work and be middle class. I don't have goals of making a million or anything, just make a living.	I would like to be free of drugs. I would like to not even have to put a grape pop in my mouth if I didn't want to. Right now I'm taking vitamin D and taking grape ice pops. I'm playing with kids. I bought a yo-yo yesterday. I'm laughing a lot and enjoying life.	I would like to be in flow with the forces of the universe . . . to experience oneness with people and nature . . . to merge with the cosmos.

Note: Adapted from H. Milkman and W. Frosch, On the preferential abuse of heroin and amphetamines, *The Journal of Nervous and Mental Disease* 156: 4, 242–48 (1973).

The Beacons of Compulsion

After studying the life histories of drug abusers, we have seen that drugs of choice are harmonious with an individual's usual means of coping with stress. The discovery of a need-fulfilling drug is usually a serendipitous event; the novice becomes infatuated because of the immediate reduction of stress achieved through the experience. Incipient addicts usually experience behavioral compulsion and loss of control before ever ingesting a psychoactive substance. Juvenile delinquency, persistent and vicious family struggles, and inability to adequately cope with everyday demands are common childhood precursors to drug abuse. Heroin users often show histories of passivity alternating with uncontrolled rage; stimulant users describe multiple episodes of life-threatening impulsiveness; those who rely on hallucinogens report that they regularly avoided problems through fantasy during prolonged periods of their childhood.

We repeatedly pursue three avenues of experience as antidotes for psychic pain. These preferred styles of coping—satiation, arousal, and fantasy—seem to have their origins in the first years of life. Childhood experiences combined with genetic predisposition are the foundations of adult compulsion. The drug group of choice—depressants, stimulants, or hallucinogens—is the one that best fits the individual's characteristic way of coping with stress or feelings of unworthiness. People do not become addicted to drugs or mood-altering activities as such, but rather to the satiation, arousal, or fantasy experiences that can be achieved through them.

Addicts whose basic motivation is satiation, for example, are likely to binge on food or television watching or to choose depressant drugs such as heroin. Psychologically, they are trying to shut down negative feelings by reducing stimulation from the internal or external world. The life of the satiation type of addict bears striking similarity to that of a child during the first year of life. The mouth and skin are the primary receptors of experience, and feelings of well-being depend almost completely on food and warmth. Harvard Medical School's Edward J. Khantzian and Howard Shaffer suggest that depressants provide a pharmacologic defense against the user's own aggressive drives. Binge eating or excessive television watching may fulfill the same adaptive role by helping people quiet strong hostile impulses. On a biochemical level, the effect of satiation activities may be similar to that of opiates. Growing dependence on behaviors such as overeating and watching television may be analagous, though more subtle, versions of opiate addiction.

While satiation addicts try to avoid stimulation and confrontation, others actively seek it. The behavior associated with the arousal mode of gratification includes crime, gambling, risk taking, and use of stimulant drugs such as amphetamines or cocaine. These addicts seek to feel active and potent in the face of an environment that they view as overwhelmingly dehumanizing. They are often boastful about their artistic talent, intellectual skill, and sexual or physical prowess. Their vast expenditures of mental and physical energy are designed to deny underlying fears of helplessness. This posture is reminiscent of two- and three-year-olds coping with the world of giants in which they live. Asked, "Who is biggest or toughest?" they often reply, "I can beat up Daddy." They protect themselves through the defense of magical denial: "I am really not helpless and vulnerable; I am powerful and feared."

The third type of addict, who uses fantasy as the preferred way of dealing with the world, favors repetitive activation of what some researchers refer to as right-hemisphere thinking. Thoughts become dreamlike, with rapidly shifting imagery and illogical relations between time and space. This style of coping often includes preoccupation with day or night dreams, compulsive artistic expression, or various forms of mystical experience, sometimes expressed as a quest for the feeling of oneness or cosmic unity. People who rely on this style partially overcome their fears by creating fantasies in which they are effective and important. They may travel with extraterrestrials, encounter the "Grim Reaper," or have their body entered by a supernatural entity.

These addicts favor hallucinogens such as LSD, mushrooms containing psilocybin, or peyote. Interestingly, the two basic types of chemical molecules—variations of indole and phenylethylamine—present in nearly all hallucinogens are also found in many compounds that occur naturally as neurotransmitters. For example, dopamine and norepinephrine have the basic phenylethylamine structure, whereas serotonin has the indole structure. The fantasy aspects of some artistic, romantic, or spiritual activities may be brought about by conversion of the brain's own indole or phenylethylamine compounds into hallucinogenic variations of these chemicals.

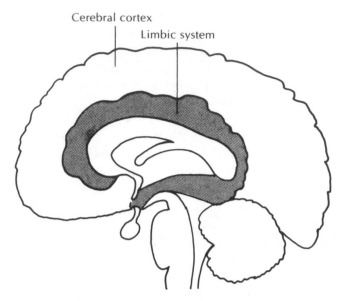

Figure 1–6. STRUCTURES OF THE BRAIN

Adapted from Kagan et al., Brain and body: The physical foundation of human behavior, in *Psychology: An introduction* (New York: Harcourt, Brace, Janovich, 1984), 62.

Limbic Sensation and Cortical Content

In addition to producing different patterns of neurotransmission, the three types of addiction seem to involve different parts of the brain. Mood shifts appear to be influenced by the limbic system, located near the middle of the brain. This system is associated with emotions and with sexual, feeding, and aggressive responses. As arousal decreases, moods may downshift from relaxation to tranquility and finally to a state of blissful satiation. Conversely, increases in arousal are accompanied by changes in experience from ordinary alertness through creativity and ultimately manic states.

While the limbic system appears to play a major role in pleasurable sensations connected with altered levels of arousal, the convoluted outer brain known as the cerebral cortex is an important determinant of mental content. Excessive activity in the cortex of the right hemisphere may help explain the uncontrolled imagery found in the fantasies of cocaine users, mystics, and schizophrenics. Similar cortical activity in the left hemisphere may be responsible for feelings

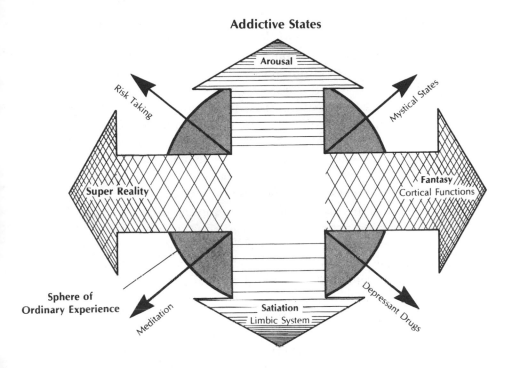

Addictive States

Figure 1 7. ADDICTIVE STATES

While the brain's limbic system appears to play a major role in the pleasurable sensations of addiction, the cerebral cortex influences mental content. Its right hemisphere may be involved in fantasy experiences such as those achieved through LSD or other imagination-oriented activities. The heightened sense of reality experienced during compulsive risk taking or work may be linked to activity in the left hemisphere.

of superreality that some individuals report during high-risk activities such as rock climbing and skydiving, which require an accurate and logical appraisal of one's options.

Society and the Deviant Career

Differences in neurotransmission, influences from the limbic and cortical systems, and the effects of various brain enzymes all interact with powerful social forces that can push susceptible individuals toward activities that have a high dependency potential. Computer games, public lotteries, and telephone escorts are just a few examples of widely available escapes from routine existence. Advertising plays on the human quest for effortless, impersonal reduction of stress. There is an implicit promise that participation in activities with high dependency potential will diminish the discrepancy between actual self-concept and ideal self-concept. Tobacco and alcohol propaganda provide the most blatant examples of this phenomenon. A visual, ego-ideal fantasy is provided in association with the product, often accompanied by a verbal suggestion for indulgence: "Come to X-Brand country." In this context of promoted immediacy, the individual moves through a network of social interactions that may influence his or her reliance on particular channels of behavioral excess.

In the earliest phase of preaddict development a child may possess a subtle yet identifiable characteristic that steers him or her in the direction of addiction. Consider the two-year-old who enjoys his or her first taste of beer, or the young boy whose nickname is "Lucky" or "Romeo." The young person may be valued conditionally, so that parental affection depends on performance of expected behaviors. Further channelization occurs when an early sense of low self-worth is relieved through rewards associated with a specific activity. The dejected child may begin to feel potent on attaining external reinforcers such as drugs, money, or sex.

Although parental role models and styles of child rearing are viewed as important contributors to future coping patterns, adolescent adjustment is inextricably bound to peer influence. According to Denise Kandel of Columbia University, the most reliable finding in drug research is the strong relation between one person's drug use and concurrent use by friends. The strength of the adolescent's motive toward peer conformity is symbolized by the flamboyant dress rituals among punks.

If a person's channelization toward problem behaviors continues into early adulthood, opportunities for success diminish as he or she is increasingly imprisoned, both socially and personally, within a deviant role. The adolescent reaches a point of no return when the social and personal costs of changing life-styles seem to outweigh the benefits. Imagine the difficulty of a seventeen-year-old high school dropout and long-standing street gang member suddenly attempting

Figure 1–8. FLAMBOYANT DRESS RITUALS AMONG PUNKS

to become an athlete or college student. Eventually the young addict is labeled by those around him or her as a member of a deviant subgroup such as alcoholic, obese, or criminal. This stigmatization tends to further decrease the addict's sense of self-worth. A youngster may begin to enact socially expected roles such as being irresponsible, noncomforming, or impulse-ridden. The stereotyped individual thus becomes further engulfed in a pattern that restricts his or her life opportunities. As the addict now drifts from stable family and love relationships, social settings are increasingly selected because of their potential for immediate gratification. The bar, sex parlor, discotheque, or video arcade may become important islands of alienated comfort.

The addictive progression often culminates in dramatic conflict with the environment. Heightened environmental demands and repeated personal failures require increasingly severe efforts to recoup self-esteem through excessive activity. The downward spiral of functioning may lead to a variety of social-service interventions, includ-

ing hospitalization, incarceration, or both, often occurring on a cyclical basis. What social scientists have labeled as relapse may simply
reflect another episode in the naturally oscillating course of the addict's futile struggle to regain control.

As schematized in figure 1–9, the process of becoming addicted
may be conceptualized as a "deviant career." Novices advance
through a series of social stages as they progress to full status in their
offbeat professions. The ripple effect from being labeled or stigmatized as a type of addict—fatty, junkie, alcoholic, and so on—may
last throughout a person's lifetime.

Multiple Disciplines: The Cutting Edge

Considering the complex biological, psychological, and social forces
that promote behavioral excess, it is not surprising that those who
attempt treatment for their compulsions usually fail. From 60 to 80
percent of all addicts who attempt abstinence relapse within six
months. It can be excruciatingly difficult to overcome renegade biological processes that are further encouraged by powerful social and
psychological influences. Yet it can be done.

Biologically, the question is: Can the human brain gain control
over inherited impulses that were appropriate for prehistoric man
but are inappropriate in the twentieth century? We know that activities that lead to compulsive life-styles are self-induced and are under
both cortical and limbic system control. We also know that the cerebral cortex, the center of thought and memory in homo sapiens, is
much larger in humans than in other animals. With this great rea-
soning capacity, we should be able to exercise more control over the
basic emotions directed by the lower brain centers. A multidisciplinary understanding of addiction should provide the conflict-solving
ability of our cortex with the power it needs to control our lives more
successfully.

The term *dharma* is used in Hindu philosophy to describe a person's free will or ability to control *karma*, that which an individual
brings into the world when born. In today's terms we may look at
dharma as cortical control and karma as the inner brain inheritance.
Clearly, humankind has the ability to exercise dharma over karma:
We need not be slaves to our compulsive behavior.

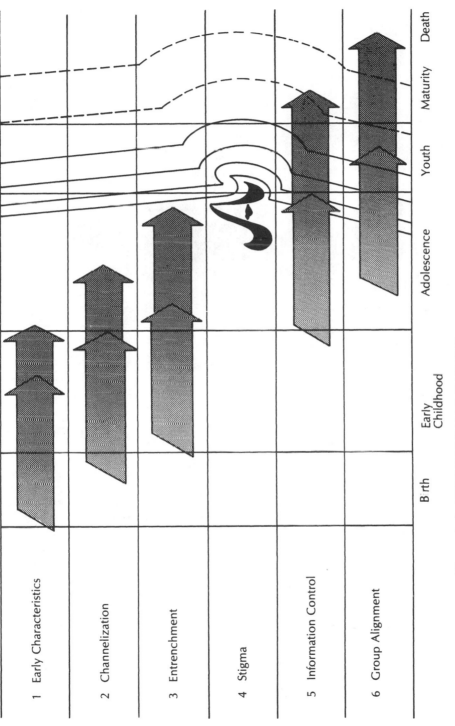

Figure 1–9. THE DEVIANT CAREER

Adapted from E. Goffman, *Stigma: Notes on the management of spoiled identity*, (Englewood Cliffs, N.J.: Prentice-Hall, 1963).

2

Substitutes for Your Thumb

A magical movement of the hand introduces a magical substance, and behold, pain and suffering are exorcised, the sense of misery disappears and the body is suffused by waves of pleasure . . . the ego is, after all, the omnipotent giant it had always fundamentally thought it was.

— Sandor Rado
The Psychoanalysis of Pharmacothymia

G ROWING up consists of finding the right substitutes for your thumb. From the cradle to the crypt, we discover various means—some socially approved, others highly disdained—for coping with the inevitable stress of walking through life's corridor. As infants we have limited resources for dealing with repetitive swells of physical or emotional discomfort. Whether we survive depends on adult caretakers. We require proper nourishment, safety, and love. From the newborn's perspective, the universe is benign or malevolent depending on his or her experience with feeding and forming intimate emotional bonds. The suckling's knowledge that he or she will be lovingly fed allows baby to develop a basic trust in other human beings.

An infant's tension is reduced through the kind deliverance of food and touch. Misery and despair soon fade into gurgles and coos as the baby swoons in a state of blissful delight. Food, touch, and novelty become associated with love and the pleasures of being unshackled from disquieting physical sensations. A soothing influence appears from the outside world and suddenly baby feels better. A flailing state of alarm melts into passive euphoria. As Sinbad on his magic carpet, the nursling simply forms a whimper and a wish and "zam-zam alacazam," a Shangri-La of nurturance and affection quickly unfolds: mother's breast, mommy and daddy's bed, a kiss, a caress, sumptuous creamy food; behold, the Garden of Eden. All this for some rapid breathing, a few tears, and several whining screams. The infant soon discovers that a measure of tension can also be regulated through self-stimulation. Syllabic babbling, masturbation, and thumb sucking become important means for reducing stress. As quoted by Freud in *Three Essays on the Theory of Sexuality*, "It is impossible to describe what a lovely feeling goes through your whole body when you suck; you are right away from this world. You are absolutely satisfied and happy beyond desire. It is a wonderful feeling; you long for nothing but peace—uninterrupted peace. It is unspeakably lovely: you feel no pain and no sorrow, and ah! you are carried into another world."

As adults, we repeatedly seek passage to the infant's heavenly retreat. Wistfully lamented Peter, Paul and Mary, "A million dollars at the drop of a hat, I'd give it all gladly if life could be like that." Life's stressful and perilous journey is made more bearable by brief excursions into pleasurable moments that we have dubbed "substitutes for your thumb." Yet, as the poet John Milton sagely advises: "The mind is its own place . . . It can make a heaven of hell or a hell of heaven." The same stimulus—whether a mood-altering drug or an activity like sex—can evoke paradise for one person and a fiery inferno for another.

An individual's unique combination of genetic characteristics and early childhood experiences determines his or her specific inclinations toward pleasurable activities. Some patterns emerge as early as the first year of life, while others are spawned during critical periods after many years of social learning and personal development. Quite naturally, need-gratifying behavior of any kind tends to be repeated because it continues to reduce conflict and tension. However, it is our biological adaptation to repeated mind-affecting stimuli—whether food, activities, or drugs—that requires increasing levels of exposure to achieve comparable feelings of pleasure. Any activity that produces salient alterations in mood (which are always accompanied by changes in neurotransmission) can lead to compulsion, loss of control, and progressively disturbed functioning.

Although the consequences of overeating, compulsive TV watching, and heroin addiction are obviously not the same, several commonalities exist between these and other tranquilizing behaviors. Subjectively, there develops an irresistible craving for food, drink, or activities that appear to lessen the impact of physically or psychologically arousing stimuli. Behaviorally, there are recurrent attempts to recreate placid childhood feelings that have their origins in the calming effects of early parental care. Psychologically, satiation seekers reduce stress by adopting a stance of passive withdrawal from internal or external conflict.

Many of us, for example, find soothing relief through the ubiquitous surrogate parent of color TV. Parents enjoy hours of peace as their children remain quietly glued to a plethora of cartoon and kiddie shows. For adults, soap operas provide temporary relief from unpleasant emotions, thoughts, or circumstances in daily life. Compulsive viewers eagerly await the times of day when they can watch the tormented lives of television performers who, in fantasy, become substitute members of their own family. During the interim week the viewers' attention remains, on some levels of consciousness, focused on an artificial, pre-scripted crisis.

A humorous example of how TV can become addictive is taken from one of Howard's "Sally Forth" cartoons: "Listen Carol, just don't get yourself into the kind of trouble I did when I was on maternity leave. One day when I was nursing Hilary I turned on a soap opera just for fun. Within a week I was mainlining. I was doing four hours of soaps a day. Then I really flipped out and started to mix soaps and game shows. Finally I had to quit cold turkey. It was awful! Do you know I still get occasional flashbacks from General Hospital?"

The Chemistry of Contentment

Heroin is said to be king of the opiate-mediated sensations. Similar feelings, however, may be subtly achieved through overeating or watching TV. Indeed, the quiet lethargy induced by heroin is reminiscent of the infant's calm, sleepy satisfaction after being breastfed. Are we then to assume that the world's most infamous narcotic and mother's milk have a chemical similarity? Is there an underlying biochemical thread that can explain the common reaction to these very disparate yet similarly satisfying substances? At first even the suggestion of some commonality between milk and heroin seems ridiculous, even sacrilegious. Yet these seemingly diverse substitutes for your thumb trigger similar changes in the brain's reward system. Similar biochemical principles may be used to account for progressive dependence on a wide spectrum of mood-calming activities—taking sedative drugs, listening to music, watching television, undergoing massage, or eating your grandmother's chicken soup—and yes, it is possible to develop a growing dependence on these chemically similar though more subtle versions of opiate addiction.

Enkephalins and related compounds, the endorphins, occur naturally in the brain and mimic the effect of morphine. They decrease the number of neurotransmitter molecules released into the synapse, or the space between neurons, which ironically increase dopamine in the nucleus accumbens, the brain's reward center, with a resulting decrease in the rate of neurotransmission in the pain pathways of the central nervous system.

Both internally produced endorphins and ingested opiates occupy neuronal receptor sites that regulate neurotransmitter release. The greater the number of occupied sites, the fewer the neurotransmitters that are released into the synapse. When there is a dramatic decrease in the number of neurotransmitter molecules released into the synapse, neuronal impulses become insufficient to support vital functions such as breathing, heart beat, and blood pressure. Fatal heroin overdoses are the result of exceeding the body's capacity for occupation of opiate receptor sites in the central nervous system. Fortunately, the probability of overdosing on endorphins as a result of non-drug-induced ecstasy is very remote.

Endorphins and enkephalins are opiates produced by the body to control pain. Without them we would constantly suffer from the slightest injury. The Spanish conquest of Mexico, as recorded by Bernal Diaz del Castillo, provides an excellent example of the body's ability to carry on in spite of serious and painful injuries. In the attack by Hernán Cortés on the Aztec capital of Tenochtitlán, Diaz records that there were no noncombative casualties as a result of injuries to the often-outnumbered conquistadors. The Spanish were either fighting or dead, even if the injuries were of such a serious nature that death ultimately followed.

Not only do the endorphins and enkephalins reduce pain, they produce a euphoria much like that of opiates. It is known that neuronal pathways associated with pain pass through that portion of the brain known as the limbic system, which is also the seat of emotion and feeling. Therefore, any substance that tends to reduce pain has a soothing effect on our emotions. Mood-calming activities also have the effect of releasing endorphins, which in turn decrease the number of neurotransmitter molecules released into the synapse. This, in turn, results in the feeling of well-being experienced during and immediately following these activities. For this reason opiates, as well as our own endorphins, produce both analgesia and euphoria. One well-known endorphin-releasing activity is eating warm and pleasant-tasting food. The relief from a cold, sore throat, or other minor pain upon eating warm soup (chicken or otherwise) is familiar to us all. It is the body's own endorphins, which mimic the effect of opiates, that bring about the desired satiation effect. Since pain relief and emotional soothing are both mediated by the occupation of opiate receptor sites on certain neurons of the brain, we have coined the term *opmex* (from opiate-mediated experience) to refer to the set of behaviors that include the ingestion of opiate drugs and also nondrug activities that release the body's internal opiates, the endorphins.

Before proceeding too far into a discussion of the chemistry of contentment, we should remember that the brain also has neuronal connections that decrease, rather than increase, neurotransmission in nerve pathways associated with emotions, feelings, and pain. These synaptic connections are referred to as inhibitory, whereas those that are associated with an increase in neurotransmission are called excitatory. Under normal conditions, the brain maintains a fairly constant rate of neurotransmission through the combined effort of the inhibitory and excitatory neurons.

The importance of the regulation of neurotransmission can be seen in those neuronal disturbances that often result in bizarre behavioral changes. Most people are familiar with the late folk singer Woodie Guthrie, who developed a disorder known as Huntington's chorea in the prime of his life. This disease is caused by a deterioration of inhibitory synapses with the resultant loss of control of neurotransmission. The fact that Huntington's chorea is an inherited disease is all the more reason to pick your parents carefully. Another disorder known as Parkinson's disease is caused by a deterioration of those cells in the brain that produce dopamine, a neurotransmitter in the excitatory pathways. The well-known photographer Margaret Bourke-White suffered from this disorder. On another level, psychotic disorders such as mania, depression, and schizophrenia are the result of an imbalance between inhibition and excitation in the brain. In addition to these internal factors, we have seen that drugs and activities can create aberrant neurotransmission with resulting abnormal behavior.

This brings us back to the baby's warm milk opmex. The act of eating or drinking pleasant-tasting food, such as warm milk, releases endorphins, which decrease the release of excitatory neurotransmitters. This results in a decreased rate of neurotransmission in the excitatory pathways, which soothes and calms the infant. Warm milk also contains another ingredient that brings about a soothing effect on the central nervous system. This substance is the amino acid tryptophan, which enters the brain through the blood-brain barrier. Once inside the brain, tryptophan is converted to serotonin, which also decreases excitatory neurotransmission. This contributes to the overall relaxing effect of the warm milk and helps the baby to sleep. Hence the old folklore of drinking warm milk to aid sleep is valid in terms of modern brain chemistry.

An empirical relationship between eating and endorphins has recently been demonstrated by Daniel Porte at the University of Washington. She showed that in some cases, giving endorphins to laboratory animals caused them to eat uncontrollably. In an experiment at the National Institute of Mental Health, Martin Cohen showed that administration of naloxone, a drug that blocks endorphin action, caused a 28 percent decrease in the amount of food consumed by volunteers who were furnished with ample amounts of their favorite foods.

Endorphins and enkephalins have been referred to as the "keys to paradise." However, many people who seek paradise through drugs or activities soon find that heaven transforms into a living hell of uncontrolled craving. How can the pleasures associated with eating, opiates, or watching television turn into such a Dr. Jekyll and Mr. Hyde experience?

We have briefly described how the brain contains regulatory mechanisms that maintain a relatively constant level of neurotransmission. Externally induced variations in this level, which account for our mood swings, bring about a counterreaction as the brain attempts to return neurotransmission to a normal level. This regulatory mechanism is essential for general health maintenance and is, in fact, necessary for our very survival. An overproduction of endorphin or excessive opiate ingestion would lower neurotransmission and pain perception to the point at which slowed physical reactions could endanger our lives. Placing your hand on a hot stove, for example, would result in serious injury were it not for the phenomenon of pain. Therefore, it is essential that the brain have a mechanism to maintain a "normal" level of neurotransmission. This natural, life-sustaining, internal regulatory mechanism accounts for dependence, tolerance, and addiction.

Dependence means that after repeated exposure to an event that decreases neuronal activity in the brain, a person leans on that experience in order to feel adjusted or normal. The rate at which one becomes dependent is variable, depending upon the type of experience, amount of exposure, and individual differences among users. All things being equal, a user can become dependent on morphine, using a typical dose once daily, in about a week. With heroin, on the other hand, typical doses must be taken about twice daily for dependence to occur. At present, the parameters of dependence for activities such as watching TV and eating mood-modifying foods are not known. When prolonged participation in behaviors associated with the ingestion of opiates or release of endorphins is abruptly discontinued, a characteristic disturbance known as withdrawal or abstinence syndrome begins to occur. The phenomenon of dependence is best understood as a biochemical rather than psychological process. Even addicted animals who have had the thinking portions of their brains removed, and babies who have inherited opiate dependence from their mothers, will experience acute physical symptoms, without conscious awareness.

The amount of subjective distress that occurs during withdrawal, however, is very much a function of the user's beliefs and life circumstance. Those who insist, for example, that they will endure incredible torment if they discontinue heroin will undoubtedly report acute psychological and physical suffering. Part of being "hooked" on a satiation experience—whether shooting heroin or listening to classical music—is the phenomenon of self-identification as an addict. The belief, "I need to have (opium, TV, or grandmother's chicken soup)," is no doubt influenced by the biological fact of dependence, but the intensity of subjectively perceived pain is very much influenced by psychology and circumstance.

Tolerance of the opiate-mediated experience develops much more slowly than dependence. The tolerant heroin addict can safely ingest a far greater amount of opium than the nonaddict, for whom a large dose might cause coma or death from respiratory inhibition. Tolerant satiation addicts can avoid becoming ill or physically distressed by maintaining a constant dose of their preferred drug or activity. Feeling high is a different story. To achieve pleasurable sensations, the addict constantly must increase the frequency or amount of opmex. In the lingo of the street, "He can stay normal, but he can't get high." Some addicts continue their habits for months or years, resigned to the fact that they will no longer get high. As soon as withdrawal symptoms begin, they will administer an accustomed dose and take pleasure in simply having achieved relief from the sufferings of abstinence.

Under increased internal or external stress, however, staying normal is not enough; the addict once again craves the feeling of getting high. At this point he or she must again increase his opmex, either in frequency or quantity. A common experience among addicts when they can do nothing more than stay normal is to construct their lives around "getting straight." They self-impose a period of abstinence, which usually involves an initial period of acute withdrawal and at least a few weeks of recuperative discomfort. Tolerance is lowered and the satiation addict may once again experience the precious high, which, for many, stands out as the most salient experience of their lives.

Patients in the Street

A complicating feature of the drug scene is that addicts often appear to have more practical information about the effects of mind-altering drugs than the physicians who prescribe them. An old adage is: "The doctor who treats himself has a fool for a patient." Deep in the gutter of the treatment community, a group of patients prescribe and administer their own medications. Through rumor and experimentation, they discover an illegal, mood-affecting drug, which appears to subdue, magically, undesired emotions. Through trial and error and various social influences, the novice learns to procure a host of substances that are known among street users to influence or improve painful emotions. Illicit drugs serve as prosthetic devices that temporarily reduce discomfort from feelings such as anxiety, rage, hurt, shame, and loneliness. Addicts select their drugs of choice based on an interaction between street mythology, the chemical action of the drug, and the nature of their particular emotional disturbance.

This perspective, known in scientific literature as the "self-medication hypothesis," has been recently delineated in *The American Journal of Psychiatry* by Edward J. Khantzian, a psychiatrist affiliated with Harvard Medical School. On the basis of observations and interviews with hundreds of addicts, Khantzian is convinced that opiate users are particularly compelled by the antiaggression and anti-rage action of narcotic drugs. He reports that addicts' life histories reveal prolonged periods of uncontrolled rage and anger, replete with horrifying accounts of violent episodes that predate their drug experiences. The addicts themselves were often victims of unusual levels of aggression in their family, their community, or both. During treatment, opiate-dependent patients repeatedly explained their compulsion for narcotics on the basis of how it made them feel in relation to their anger. They frequently used such terms as mellow, soothed, normal, calm, and relaxed. Khantzian also reported his observation that patients who often appear hyperaggressive, restless, or even assaultive in group therapy become more relaxed as they adjust to a therapeutic dose of methadone. Many patients seem to switch to heroin as their drug of choice when they repeatedly experience uncontrolled fits of violence or rage under the influence of alcohol, sedatives, amphetamines, or cocaine.

Philip is an example of an addict who switched his drug of choice from cocaine to heroin after discovering heroin's soothing and antiaggression effects. When interviewed, he was twenty-nine years old and he had been in drug-free treatment for nearly fourteen months. He began smoking pot and using amphetamines at thirteen years of age and maintained a $100–$200 per day heroin habit for five years, prior to his conviction and mandatory treatment. He supported his addiction primarily through the sale of marijuana and cocaine. In lieu of prison, Philip opted for placement at a residential drug treatment center after having been arrested for possession and attempted sale of ten grams of cocaine.

In his fourteen-year history of experimentation, use, addiction, and sale, Philip became extremely knowledgeable about the commodities and characters in the drug world. In the following discussion we shall "inject" Philip's understanding of his progression from heroin use to addiction with an explanation of the biochemical substratum of his progressively disturbed functioning. His case illustrates how an addict learns to regulate his physiology through a well-planned self-medication schedule. His skill reflects a high level of street knowledge of how to cope with the medical issues of dependence, tolerance, and withdrawal.

Philip is the only male in a family of eight children. He felt "robbed" at the age of nine when his father suddenly died of a heart attack while serving in the military. During adolescence, in the mid-1960s, he lived in a large metropolitan area where illicit drugs were readily available. He started experimenting with marijuana and amphetamines at the age of thirteen. At the age of fifteen he began to sniff cocaine and would sell grams of coke to his friends and school contacts. He first sniffed heroin at seventeen, recalling that he was tricked by a friend who told him it was cocaine. He was initially angry because he had heard about the perils of heroin on the street. He ignored the warnings, however, as he enjoyed the soothing sensations brought on by the drug. He continued to use heroin, blocking from his mind any thoughts of becoming "strung out."

Through sniffing heroin, Philip brought about a temporary decrease in the rate of neurotransmission in his central nervous system, which was precisely the effect that he enjoyed. However, in a few hours the drug sensations wore off, and his level of neurotransmission returned to normal. Subjectively, he experienced a return to his customary state of loneliness and tense depression. He continued to episodically sniff heroin for the next six months, when the drug was available and when inner distress and anxiety seemed unbearable. Although the filling of the opiate receptor sites in the brain by the ingested heroin caused a corresponding decrease in neurotransmission, the brain would automatically initiate a self-regulatory process to reinstate normal neuronal activity. Enzymatic changes occurred in an attempt to accelerate neurotransmission to offset the decrease brought about by heroin.

When he first began to use heroin, Philip could be satisfied with an amount about the size of one match head. It would "nod him out" for about six hours. Between irregularly timed doses, which he ingested two to three times weekly, his functioning seemed unimpaired. In only a few hours the drug sensations seemed to wear off and Philip could conduct his business as usual. He was able to eat and sleep regularly. Yet the immediate soothing effects that he derived from ingesting heroin were slowly being challenged by longer lasting changes in the brain chemistry responsible for regulating neurotransmission. Although he continued to use heroin at the initial match-head level, the intensity of his feeling was being eroded constantly by these insidious chemical changes that attempted to return his neurotransmission to a "normal" level.

After several weeks Philip noticed that he needed an increased amount of heroin to feel high. His required dose began to swell, to two, three, four, and still more match heads. Even at higher doses, however, he began to recognize that he wasn't getting the same feeling of pleasure. He recalled that after about six months of frequent and escalating use, he woke up one morning "feeling shitty." Philip had become physically dependent on heroin and required it regularly just to feel normal. He was getting strung out.

About two months later, he allowed a crony to "geez" him with a hypodermic syringe. "Hitting-up" was like nothing he had ever experienced before. To Philip, it was "heaven . . . like everything in the world had just been taken care of." He quickly learned to self-administer the drug and began to use it on a daily basis. Without heroin he would anticipate becoming sick. During this period his thoughts became obsessed with when and how he was going to "do some stuff." He would attribute all unpleasant bodily sensations, even hunger, to the absence of heroin in his system. His body weight decreased from 150 to 118 pounds. When heroin wasn't readily available, Philip would use prescription narcotics. He knew a physician who, in exchange for cocaine, would allow him to browse through the PDR (*Physician's Desk Reference*) and pick out any drug he wanted. He would select Dilaudid to avoid being sick, but always preferred heroin, which didn't seem to have negative side effects like headaches or ringing in his ears. At this point in his addictive "career," his entire life began to revolve around not being sick. His tolerance was so great that he could get normal, but he couldn't get high. Philip was deeply entrenched in the maintenance phase of his habit. The enzyme levels in his brain had changed so drastically due to his drug habit that even large doses could not counteract the brain's unwillingness to accept repeated attempts to alter "normal" neurotransmission.

After two to three years of regular use, Philip recalls having to wake up every three or four or five hours to inject himself with heroin. When he was without the drug for more than eight hours, his withdrawal symptoms would become very severe. He remembers his skin becoming blotchy; breaking out in cold sweats; shaking all over; getting cramps in his legs, back and stomach; and sometimes vomiting. In the absence of the drug, his neurotransmission did not return to normal, but became accelerated because of the semipermanent enzymatic changes brought about to offset his drug-induced attempts to lower neurotransmission. Somehow he would manage to get some heroin from a spoon into a syringe, then into a vein. Within about thirty seconds, he felt as if heroin were "filling all the gaps" in his body. Sometimes he would "jack-off" with the needle by pulling up blood into the syringe and then injecting it back into his vein. For the most part Philip found this practice repulsive and he did it infrequently. He remembered a female addict, however, who would sit, sometimes for twenty minutes, "pulling it up in the syringe . . . in and out."

During the lengthy maintenance period, Philip was nearly always obsessed with the functioning of his body. He recalls being regularly constipated from the effect of heroin on his digestive system. When several days passed without a bowel movement, Philip would interpret being constipated as "something wrong." His remedy was based on practical experience with a range of pharmacological effects. He would sit on the toilet, get some cocaine, then "hit it up." By repeating this procedure at least two times per week, Philip was able to "clean himself out."

After five years of living in this hellish state, Philip was ordered by the court to choose between jail and treatment for his drug problem at a therapeutic community (TC). Therapeutic Communities of America Inc. is a 120-member consortium that represents over 12,000 drug-treatment slots throughout the United States. Philip, like thousands of other junkies who have faced prosecution for drug-related offenses, opted for treatment rather than incarceration.

The theory underlying the traditional TC views drug addiction as a symptom of weakness in character, usually associated with alienating childhood circumstances. The addict chronically avoids dealing with conflict by withdrawing into a protective shell. This self-destructive pattern is interpreted as a response to feelings of incompetence and inadequacy. While using drugs to escape from stress, the addict denies personal problems and hides behind a criminal mask of toughness and superiority. Under the guise of sincere friendship and urgent need, addicts manipulate others to assist them in gratifying their infantile wishes.

The therapeutic community strives to provide a positive family atmosphere in which self-realization can occur. In a setting where drug inaccessability is strictly enforced, addicts are given the opportunity to clarify their values and goals in life. They are expected to move toward the development of a greater sense of moral responsibility. These opportunities are possible largely because the addict has been removed from the environmental stimuli—drug access, recurrent stress, and drug-using friends—that have surrounded and fostered his compulsive drug-using behavior. Correspondingly, TC graduates are expected to eliminate drug use, learn adaptive responses to stress, and readjust to the outside world as comfortable and responsible citizens.

The new resident's involvement in the TC program is strongly influenced by his experience during the initial or "prospect" phase of treatment. Philip was tempted to "jump" several times, but each time a senior resident talked to him, and he decided to stay. He remembers feeling completely disoriented during the beginning of treatment, when he was required to wear pajamas, work at menial chores, and sit in groups with fellow residents who "yelled and screamed their guts out at each other."

A hierarchical arrangement of leadership roles within the resident group is an integral part of the TC treatment approach. Residents take on increasing responsibility for operating the facility as they earn status as reliable and trustworthy members of the community. Conversely, verbal reprimands, role demotions, and increased work assignments are directed toward shaping and directing clients who have been observed to "slip."

As time went on Philip began to realize the importance of being in treatment. In the beginning he remembers feeling that it didn't matter how he acted; he would get accused, insulted, and questioned anyway. He felt "damned if you do, damned if you don't." He later understood that the purpose of frequent personal confrontations was to promote healthy responses to stress. "No matter what situation you were in; no matter what you tried to work out; you could always do it without stickin' a fucking needle in your arm." He remembers always being scrutinized and challenged by other members of the group about minute details of his demeanor. After several months of being constantly and thoroughly checked for his motives and attitudes he noticed that he began checking himself. "All of a sudden you caught yourself like, I'm doing something wrong. I shouldn't be doing this . . . you started to feel guilt. For once you started feeling happy. You noticed the birds singing and the sun's shining, and they're gonna let us out in the park to throw the football around."

When positive experiences such as these occur, the result is often enhanced self-esteem and a corresponding reduction in alienated-alienating behaviors. Philip now regards having "stuck out" the therapeutic community as the best decision of his life. He views the TC as the only place where a hard-core drug abuser can have a chance at getting his life together. He feels that in the course of treatment, he came across many people who helped him to "clean up," but the person he thanks most is himself. After fourteen months of complete abstinence, Philip reported that he reached a point where he made the decision to stay clean permanently. He realized that there was no way that he could continue doing heroin and be a normal human being, "and what I want to be is a normal human being, so I decided never to do it again."

Philip was hired as a counselor in the therapeutic community. He has been able to use his drug abuse and treatment experiences to guide others through the recovery process. At the time of this writing he has been entirely drug-free for six years.

Love Jones

Some addicts, particularly ghetto blacks, describe the insatiable craving for an elusive, unattainable, yet tantalizing lover as a "jones." A jones means that you've got a habit—a bad habit. Eventually, it might even do you in. As with uncontrolled dependence on heroin, no matter how much you get, you always want more. Like an infant who has been abandoned by its mother, you fall to pieces when "mamma" won't give you a "fix."

We can all catch a glimpse of ourselves in this grim, shadow side of romance. In proper proportion, the majestic clockwork of love—a synchronized blend of arousal, satiation, and fantasy—gives rise to

Figure 2–1. LOVE: PIÈCE DE RÉSISTANCE
OF THE ADDICTIONS.

life's most fulfilling experience. By nature, we become impassioned by elements that create or sustain life. But all too often the delicate process goes amiss; angels transform into devils, joy becomes jealousy, and heaven changes to hell. The nightmare of tormenting love is nothing but a miscarriage of our natural attraction toward people who evoke feelings of safety and pleasure. And so it is with all addictions; they are self-destructive outgrowths of adaptive, life-enhancing behaviors.

Indeed the phenomenon of infatuation is so powerful that some people compulsively attempt to recreate the experience, time and time again. In simplest terms, falling in love means thinking about another person all the time. In *Love and Limerence: The Experience of Being in Love*, Dorothy Tenov describes the symptoms of romantic love, which she collectively calls *limerence.* In limerence there is constant thought about one person, to the exclusion of all others, as a possible sex partner. When for some reason the prospective lover is not readily taken, romantic sentiments are further intensified. Obsessed suitors are able to achieve some degree of solace through rich and elaborate fantasies of lovemaking and courtship. If the "chosen" shows even the slightest inclination toward amorous reciprocation, feelings of elation are likely to follow. For a state of true limerence to exist, at least the potential for mating must exist, tinged with an umbra of uncertainty or doubt about the future of the relationship. Therefore, the answer to your question is, yes—do play "hard to get."

A brief excursion into the legend of St. Valentinus, the unofficial patron saint of romance, will illuminate Tenov's portrait of limerence. During his reign, the Roman Emperor Claudius Gothicus issued a decree that all Roman citizens must worship and pay homage to the twelve Roman gods. Valentinus is said to have been a man of learning and a devout Christian. He refused to forsake his religion and was arrested for disobedience, a crime analogous to treason and punishable by death. He was kept in prison until the date of his scheduled execution.

During his captivity, Valentinus met a beautiful young woman named Julia, who, like love itself, was completely blind. She was the daughter of the jailer, who recognized Valentinus as a learned man. He appealed to Valentinus to provide Julia with an education. She was delighted by Valentinus's teachings and cherished his accounts of nature and God. Julia confessed to Valentinus that each day she prayed for sight so that she could discover all the beauty that he had described. Valentinus is said to have assured her, "God does what is best for us only if we believe in Him." As the story goes, they sat quietly in prayer when suddenly the prison cell was enveloped by a brilliant white light. Julia's shrill voice pierced the air. "Valentinus, I can see," she shrieked, "I can see!"

On the eve of his death, Valentinus wrote a note to Julia urging her to remain close to God, even in his absence. He signed it, "From Your Valentine." His death sentence was carried out the next day, February 14, 270 A.D., near a gate that was named Porta Valentia, in his honor. He was later buried at what is now the Church of Praxedes in Rome. According to the legend, Julia planted a pink-blossomed almond tree near his grave, which has endured as a symbol of abiding love and affection.

Undoubtedly if Tenov, or her soul from a previous life, could have observed the legendary courtship, she would have concluded that indeed a strong state of limerence had occurred. Julia, the blind child of a watchful father, presumably had little opportunity for intimate male contact. Valentinus, even though he was a prisoner, was as close as she might ever come to an attainable lover. Admittedly, the probability of actualizing a sexual relationship was quite remote, but Julia's blindness might have intensified her romantic fantasies. Valentinus, knowing that he was to die, might well have telegraphed his natural desires to be wanted and loved. Of course the slightest hint from Valentinus that Julia's affection might be reciprocal would fuel her desire even more. Finally, the impending execution—particularly when we consider that Julia must have prayed for Valentinus' life, and on some level must have believed that God would spare him—most definitely meets Tenov's criterion of uncertainty regarding the future.

In some sense, the abrupt curtailment of Julia's short-lived romance was a blessing in disguise. Had Valentinus's sentence been commuted to life imprisonment, we can speculate that Julia would have inherited an even more difficult predicament. She would have continuously longed for the love of her life: the unattainable soul mate who helped her to see beauty in nature and affirmed her faith in God. The limitations of her childhood, coupled with the incomparable joy that she experienced with Valentinus, would etch a permanent imprint on her psyche. The fleeting moments of pleasure that she could extract from periodic visits to his cell would only enlarge her desire and prolong her suffering. Indiscretion would surface, as rationality would eventually dwindle to a mere silent observer. The folly of love would progressively erode her happiness, and eventually she would reach the same tortured state that many of us have endured—feeling desperately entrapped in love's crushing grip. Her behavior might well have been characterized by compulsion, loss of control, and continuation despite harmful consequences.

We can all identify with Julia's hypothetical plight. The combination of psychological need and social pressure "to be in love" is so great that we compulsively hang in, even after the game is over. In the short run, having a lover, no matter how problematic the relationship, serves to deflect the ubiquitous existential concern: "I am afraid to face my life and death alone." Objectively it is not whether two people stay together, but how they stay together, that separates genuine intimacy from love addiction. In a healthy love relationship both members strive to enrich and fulfill their lives through intense, mutual involvement. The love addict, despite a multitude of protestations to the contrary, cares little about the well-being of his or her partner. Romance junkies demand or beg for approval and affection, in an escalating cycle of disappointment and reprisal. Eventually harmful consequences result, including deterioration of work, social, or health functions. Alcohol, for example, may be used as a temporary stopgap for feelings of anger and despair. Unfortunately, most demoralized lovers who take refuge in the womb of spirits cannot honestly echo the famous boast attributed to W. C. Fields: "It was a woman who drove me to drink and I haven't had the decency to thank her."

Those who become addicted usually lack confidence in their ability to cope without some form of support, either real or imagined, from a love object. Donald Klein and Michael Liebowitz of the New York State Psychiatric Institute have proposed the term *hysteroid dysphoria*—a chronic and intense form of lovesickness—as a new category of mental disturbance. The disorder, which they have observed with surprising frequency in the course of their psychiatric practice, is characterized by depression, depletion of energy, and increased appetite in response to feelings of rejection. Conversely, when a romantic figure shows only minimal signs of approval, hysteroids react with increased energy and euphoria. People who suffer from this disturbance seem to fall in love more easily than others, and with less discretion. Their moods are marked by great sensitivity to even the slightest sign of disapproval, particularly from people in whom they have made romantic investments.

If you seem to have more than an academic interest in this syndrome, then perhaps you may be questioning your own propensity as a love addict. Fear not, nearly everyone has a similar reaction: "Is that me?" Don't forget, however, that you can have mild, moderate, or severe degrees of love dependence, as with addiction to food, drugs, or alcohol, and the symptoms are remarkably the same. If your relationship meets three or more of the criteria listed below, then love may be your Achilles heel.

Denial. Your friends and family say you're in a bad relationship, but you don't agree.

Immediacy. You require frequent emergency "pow-wows" with your lover in social and business situations.

Compulsion. You've broken up (seriously) at least twice, yet you always make up.

Loss of Control. You often feel powerless to control your feelings or behavior with regard to your lover.

Progression. Over time you suspect that your relationship has been on a downward spiral.

Withdrawal. You become depressed and experience physical disturbance (loss of sleep or altered eating and drinking patterns) when distanced from your lover.

It is love's unequaled capacity to profoundly influence each of the three pleasure planes—arousal, satiation, and fantasy—that qualifies it as the pièce de résistance among the addictions. While the human inclination toward intimate pairing affixes a territory within which mating can occur, it also holds the trigger to the most primitive impulses on earth. An instant of reflection on love's hearty contribution to homicide and suicide reminds us of the horrifying consequences of uncontrolled passion.

Poetry, the language of <u>love</u>, has been used for ages to express the agony and ecstasy of <u>life's most exalted emotion</u>. Untimely death, the ultimate consequence of a disturbance in nature, has been a central theme in love stories since time immemorial. In his classic poem, "Porphyria's Lover," Robert Browning encapsulates a man's compulsion to murder his sweetheart. Suddenly realizing the impermanence of Porphyria's affection, her lover is overwhelmed by an impulse to preserve forever his moment of ecstasy.

> Be sure I look'd up at her eyes
>   Happy and proud; at last I knew
> Porphyria worshipp'd me; surprise
>   Made my heart swell, and still it grew
>   While I debated what to do.
> That moment she was mine, mine, fair,
>   Perfectly pure and good: I found
> A thing to do, and all her hair
>   In one long yellow string I wound
>   Three times her little throat around,
> And strangled her. No pain felt she;
>   I am quite sure she felt no pain.

And few have ever savored a romantic rhyme without being touched by Edgar Allan Poe's masterpiece of morbid obsession, "Annabel Lee":

> For the moon never beams without bringing me dreams
>   Of the beautiful Annabel Lee,
> And the stars never rise but I feel the bright eyes
>   Of the beautiful Annabel Lee.
> And so, all the night-tide I lie down by the side
> Of my darling, my darling, my life, and my bride,
>   In her sepulcher there by the sea,
>   In her tomb by the sounding sea.

While the language of love is undoubtedly poetry, the language of the brain where love abides is chemistry. In this sense the language of love is chemistry. We respond chemically to other human beings. At the level of the neuron, our synapses are stirred by a lover's furtive glance. Love itself has become a legitimate target for neurochemical analysis. And why not? Through the use of positron-emission tomography (PET), scientists can now take pictures of the brain at work. It has been shown that emotion-laden events trigger the release of neurotransmitters that affect particular regions of the brain. In anxious people, for example, neurochemical activity increases in the right brain hemisphere. Altered neurotransmission in people with severe depression or schizophrenia has been the focus of intensive brain research for the past three decades. Some neuroscientists have now turned their attention to the study of positive feeling states.

According to Michael Liebowitz, author of *The Chemistry of Love*, a substance known to biochemists as phenylethylamine or PEA is released in the brain when we fall in love. The PEA molecule, which is considered an excitatory amine, bears striking structural similarity to the pharmaceutically manufactured stimulant amphetamine. Liebowitz regards the accelerated use of PEA, which occurs during infatuation, as the key to feelings of excitation, exhilaration, and euphoria.

An important similarity between PEA and amphetamine is that the benzene ring is basic to each of their molecular structures. The nineteenth-century German chemist Kekule, who dreamed about the chemical composition of benzene, may have been even more of a seer than anyone has yet realized. Kekule had spent many hours trying to discover the structure of the benzene molecule. One evening while dozing in front of a fire, in a half-dream state he imagined the leaping flames to be snakes which twisted and turned. Suddenly the snakes curled around and held onto their tails with their mouths. In this moment Kekule awoke and realized that he had visualized the structure of benzene, which is a closed carbon ring, as he had imagined the snakes to be. He is now credited with having discovered the chemical structure of benzene. Until now, however, Kekule's snake has evaded recognition as the same cunning serpent who tempted Eve to eat from the Tree of Knowledge. Indeed, there is the sense of having violated our own innocence as we trespass on the heretofore unspoiled Garden of Romance. We feel unprecedented shame as we reduce one of life's most exalted experiences to measurable fluctuations in brain chemistry.

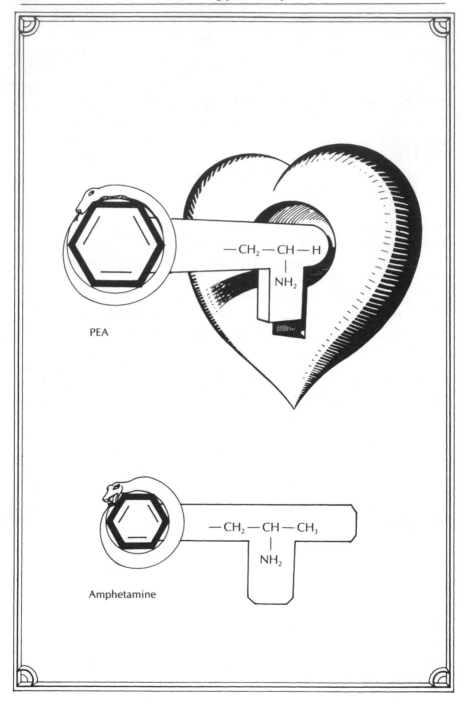

Figure 2–2. THE LOVE MOLECULE

Yet rapidly advancing brain science will not be slowed by the sentimental reigns of romance. No matter how mystical we perceive love to be, we are now aware of its neurochemical aspects. Indeed, remarkable biological parallels exist between pathological drug use and the unhealthy need for affection. Becoming dependent on love may be described as a dynamic process with two distinct biochemical phases: infatuation and attachment.

Infatuation is usually an experience of heightened energy and feelings of euphoria. According to Liebowitz, the initial period of psychosexual attraction produces increased concentrations of the neurotransmitter-like substance phenylethylamine. The brain responds to this chemical in much the same fashion that it would to amphetamine or cocaine; infatuated lovers seem to experience boundless energy, elation, and a remarkable sense of well-being. They have no problem in "painting the town red," then going to work, then going out the following night and doing it all over again.

After a short time, however, the speedy feeling appears to reach a maximum level, and lovers begin to recognize that their relationship is on a plateau. The romance remains exciting, yet the remarkable sensations of invigoration and euphoria appear to be dwindling. In chemical terms, the pleasure of falling in love is derived not from increased production of PEA, but rather from steady increases in the rate of PEA production. When PEA acceleration reaches zero, that is, when increments in the rate of chemical reward have stopped, the honeymoon is over.

At this juncture, one of two possible biochemical processes becomes operative: amphetamine-like withdrawal, or a shift to an endorphin-mediated relationship. Long-term lovers are able to make the transition from zooming around in the fast lane to enjoying cuddles and quiet evenings at home. But recall the chemistry of contentment. The prolonged love-swoon is, after all, an opiate-mediated experience. The addictive quality of romantic attachment becomes painfully obvious during periods of separation. As in the examples of Browning's "Porphyria's Lover" or Poe's "Annabel Lee," sudden or prolonged abstinence can cause paranoid thoughts and deranged conduct. Forlorn satiation types may become as pathetic as any heroin junkie who suddenly finds himself without a fix. Love addicts may survive for years, completely undetected, so long as there is a constant drug supply. However, they may cheat, lie, steal, or kill—even for a minimal dose—to avoid the dreaded pain of withdrawal.

Some people become so dependent on the rush of increased concentrations of PEA that they encounter severe depression, fatigue, and lethargy as their rate of excitatory neurotransmission begins to level off. People who compulsively seek new lovers are likely to be arousal types who require increasing levels of neuronal excitation to feel intact. They find it excruciatingly difficult to adjust to the endorphin phase of love. From a biological standpoint, the frequently held belief that sex is the most important part of a person's life is little more than a self-serving justification for poorly modulated excitatory biochemistry. While nature sets a biochemical predilection toward arousal, personal history directs the development of more or less successful styles of coping.

Patrick Carnes, author of *The Sexual Addiction*, portrays the promiscuous love addict as a man who spends his last few dollars for half an hour with a prostitute, even though his child needs a pair of shoes; or as a salesman who earnestly begins each day trying to peddle his wares, but frequents the local porno shop instead. The sex addict may also be a woman whose job as an intercity conference coordinator serves as a cover for bar and bed hopping in nearly every location she visits. Consistent with Liebowitz's theory of neurochemical adaptation, sex addicts report the need for continuous escalation in the intensity of their sexual encounters.

Peter recalls being severely reprimanded for thumb sucking as a small child. While in junior high school he discovered that masturbation while gazing at pictures of women could provide some relief from his feelings of anxiety and basic unattractiveness to girls. Throughout high school he felt awkward and isolated from his classmates. Compulsive masturbation became Peter's preferred means to cope with even the slightest degree of stress.

At the age of twenty-one he married the first girl he had sex with and experienced a short flight into health until his wife became pregnant. Shortly thereafter he began prowling the bars, searching for any female who could offer him novel stimulation. By the age of twenty-six he had his first adulterous affair and soon afterward had intercourse with a prostitute. He became immediately "hooked," and by the age of thirty-three he described himself as a compulsive "trick"—the term prostitutes use for their paying customers. At first Peter would always use protection against venereal disease, but as his addiction progressed he became more and more indiscreet about the time, place, and people with whom he would have sex.

After twelve years of marriage and three children, Peter felt so guilty about his compulsion for sexual excitation that he asked his wife for a divorce. He quickly remarried, however, wanting to believe that if he could only make an honest commitment to a different partner, he would then gain control over his sexual appetite. Within days after the wedding, Peter found himself back to masturbation, and within months he returned to cruising the streets and bars. At this point, even the thought of sex, or look at a girlie magazine, would ignite his compulsion to score. Finally he reached a state of "incomprehensible demoralization," as he began to have fantasies of suicide and was willing to become a pimp in order to have ready access to prostitutes.

At this time, Peter found his way to Alcoholics Anonymous. He began to work on the AA Twelve Steps, recognizing that sexaholism and alcoholism are virtually the same disease. He completed the first step when he admitted that he was powerless over lust—that his life had become unmanageable. He completed the second step when he slowly came to believe that a power greater than himself could restore him to sanity. With the help of AA, Peter began to feel an unprecedented release from sexual compulsion. He felt teachable for the first time since childhood. He became willing and committed to stop changing sex partners, even in fantasy.

After seventeen years of sexaholic sobriety, Peter now views his previous existence as a life of slavery, when he was emotionally and spiritually dead. He regards the years of compulsive searching as a period of running—running from others, himself, and God. He now believes that his continuing freedom is predicated on maintaining a spiritual program and never forgetting that although he has been set free, he will never be cured. He lives one day at a time, constantly subduing the wayward sexual impulse. He intends never again to allow himself even a "nip."

There comes a turning point in the life history of many cocaine abusers when they make a switch to opiate drugs. Peter's transition from a raging sexaholic to a person who has rediscovered himself, his family, and God may be a subtle version of changing from stimulant to narcotic drugs. Most of us can identify with Peter's experience, particularly during adolescence, when arousal seems to be the driving force for interpersonal attraction. Many of us also recognize that at the onset of most of our love relationships, we were far more excited and sexually active than we are now. Liebowitz's interpretation is extremely appealing when we try to understand the inevitable transition from a whirlwind romance to the more relaxing, but less exciting, posthoneymoon period.

Yet somehow, arousal and satiation—extremely important aspects of love—just don't seem to describe its spiritual quality. What of the times when you gaze into your lover's eyes and all of infinity opens before you; you feel one with your partner and at one with the world around you, as if time itself has stopped. Your aesthetic senses suddenly explode—art, nature, theater, and music become havens for your courtship.

It would seem that there must be yet another chemical mediator, even more potent than PEA or endorphin, to account for these transcendent experiences. In fact, Liebowitz postulates that there is "some additional neurochemical reaction . . . which may be similar to (although usually briefer than) whatever the psychedelic drugs do to our brains" that is responsible for the spiritual wonders of love. Liebowitz suspects that there is a psychedelic version of PEA that endows transcendent love with its mystical quality. As William Shakespeare wrote in Sonnet 29:

> Haply I think on thee,—and then my state,
> Like to the lark at break of day arising
> From sullen earth, sings hymns at heaven's gate;
>> For thy sweet love remember'd such wealth brings
>> That then I scorn to change my state with kings.

If Liebowitz is correct then perhaps there is a synthetic drug that mimics the action of the suspected neurochemical Aphrodite. It has long been recognized, and particularly underscored by the discovery of endorphin, that addictive drugs are structurally quite similar to naturally occurring brain chemicals. Is there a man-made drug that opens the combination to the vault of mystical love?

On the street, they call it Ecstasy; in the laboratory it is properly referred to as 3,4-methylenedioxymethamphetamine, or MDMA. Advocates claim that it produces a pleasant two- to four-hour high that dissolves anxiety, makes people less defensive, enhances communication and insight, and leaves people more emotionally open. MDMA is less potent and differs only slightly in chemical structure from the psychedelic MDA, known in the 60s as the "love drug." Ecstasy seems to combine some of the hallucinogenic effects of mescaline with the stimulant effects of amphetamine. Those who endorse Ecstasy cite hundreds of case histories where MDMA was used as a tool in psychotherapy by releasing patients from the fear of emotional injury.

Opponents believe that the drug effects are unpredictable. Increased blood pressure, sweating, blurred vision, involuntary teeth clenching, and biting of the inside of the cheek have been observed during experimental trials. Psychopharmacologists Lewis Seiden and Charles Schuster of the University of Chicago have reported alarmingly low levels of serotonin (a neurotransmitter involved in the regulation of sex, aggression, sleep, and mood) after analyzing data from their studies conducted on rats and guinea pigs. Ronald H. Siegel, a psychopharmacologist at UCLA, finds that under high doses people may become insane rather than ecstatic; some may assume a fetal position for several days. The dose levels that Seiden and Schuster have associated with brain damage are only two to three times greater than the average street dose. Meanwhile, U.S. officials claim that drug treatment programs around the United States have reported numerous cases of psychotic episodes among MDMA users. The Drug Enforcement Agency views Ecstasy as a rapidly spreading recreational drug that can cause psychosis and permanent brain damage. In June 1985 Ecstasy was banned from medical use via a one-year emergency Schedule I controlled-substance classification, the same classification used for heroin and LSD.

Basement chemists, however, scoff at the government's effort to abolish MDMA. Current drug laws define drugs by their precise chemical structure. "Designer drugs"—compounds that preserve the psychoactive quality of the drugs but slightly alter their molecular structures—have become devious ways to skirt the law.

On counterpoint, Congress is now considering legislation that would prohibit the manufacture and distribution of drugs similar to those previously placed on Schedule I. All this seems terribly déjà vu. Wasn't love already criminalized in *1984* by George Orwell's Big Brother?

The Great Psychiatric Tavern

Alcohol and not the dog is man's best friend.
                                                    — W. C. Fields

The bar serves an important function as a center for relaxation, interpersonal encounters, and casual business negotiations. However, the role of the tavern as an informal psychiatric clinic that ministers to a sizable population of emotionally disturbed clients remains largely unrecognized. Indeed, a striking parallel exists between the omnipotent psychiatrist and the bartender, who also controls a multitude of psychoactive substances. This tavern "doctor" conducts individual and group treatments, assisted by a team of "nursing" waitresses and other support staff. Recreational devices include music, dancing, darts, billiards, TV, and video games, geared toward a broad spectrum of consumer interests and needs.

"Treatment taverns" exist in most societies, cutting across ethnic, gender, social, and religious boundaries. Affluent clients enjoy therapeutic atmospheres that are aesthetically designed and immaculately maintained. In establishments such as these, "medicines" are fashionably delivered,' meeting rooms are filled with artistic splendor, and meals are served with elegance and charm. In more pedestrian locations, "bar-patients" are coaxed to achieve optimal dose levels through seductive devices such as "Happy Hour" and "Buy Backs." "Prescriptions" are self-selected on the basis of the customer's perceived state of psychological need. Provocatively named concoctions like the Screaming Orgasm, Zombie, or B-52 invigorate erotic, masochistic, or power fantasies: "I am feeling a bit horny tonight . . . why not a Screaming Orgasm," and so on. Herds of bar-patients revel in orgiastic delight as they discuss forbidden desires in a highly permissive environment that encourages childish fantasy and adolescent bravado.

A most intriguing similarity between the mental hospital and the tavern is the illusion of familiar family setting. In atmospheres such as these, where childlike behavior is expected, staff become symbols of parental authority. The alluring waitress delivers the "milk of human kindness" in an atmosphere of heightened stimulation and increased vulnerability. Like the Oedipal boy, the incipient "bar-patient" naturally develops amorous feelings toward the seductive beauty who has triggered his sexual fantasies. He harbors secret wishes that the barman—who symbolizes his father—would either cease to exist or at least temporarily disappear. Yet sexual intimacy is forbidden. When the admixture of intoxication and libido erode his dignity, the love-struck patron is doomed to rejection. A hassled waitress will first avoid personal contact, then she will limit service availability. Disorderly conduct may ultimately be reported to that awesome symbol of patriarchal authority, the bartender. Anxiety caused by the fear of being rejected is conveniently blunted through increasing doses of alcohol. When sex or aggression become seriously unbridled, the waitress on orders from the chief may deliver the humiliating sentence, "You're cut off!" At this point, the emasculated patron is denied service for the duration of the evening. More reprehensible behavior, sometimes based on a cumulative record of misconduct, will ultimately result in the penalty of being "eighty-sixed," or thrown out. Customers such as these unwittingly recreate their own Oedipal disappointment; they experience unrequited love and reprisal at the hands of a surrogate mother and father.

Full-time inhabitants of the local pub learn to repress their sexual impulses, while forming amicable relationships with the barman and staff. Day into night, the "revolving door" tavernite looks toward the barkeeper for his attention and counsel. Increasingly, alcohol releases private fantasies of power and control; these serve in the struggle against deep-seated feelings of inadequacy and sexual unfulfillment. The bartender performs a dual role: he provides psychoactive medicine, enabling partial relief from suffering and rage; he also functions as a limited yet reliable source of human relatedness. He becomes a kind of adjunct personality through which the patron, bearing the load of a clouded sensorium, maintains some contact with the real world. The situation is described by Paul, a bartender employed by day as a psychiatric nurse:

> They could be looking directly at a mirror. Most bars have mirrors so you can look at your own reflection . . . I do it myself. I've sat down in bars when I'm by myself and I don't know the clientele or the barman, so I will stick to him—probably in fleeting moments—exactly as they do. And I can sit at the bar and look in the mirror, and let my mind wander . . . what they do when I'm on

the other side of the bar. And of course when you walk past there's an exchange of conversation, which can be short, depending on the business at the bar. When I walk away, you can see the customer drift off into fantasy. When I return, it gives him the opportunity to respond to his own thoughts. You might be a Christmas tree but he thinks that you are listening.

When a customer telegraphs potential danger, the bartender becomes a crucial source of control. He signals the inebriated patron to regain composure using facial expressions, direct commands, or outright discontinuance of service. Paul recounts his experience as a bar disciplinarian:

> There's the younger ones and the older ones. Some will tap on the bar. . . . One thing I can't stand is whistling. If someone whistles, I just say, "I'm not going to serve you—I'm not a dog." So I wait . . . if they whistle twice, I won't serve them for a little longer. And so there you see. They've got to behave or leave it as you please. You train the client to your own pace because you're in control. . . . You can always turn around and say, "You're the drunk and I'm sober."

As a last resort the barman may discontinue service and defer "treatment" until the following day. Like the unfortunate hostage who develops the so-called Stockholm Syndrome (feeling affection for one's captor), tavern regulars eventually feel gratitude and devotion toward the bartender. They murmur platitudes of respect, tipping lavishly, existing in drugged anticipation of a few sporadic moments with a longed-for father. Taxis run ambulance from hospital to home.

Despite the watchful eyes of saloon personnel, some patrons have a repeated history of acting out bizarre impulses while intoxicated. Roger, for example, is a successful young lawyer with a boyish face and contagious smile. He enjoys a lucrative corporate practice in a large metropolitan area. His favorite tavern is designed for the more impulse-ridden patron—waitresses allow physical contact, and the floor manager has been known to drink and share drugs with customers. One evening when Roger was feeling particularly alone—and very intoxicated—he quietly stood on the bar stool and urinated on the counter. He was immediately "cut off" and "eighty-sixed" from the premises.

Prior to the incident, Roger had a history of being unable to form intimate relationships with anyone but his mother. He was an only son, and when he was six years old his father died suddenly. Roger's mother assuaged her intense mourning by encouraging undue physical contact and a deepening emotional dependence. The actualization of Oedipal conquest left the young boy with a great sense of guilt. He had unconscious wishes for male domination, paternal reprisal, and ultimate forgiveness. As a young lawyer Roger symbolically performed penance by impressing the judge with his sincerity and hard work; as an intoxicated tavernite, he yearned for punishment and pardon from a substitute father—the bartender. His wish-fulfilling choreography was so adept that the sympathetic manager, who had been abandoned by his father early in life, reinstated Roger with full "treatment" privileges within six months of the dramatic incident.

For many like Roger, with acute sexual unrest, specialized sex "clinics" have become widely available. Clients may choose from a variety of centers, ranging from lively pick-up spots to rugged S & M hangouts. In the most prevalent type of sex-bar facility, heterosexual anxiety is handled routinely by a cadre of fantasy lovers. Striptease dancers perform erotic movements before a male audience who experience varying degrees of sexual frustration, confusion, and fear. Heavily medicated patrons witness female genitalia without their usual worries of inadequacy or rejection. While "ladies nights," featuring male strippers, are occasionally scheduled, sex-bars cater primarily to a male clientele. Aided by the sedative effects of alcohol, sex-bar patrons may indulge in any manner of erotic fantasy: they may whistle and shout, grimace and groan, even convey a dollar bill held between their teeth to the forbidden ecstasy beneath a dancer's G-string. Activities such as these allow for a kind of limited sexual pleasure, without the interpersonal demands, anxiety, guilt, and fear that have accompanied more authentic sexual encounters. Some men become so dependent on the sex-bar milieu that they journey to Patpong Road in Bangkok for proper case management. There, Thai strippers are readily solicited as surrogate lovers; they may be available for a given evening, as weekend partners, or even as long-term, live-in companions. A number of entrepreneurial travel agents have built surrogate lovers into special vacation packages.

Sex-bar recreation bears striking similarity to a widely used psychological strategy, known as sensate focus, for the treatment of sex-

ual dysfunction. The basic premise of this technique is that appre-
hension during intercourse interferes with sexual excitement and
pleasure. In the female, anxiety blocks the lubrication and swelling
phase; in the male, it suppresses erection. The goal of treatment is
to reduce tension and to restore confidence. This may be achieved
by promoting sexual enjoyment while minimizing the demands associated with arousal and intercourse. In the "pleasuring phase" of
sensate focus, couple are instructed to avoid having intercourse or
orgasm, while actively appreciating the erotic sensations of nonde-
mand sensuality.

But what of the multitude of alcoholic patrons who establish un-
wrinkled residence in the mainstay of the great psychiatric tavern,
the neighborhood bar? Eventually, "regulars" understand that continued attempts to seduce female employees are destined for failure
and possible reprisal. Erotic or hostile impulses toward parental figures gradually fade into feelings of affection and respect. Interpersonal relationships become increasingly centered on daily encounters
between regulars and staff. The function of the tavern begins to
merge with a traditional family unit. Cohorts of alcoholics develop
tight sibling bonds, while humor and wit become the currency for
fraternal affection and staff approval.

Below the surface image of happy-go-lucky rogue, the chronic
alcoholic suffers from profound feelings of worthlessness and despair. His equilibrium and composure depend on the firm guidance
and external support of a professional team of tavern personnel. The
bouncer (or hospital guard), who represents a visible extension of
paternal authority, must be vigilant and instantly available to quell
primitive expressions of lust or rage that may surface during the intoxicated state. Because machismo and stupor barely soften the horrendous bludgeons of self-perceived failure and ineptness, minor interpersonal confrontations can acquire the intensity of powerful
sibling rivalries—rivalries that may even explode into fits of homi-
cidal rage.

"Spoons" is a bar game that exemplifies the breakthrough of sa-
domasochism in the absence of adequate parental controls. A naive
patron enters a tavern patronized by a cohort of well-established
chronics. The newcomer becomes chatty, has a few drinks, and begins to enjoy a sparring camaraderie with several well-established

Figure 2–3. SPOONS

group members. Under the pretense of fair game, the initiate is invited to partake in a unique sporting competition known as "spoons." The newcomer is cajoled into watching a round and then having a go. Two of the regulars pull their bar stools to within a foot of one another. Each places the handle of a tablespoon solidly between his teeth with the ladle turned upright. To the crowd's seeming delight, one bows his head forward, inviting the other to serve him a crown. Amidst great oohs and hollers the attacker twists his head up, musters maximum torque, and delivers the first blow. Players alternate between banger and taker while the crowd roots them on. After several exchanges, the novice is invited to give it a try. "No harm can be done with a slight knock on the head. . . . The spoon is so close . . . go on, give it a try . . . see who hits harder." Aiming to please, to be a good sport, to belong to the group, the novice takes up the dare. What he fails to suspect is that when he courageously lowers his head, a conspiring group member—who has concealed his own spoon—will blast him unmercifully.

The scheme is unraveled as a member of the group mischievously directs the "pigeon" or "chump" to the sight of three spoons placed on the bar. "Now how many spoons do ya see there?" Amidst the cackles and squeals of an ecstatic crowd, it dawns on the victim that he has been duped. The newcomer's ability to handle humiliation and deceit will ultimately determine whether he is permitted to join the fellowship of chronics.

In a properly managed tavern, primitive expressions of anger or uncontrolled sexual breakthroughs rarely occur. The well-behaved chronic accepts medication beyond the point of disinhibition and impulsive breakthroughs; he welcomes sedation and stupor. Like the schizophrenic zombie who paces the ward, the intoxicated regular staggers from bar stool to toilet, and eventually goes home. The abrupt declaration of "Last call for alcohol" pierces through ethanol's cushion of befogged escape. The noise level soars as drunk conversations become louder and more intense. The vociferous flurry, just before closing, represents an emergent awareness that the sleep which follows will be on a pallet of loneliness, discomfort, and desperation. At the notorious Black Banana of Philadelphia, the announcement of last call is, "If you're not fucking the help, please leave."

The past decade has borne witness to a shift in the management policy of the Great Psychiatric Tavern. Traditionally, residents have been mostly male, skillfully maintained on massive doses of psychoactive substances. Women were sporadic visitors who, by and large, have had only limited access to the tavern as a means of coping with stress. Compared to men, females who abuse alcohol are reported to have higher levels of emotional distress. While male alcoholics are often described as impulse ridden and tending toward a criminal life-style, females tend to be perceived as more depressed, angry, anxious, lonely . . . and not as likable. Female alcoholics are often emotionally ill and tend to display more suicidal behavior than their male counterparts. Women are said to resort to alcohol and drugs from the desperation of trying to cope with guilt, anxiety, anger, and stress in their daily lives. Many experience difficulty in adhering to traditional role expectations concerning nurturance, motherhood, and sex. Increasingly, women rely on the tavern as a socially approved means of coping. The "white wine syndrome" has become an occupational hazard for executive females, particularly those between twenty-one and twenty-four years of age. Young professional women have discovered the "businessman's lunch," which may continue after work, through dinner, and on into the evening.

Meanwhile, fraternal excess, which has been encouraged for decades, appears to have reached a point of social disfavor. It appears that the alcohol industry has taken an "If you can't beat 'em, join 'em" stand on the issue of health promotion. It is common knowledge that heavy drinking can lead to liver, heart, and kidney problems and increase the risk of cancer. But, according to Robert Niven, director of the National Institute of Alcohol Abuse and Alcoholism, at least ten studies point toward a life-enhancing effect of drinking one or two drinks a day. Increasingly, wine or beer are considered better choices than hard liquor; and moderate, relaxed drinking is in vogue as a constructive means of reducing stress. The Cooler, a low-alcohol mixture of wine, fruit juice, and carbonated water, is consumed by a growing number of female tavernites.

Yet, the Great Psychiatric Tavern remains a bastion of male camaraderie and psychological support. Thousands of neighborhood saloons continue to function as informal mental health centers that provide short-term relief for a vast clientele of lonely and emotionally disturbed patrons. In the long run, multitudes of "regulars" exist in progressive deterioration as they become hopelessly entrenched in alcohol maintenance, a miscarried form of self-repair. Caring communities are challenged to develop alternative means for gratifying the needs that have been previously met through tavern life. Atmospheres must be created where surrogate family networks promote constructive measures for coping with internal conflict and social stress. The sense of adventure, spontaneity, relaxation, and human relatedness, all within reach at the pub, must somehow be preserved, without the unwanted consequences of repetitive intoxication.

Drinking Alone

Depending on how one defines alcoholism, it will afflict between 3 and 10 percent of all Americans at some time in their lives. Estimates of the number of females who abuse alcohol vary widely. Private physicians have estimated that among their patients, the ratio of male to female alcoholics is 3:1. In police custody, the ratio of men to women alcohol abusers is believed to be 11:1. There is consensus that because of harsh social judgments and persistently strong taboos, a larger number of female alcoholics remain undetected and untreated. Extrapolating from these calculations and considerations, we conservatively estimate that one million American women have serious problems with alcohol. The actual number may exceed this by as much as 100 percent.

In a study of sixty-nine female alcoholics, Wood and Duffy found that none were "happy drunks." Instead, alcohol was reported to release rage and reduce anxiety caused by failure to attain female role expectations. Unlike the sizable proportion of men who drink to induce power fantasies, women drink to diffuse a generalized sense of malaise. The dual challenge of succeeding as good mother and career woman often contributes to profound feelings of helplessness and despair.

The case history of Bernice is illustrative of a woman whose alcoholism is intimately connected with a deep sense of disappointment regarding her feminine role. Many years of hidden drinking eventually became visible through a series of emergency hospitalizations. Bernice is a middle-aged housewife who lives with her husband and twenty-three year-old son in the suburbs of a relatively large metropolitan area. During the past decade she has been hospitalized numerous times for alcoholism. When asked to describe the reasons for her recent relapse, Bernice began to reminisce about her daughter, who suffered from cerebral palsy and died more than ten years ago. She explained that the present hospitalization was precipitated by a full night of solitary drinking after she felt rejected and insulted by a female friend. Bernice called her psychiatrist and asked to be treated for alcohol-withdrawal symptoms. She said that she was frightened by the illusion of a young, dark-haired girl who appeared at the side of her bed. Bernice denied any connection between her vision of the young girl and her daughter. She felt that the underlying reason for her hospitalization was to escape from her husband's and son's anger and the feelings of loneliness she experienced at home.

Bernice was raised in a Midwestern city along with her sister, who is five years older. At the time of this writing her mother and father were still alive and in their seventies. In her early childhood Bernice remembered feeling coerced to conform to what she regarded as unreasonable parental expectations. Her earliest memory, for example, involves a trip to Baltimore, where she was required to change clothes in the woods in order to appear neat and tidy while visiting her grandmother. Her early relationship with her mother is described as "OK," but as she grew older the situation deteriorated dramatically. Bernice believes that her mother lived vicariously through her children. "She wanted me to do what *she* wanted to do." Her memory of her father is somewhat more pleasant. She describes him as an "intelligent, ingenious, fun-loving person . . . whose idealism causes him to be disappointed in people who don't live up to his standards." She also remembers being pressured by her father into living up to unreasonable expectations. "He wished more from me than could be expected of a young child."

During early childhood Bernice had only one female friend, a retarded foster child. Bernice was looked after by her sister, who resented having to take care of a child five years younger. Until Bernice was fifteen years old, they occupied the same bed. Bernice recalls the physical contact that she and her sister shared with displeasure, and her resentment at being ordered about. Teenage years are described as "ghastly," and most of her adolescent friendships were with boys. During this period her sister joined the military, and Bernice was left to care for her mother who suffered from epilepsy. She has horrible memories of her mother being stricken with grand mal seizures, sometimes becoming injured from losing consciousness, often screaming from lack of air. During this time the relationship between Bernice and her mother was most stressed. Bernice felt the brunt of her mother's frustrations. She remembers being told, "You're cold, abrupt, unaffectionate . . . contemptuous," and often confronted with her unattractiveness to men.

Bernice studied psychology in college, where she met her husband. Their courtship lasted about two years and was for the most part asexual. Her first sexual encounter occurred at about seventeen years of age although she did not have intercourse until sometime after. She had intercourse with her husband and one other man prior to marriage, and in 1950 became pregnant with her first child—out of wedlock. She and her husband went to great lengths to conceal the pregnancy from her parents until after they were married. The child was born brain-injured with a diagnosis of cerebral palsy.

At the time of hospitalization Bernice associated problem drinking with the agony of caring for her daughter, who developed allergies and asthma for which she required medication, to be administered in the early hours of the morning. Bernice would remain awake reading and drinking vodka until her daughter was sedated. She continued drinking after her daughter's death and believes that she had been alcoholic about three years prior to that.

Bernice became very disturbed at the thought of divorce. She recalled her doctor's warning that "he may have to divorce you in order to get you to stop drinking." She expressed the belief that her husband and son were angry at her for her drinking. She believed that she could use alcohol in order to avoid their anger. Her marriage was further complicated by Bernice's concern about not having reached orgasm for the past year. She wondered whether this was alcohol related. Another aspect of her problem was the loneliness that she experienced during her husband's absence from home. She resented his travel as a salesman: "I'd like to get a map of the U.S. someday and the first big black thumbtack would go into Chicago because that is where he goes most . . . then Santa Fe, Albuquerque and El Paso . . . "

At the onset of psychotherapy, Bernice had neither a strong sense of femininity nor a sufficient degree of positive self-regard. Early experiences with females were unusually stressful. One friend was mentally retarded, her mother was epileptic, and her sister appears to have been overly aggressive and demanding. Having internalized a rather strict set of parental expectations, Bernice was critical of others and of herself. The guilt engendered by a premarital pregnancy was considerable, but the feelings of worthlessness surrounding the mothering of her severely afflicted daughter were enormous. Bernice felt victimized, viewing herself at the mercy of circumstances and people—her parents, sister, and daughter in the past, and her friends, husband, and son in the present. Drinking was the vehicle through which she had been able to cope with her surroundings. She became as helpless as the people for whom she dedicated much of her life. At the same time she could use alcohol to escape from the guilt, loneliness, and anger that she was continuously plagued by. Like her mother, she was able to command assistance from those who cared about her.

In the course of psychotherapy Bernice began to assume personal responsibility for alcoholism, while she gradually revised the deep-seated view of herself as a victim. In-depth explorations of her feelings about femininity and motherhood were most profitable. In the context of a safe and caring relationship with a female therapist, she was able to disclose feelings of guilt, inadequacy, and failure. After one year of individual therapy, her husband participated with Bernice in the counseling process. The couple was helped to understand the relationship between Bernice's drinking and her husband's moods and absence. Although Bernice was the "identified patient," her husband also benefited from treatment. They made a commitment to spend more time together in mutually satisfying activities. Bernice and her therapist explored her relationship with her son, specifically how she would cope with separating—if and when he would leave home. She began to realize that her intellectual skills were sufficient to qualify her for interesting and rewarding employment; she set a long-term goal to transform from a woman feeling inadequate and victimized to one who accepts the challenge of having a comfortable and responsible life without the use of substances.

Of particular benefit to Bernice during treatment was her therapist's use of a relapse-prevention strategy developed by Alan Marlatt of the University of Washington in Seattle. By systematically reviewing and exploring with her therapist her typical thoughts and actions just before she began drinking, Bernice was able to understand the mental precipitants of previous relapses and to remain sober. The schematic diagram in figure 2-4 traces typical thoughts and behaviors that often culminate in addiction relapse. Although in this case the model was used as a tool to help Bernice to remain sober, it can be applied to the entire spectrum of addictive behaviors.

Hey, What's in This Stuff Anyway?

The Old Testament contains many references warning people of the dangers of alcohol. Proverbs 20:1 notes: "Wine is a mocker, strong drink a brawler; and whoever is led astray by it is not wise." An insightful description of the progressive effects of alcohol, including those on the central nervous system, is found in Proverbs 23:29–35.

> Who has woe? Who has sorrow? Who has strife? Who has complaining? Who has wounds without cause? Who has redness of eyes? Those who tarry long over wine, those who go to try mixed wine. Do not look at wine when it is red, when it sparkles in the cup and goes down smoothly. At the last it bites like a serpent, and

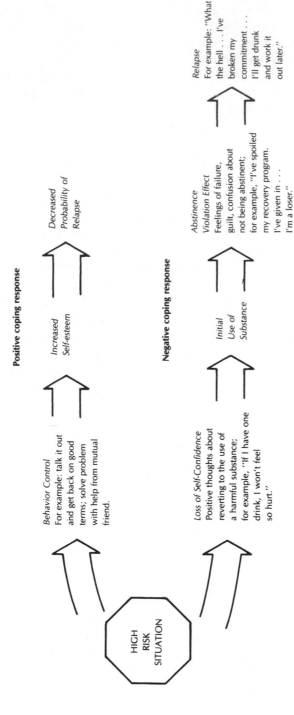

Figure 2–4. MODEL FOR RELAPSE PREVENTION

Adapted from G. A. Marlatt and J. R. Gordon, Determinants of relapse: Implications for the maintenance of behavior change. In *Behavioral medicine: Changing health lifestyles,* edited by P. Davidson. (New York: Brunner-Mazel, 1979).

stings like an adder. . . . You will be like one who lies down in the midst of the sea, like one who lies on the top of a mast. "They struck me," you will say, "but I was not hurt; they beat me, but I did not feel it. When shall I awake? I will seek another drink."

The Old Testament also clearly describes the pleasure associated with wine; a pleasure which we know today can lead to tolerance, dependence, and addiction: "Shall I leave my wine which cheers gods and men?" (Judges 9:13), and "Mark when Amnon's heart is merry with wine . . . " (2 Samuel 13:28). The writers of the Old Testament clearly understood alcohol's double-edged sword, which is the double edge of the addictive process in general. That is, it serves while it destroys.

This dual message, condemning excess while condoning controlled use, is prevalent in most countries today. Our society is bombarded by advertisements extolling the glamour and excitement of drinking, yet the unfortunate person who drinks to the point of drunkenness is looked upon with a great deal of disgust. This dichotomy was also prevalent in the Aztec city of Tenochtitlán, where drinking pulque (a very strong alcoholic beverage) was a common practice, but public drunkenness was punishable by death.

Today alcohol is clearly the most widely used substitute for our thumb. In moderation it appears to have a beneficial effect on not only the emotions but perhaps health as well. It is when the user crosses over the fine line where use turns to abuse that the devastation that destroys millions of lives and costs billions of dollars begins to occur.

Everyone has heard the statement: "Alcohol is a depressant." Why then would anyone drink? Most people drink to feel better, to be more sociable and less depressed, not more so. Indeed as we watch people who come to a cocktail party, we observe that after the first several drinks they seem to loosen up and become more relaxed. Rather than depressed, they appear to be more enthusiastic, animated, and expressive. As the party continues, and some guests are putting away their fifth or sixth drink, we notice a change in their behavior. Their speech becomes slurred and they seem unable to comprehend simple concepts. If they drive, they are more likely to become involved in accidents because of delayed reaction time. Continued drinking may result in loss of consciousness.

How can we explain this apparent contradictory effect: initial excitation of the nervous system followed by depression? To understand this dichotomy we need to go back once more to the neuronal pathways in the central nervous system. As we have mentioned, the central nervous system has many checks and balances to prevent either chronic overstimulation or understimulation. One of these regulators, which maintains a baseline level of neurotransmission, is the existence of two types of synaptic connection. One is the excitatory pathway which, as we discussed, is responsible for increasing the state of arousal. Obviously there must be some mechanism to regulate these excitatory connections, or everyone would be in a chronic state of hyperactivity. A second type of neuronal connection is inhibitory, serving as a check on neuronal overexcitation. When alcohol is ingested, the inhibitory synapses are depressed *first*. Excitation momentarily predominates, and the drinker feels exhilaration rather than depression. As drinking continues, however, the excitatory pathway is also depressed. The stupor and slowed reaction time of excessive drinking sets in.

How does this seemingly benign beverage become the self-inflicted poison par excellence? In some ways the answer may lie in the fact that not everyone who drinks, even excessively, becomes addicted. Until recently alcoholism was regarded as a sign of a weak and/or vicious personality. Consider these words from an 1897 temperance lecture, describing the behavior of someone under the influence of alcohol: "But see that fiend incarnate with loathsome breath and oath stained lips as he stumbles across the room to drag the dying wife from her last repose!"

The contemporary perspective held by the National Council on Alcoholism, Alcoholics Anonymous, and the American Medical Association is quite different. Alcoholism is regarded as a chronic and potentially fatal disease that pays little respect to strength or weakness of character. The disease concept, which has been invoked for other addictions as well, holds that addicts have inherited maladaptive biochemical responses to certain chemicals. Faulty genes lead to the production of faulty enzymes, which disturb the normal metabolism of alcohol. This in turn results in a pathological response to the drug. The most convincing research on genetic factors on alcoholism comes from adoption studies. There is considerable evidence that regardless of environmental influences the biological children of alcoholics—even when their adoptive parents abstain from drinking—are more likely to become alcoholics than are the children of nonalcoholics. The child of two alcoholic parents is reported to have a four times greater likelihood of becoming alcoholic than is average.

To understand the theory of inherited alcoholism, consider the pathway by which alcohol is metabolized in the liver (figure 2–5). In the first step alcohol (ethanol) is converted to acetaldehyde using an enzyme called alcohol dehydrogenase (ADH). This conversion requires a coenzyme, nicotinamide adenine denucleotide (NAD+), which will be important to remember when we discuss the addictive nature of alcohol. In the second step, acetaldehyde is then changed to acetate and finally to carbon dioxide and water. The conversion of acetaldehyde to acetate requires another enzyme known as aldehyde dehydrogenase (ALDH), as well as the same coenzyme (NAD+) used in the initial conversion of alcohol to acetaldehyde.

Since enzymes (in this case ADH and ALDH) are involved in the metabolism of alcohol, any alteration in their level, or the absence of these enzymes, would change the rate at which alcohol is metabolized. Further, since the formation of enzymes in the body ultimately depends on our genetic makeup, the alcoholic's known inappropriate response to alcohol may be explained on the basis of inherited irregularities of the enzymes ADH, ALDH, or both, which are necessary for the normal metabolism of alcohol. Supporting this theory are a number of studies that show that certain individuals are at genetic risk to alcoholism because they metabolize alcohol differently than others.

Mark Schuckit of the University of California in San Diego has shown that the blood acetaldehyde level is higher in those with a family history of alcoholism. He has further shown that acetaldehyde is converted into acetate at about half the rate in confirmed alcoholics as in nonalcoholics. This explains the well-known fact that acetaldehyde accumulates in alcoholics. Schuckit has also demonstrated that this metabolic abnormality may exist even before heavy drinking. That is, the children of alcoholics who, before the experiment, had never ingested alcohol, were unable to convert acetaldehyde to acetate at the normal rate. On a behavioral level, Schuckit has observed that people with family histories of alcoholism

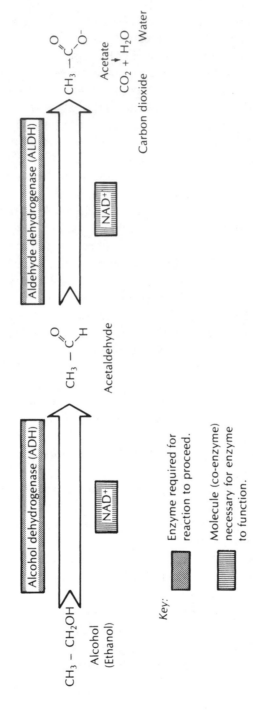

Figure 2–5. METABOLISM OF ALCOHOL

sway less after three or four drinks than those without familial alcoholism. This may be a simple test to detect a genetic predisposition to alcoholism.

There is reason to believe that genetic influences, similar to the ones identified for alcoholism, may be found for other compulsive behaviors as well. Allan Collins of the Institute for Behavior Genetics at the University of Colorado reports that, although fewer studies have been done, there also appears to be a genetic contribution to cigarette addiction.

Earlier in this chapter we described how atypical patterns of enzyme distribution cause addicts to react differently than other people to precisely the same stimuli—drugs or other. Altered enzymatic responses, however, need not always have a genetic origin. Chronic ingestion of alcohol, for example, can cause metabolic deficiencies that are characteristic of alcoholism. This does not negate the concept of addictive disease, since many illnesses related to a genetic predisposition can also be caused by environmental and behavioral factors. Diabetes, for example, is a disease whether it is inherited or environmentally induced. When the alcoholic faces potentially fatal consequences because of his or her uncontrolled behavior, altered biochemical processes may well be demanding to be treated as a disease.

The concept of alcoholism as a disease, whether environmentally or genetically induced, encourages us to examine the nature of alcohol's addicting power. Often we hear the comment that something (drug or other) is psychologically and not physiologically addicting. Such a distinction is artificial and has no place in a sophisticated discussion on addiction. The distinction implies that the central nervous system (psychological addiction) is somehow separate from the rest of the body's functions (physiological addiction)—sheer nonsense.

Many theories attempt to explain the addictive quality of alcohol. A cursory look at the molecular structures of the substances that are most addicting leaves one with the feeling that alcohol does not belong in this group. As seen in figure 2-6, alcohol is the only substance that does not contain the element nitrogen (indicated as N in the formulas). In addition, alcohol is by far the smallest of the molecules in figure 2-6. Generally one thinks of addicting molecules as those of moderate size (for example, cocaine) that contain nitrogen.

CH$_3$ – CH$_2$ – OH

Alcohol

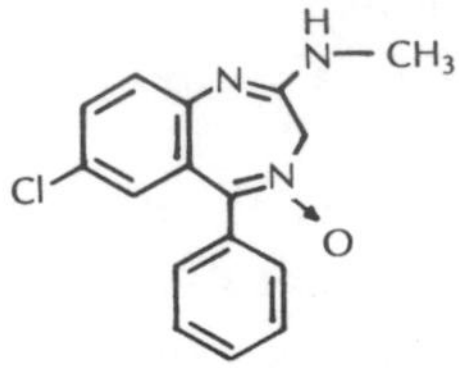

Chlordiazepoxide (Librium)

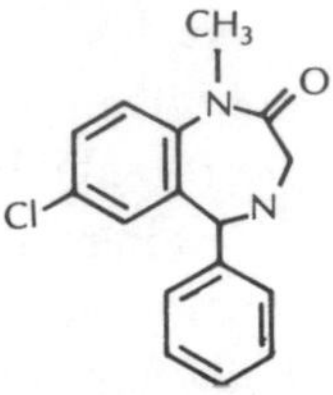

Diazepam (Valium)

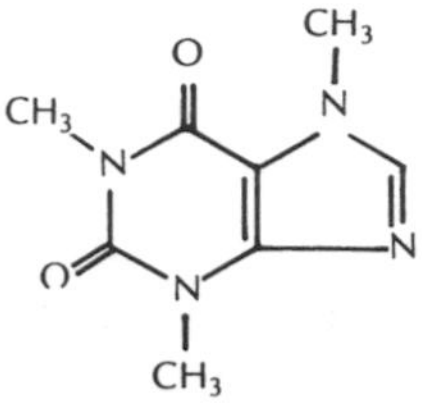

Caffeine

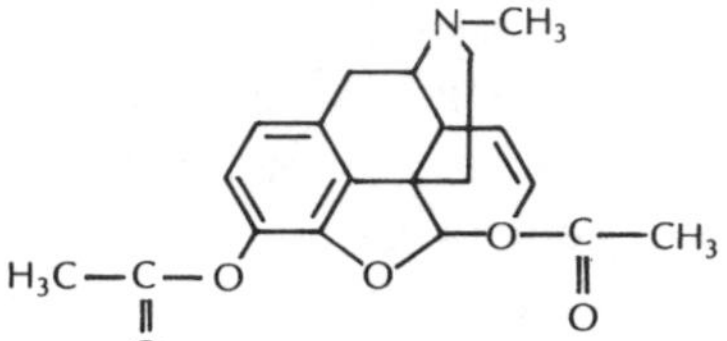

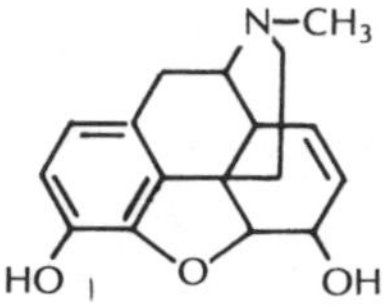

Morphine

Heroin

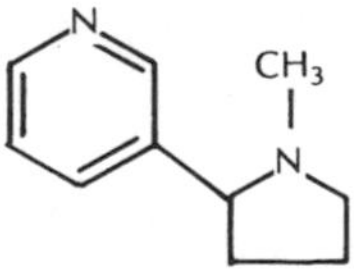

Nicotine

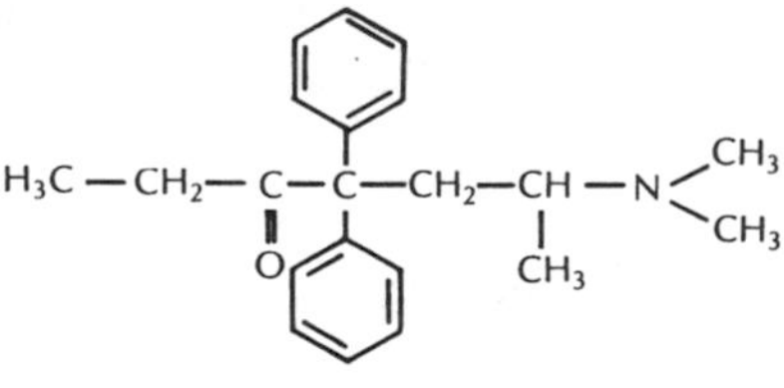

Methadone

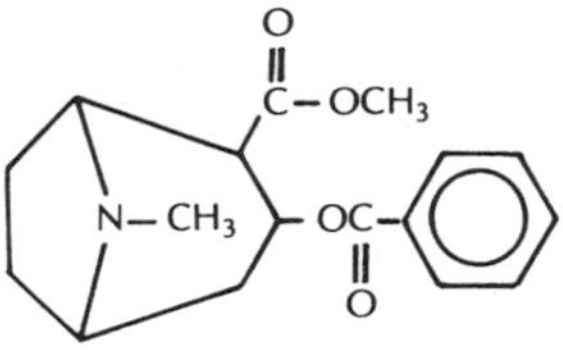

Cocaine

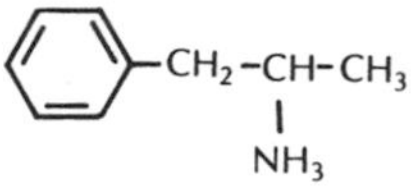

Amphetamine

Figure 2–6. CHEMICAL STRUCTURES OF THE MIND BENDERS

Since alcohol is much smaller than the other addicting molecules and contains no nitrogen, scientists have looked to other factors that contribute to its addictive nature.

One of the most attractive theories of alcohol addiction is one that involves the neurotransmitters present in the central nervous system. To understand this theory, consider the fate of the neurotransmitter dopamine. The level of neurotransmitters is regulated by their composition and degradation within the central nervous system. This process is necessary to maintain a normal level of dopamine. Figure 2-7 illustrates the usual metabolic degradation of dopamine, with and without alcohol.

In the first step of degradation, dopamine (I) is converted to 3, 4-dihydroxyphenylacetaldehyde (II). Normally this substance is then converted to 3, 4-dihydroxyphenylacetate (III). Note that this last step requires the same coenzyme (NAD+) that is required to convert alcohol to acetaldehyde (see figure 2-5). Consider the person who is a heavy drinker. To metabolize large quantities of alcohol, that person requires large quantities of NAD+. Since NAD+ is not present in unlimited amounts in the body, it is possible that the heavy drinker may not have enough NAD+ to convert alcohol to acetaldehyde and also to convert dopamine to compound II (figure 2-7). If this is the case, the body must choose at which metabolic site to use the limited amount of NAD+. The choice is easy: alcohol is very toxic. To live, the body of a heavy drinker must metabolize and eliminate the alcohol as quickly as possible. Therefore, the available NAD+ is used in the removal of alcohol from the system. This could deplete the limited supply of NAD+ to the point at which compound II is not converted to compound III. When this occurs the normal reaction flow is blocked. Just as water backs up behind a dam, compound II backs up and becomes present in excess. This excess of compound II then begins to react with unconverted dopamine (I) to form another compound (IV), which has a structure somewhat similar to opiate narcotics (see morphine in figure 2-6).

According to Robert Myers at the University of North Carolina, this compound (IV), which is an example of a class of chemicals known as tetrahydroisoquinolines (THIQ), is believed to behave much as opiates or our own internal endorphins. We would expect the THIQ's to occupy the same neuronal receptor sites as those occupied by opiates. If this occurs then the same addictive processes

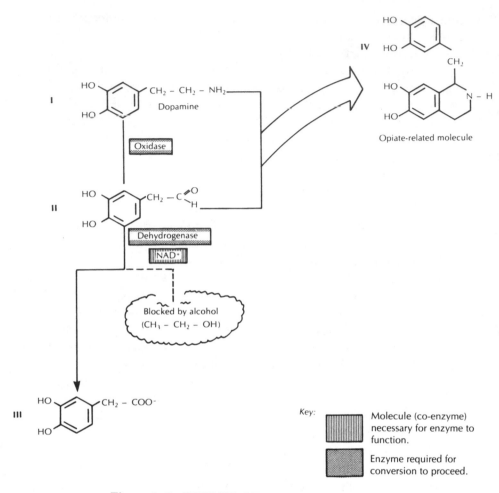

Figure 2–7. EFFECT OF ALCOHOL
ON DOPAMINE METABOLISM

discussed in chapter 1 for opiates would be operative for THIQ's. In
support of the THIQ theory, Myers created instant alcoholic rats by
injecting THIQ into their brains.

It should be noted that, as with most scientific theories, the
THIQ model is by no means the only explanation of alcohol addiction. Certainly alcohol addiction is not identical to opiate addiction.
One of many reasons for this difference is the powerful effect that
alcohol and its first metabolic product, acetaldehyde, have on many

cells in the body, including brain cells. Chronic alcohol ingestion is believed to permanently alter the membranes of nerve cells. This alteration itself could contribute to the addictive nature of alcohol. Very likely several factors together cause alcohol to be addicting. Whatever the cause, alcohol addiction remains the world's most serious drug problem.

Most alcoholics have difficulty in admitting that alcohol presents a serious problem in their lives. The questions in Table 2-1 are suggested for people who want to take an honest inventory of their current relationship with alcohol. The questions are designed to enhance self-awareness while minimizing guilt.

Table 2–1
AM I AN ALCOHOLIC?

If your answer is yes to more than two or three of these questions you are likely to be an alcoholic.

1. Do you occasionally drink heavily after a disappointment or a quarrel, or when the boss gives you a hard time?
2. When you have trouble or feel under pressure, do you always drink more heavily than usual?
3. Have you noticed that you are able to handle more liquor than you did when you were first drinking?
4. Did you ever wake up the "morning after" and discover that you could not remember part of the evening before, even though your friends tell you that you did not pass out?
5. When drinking with other people, do you try to have a few extra drinks when others will not know it?
6. Are there certain occasions when you feel uncomfortable if alcohol is not available?
7. Have you recently noticed that when you begin drinking you are in more of a hurry to get the first drink than you used to be?
8. Do you sometimes feel a little guilty about your drinking?
9. Are you secretly irritated when your family or friends discuss your drinking?
10. Have you recently noticed an increase in the frequency of your memory blackouts?

Table 2–1 *(Continued)*

11. Do you often find that you wish to continue drinking after your friends say they have had enough?

12. Do you usually have a reason for the occasions when you drink heavily?

13. When you are sober, do you often regret things you have done or said while drinking?

14. Have you tried switching brands or following different plans for controlling your drinking?

15. Have you often failed to keep promises you have made to yourself about controlling or cutting down on your drinking?

16. Have you tried to control your drinking by making a change in jobs, or moving to a new location?

17. Do you try to avoid family and close friends when you are drinking?

18. Are you having an increasing number of financial and work problems?

19. Do more people seem to be treating you unfairly without good reason?

20. Do you eat very little or irregularly when you are drinking?

21. Do you sometimes have the "shakes" in the morning and find that it helps to have a little drink?

22. Have you recently noticed that you cannot drink as much as you once did?

Note: Reprinted with permission from G. Vaillant, *The natural history of alcoholism* (Cambridge, Mass.: Harvard University Press, 1983) 296–97.

Eating Yourself Sick

Weight watching in the United States is a $5-billion-a-year industry. Nearly 90 percent of Americans believe that they are overweight, and more than 35 percent say they want to lose at least fifteen pounds. Each year the diet-conscious invest nearly $200 million in appetite-suppressing drugs containing caffeine and amphetamine-related compounds. They purchase diet and fitness guides with such regularity that at least one appears on the best-seller list each week; maintain a torrid love affair with low calorie foods; and join health spas and self-help groups like Weight Watchers or TOPS (Take Off Pounds Sensibly) by the millions. They commission an assortment of nutrition gurus including high-priced diet doctors, psychothera-pists, and religious fanatics who espouse the values of self-denial and impulse control.

Fortunately (or unfortunately depending on your viewpoint), there is a tailor-made diet for every taste. Eating fads range from high-protein to high-carbohydrate diets, with obligatory emphasis on vegetables, fruits, and high-fiber foods. Some regimens empha-size eating certain foods at fixed times of the day; others stress not mixing particular foods. Recommendations and admonitions are often contradictory and sometimes bizarre: no salt, no milk products, lots of milk products, fasting, eating as much as you like, fruit juice only, no fruit juice, no meat, all meat, drinking vinegar or your own urine (as in India)—you name it. A recent issue of a popular woman's magazine published a feature article extolling the practice of an ex-clusive rice diet. Devotees are promised weight loss of fifteen to twenty-five pounds within two weeks. It is the opinion of the au-thors of this book, both of whom have travelled widely in the Third World and observed the effects of rice-rich regimens, that this diet does indeed have the ability to produce skinny, even emaciated, people.

To be sure, the contemporary obsession with weight control—the svelte craze—is influenced by the whims of Hollywood and Madison Avenue. Among movie stars and models, thinness is not only fashionable but an occupational necessity. Since *Playboy* began publishing in 1953, centerfold models have become progessively slimmer. Those who pay little attention to fashion and fad—women from lower class backgrounds—are six times more likely to be obese than upper class women. Studies of immigrants and their descen-dants show that as new generations move up the socioeconomic scale, obesity, especially among females, declines. A simple extrap-olation from the body measurements of a child's Barbie doll reveals the tremendous social pressure toward slimness and form. As a sym-bol of femininity Barbie is not a harmless toy—not with a physique that translated into human terms measures 33-18-28½.

Anorexia nervosa and bulimia are closely related eating disor-ders, primarily found among middle and upper middle class women who appear to be victims of fad and fashion. The core symptom of anorexia nervosa is a relentless pursuit of excessive thinness. Diag-nostic criteria include self-imposed dieting; weight loss of at least 25 percent of the person's usual body weight; distorted perception of the body (she thinks she's too fat); cessation of menstruation; and no known medical illness to account for the weight loss. Approximately 50 percent of anorectics are also diagnosed as bulimic.

Bulimia is a chronic dieting disorder usually associated with binge eating. Bulimics may be emaciated, of average weight, grossly obese, or anywhere in between. Experts disagree as to whether bulimia and anorexia are part of the same disorder. In a 1981 study of 355 college students, researchers at Cornell Medical Center reported that 19 percent of the female population that was sampled experienced all the major symptoms of bulimia as described by the American Psychiatric Association. Other studies suggest that bulimia may affect as much as 10 percent of the entire college student population. Characteristically, an individual with bulimia consumes an excessive amount of food in a short period of time. Binges are usually planned and may last from several hours to several days. Food tends to be eaten very rapidly, gobbled rather than chewed. It is often very sweet and high in calories. Eating usually occurs in a clandestine manner, in which the eater experiences a sense of loss of control and an inability to stop. Binging varies in frequency between individuals, from several times a month to several times a day. Many people who indulge in bulimia, which literally means pathologically insatiable hunger, begin to induce vomiting to prevent weight gain and to decrease sensations of physical discomfort. The binge-purge cycle often includes the use of such cathartic devices as laxatives, suppositories, or enemas for rapid evacuation of the bowels. This pattern of dietary chaos is often accompanied by periods of intense, sometimes excessive, exercise, which may be interpreted as a form of penance for partaking of forbidden fruit.

Although there is much disagreement about the origins of these disorders, many personality researchers concur that women who suffer from either anorexia or bulimia (or both) may be struggling with deep-seated disappointment and frustration in relation to female role expectations. Ironically, when Karen Carpenter died in February 1982 as a result of anorexia nervosa, the very same newspapers and periodicals that covered the tragedy of her illness contained multiple ads featuring photographs of models who apeared to be thinner than normal. Can there by any doubt that these slender role models have a strong psychological influence on those who desire to be in the "now" generation, with its emphasis on youth, yoga, and reincarnation? The National Association of Anorexia Nervosa and Associated Disorders (ANAD) has set up chapters on college campuses in thirty-six states to help women who find themselves unable to manage their own nutritional needs.

Although being svelte and displaying one's aptitude for weight control is undoubtedly in vogue, large numbers of people are actually dangerously overweight. Obesity is generally defined as a body weight that exceeds the average by 20 percent. In the United States, it is estimated that somewhere between a quarter and a third of all adults fall into this category. As in other compulsive disorders, overeating usually leads to progressively impaired functioning. While the psychological and social complications are severe—interpersonal anxiety, job discrimination, sexual and social limitations—the physical dangers are even more frightening. Obese people are at increased risk for high blood pressure, heart disease, diabetes, back and joint problems, and respiratory disorders. Fat men have a higher incidence of certain cancers, including those of the colon, rectum, and prostate. Overweight women are at a greater risk for developing malignant tumors of the ovaries and uterine lining, and after menopause of the breasts. With stereotypic joviality, an obese woman whose blood pressure began to soar as her weight reached nearly 300 pounds recalls her doctor's warning: "If you don't lose weight, I'll put you in a coffin with a shoehorn."

On counterpoint, there is an alarmingly high incidence of dangerously underweight individuals in today's "slimness generation." In some cases dramatic weight loss may be attributed to a brain tumor, bowel disease, or glandular dysfunction. Recent studies, however, have identified figures as high as 1 percent of selected populations, primarily females, who for no known biological reason appear to be starving themselves—sometimes to death.

The person with an eating disorder faces a unique problem among addicts. Whether the symptom is obesity or self-induced emaciation, everyone must eat. Abstinence, the usual goal of treatment for compulsive disorders such as alcoholism, heroin addiction, and gambling, simply doesn't apply. Food addicts must learn to moderate the very stimuli that control their lives. The eating patterns of overweight people are unusual in several respects. Fat people tend to eat whenever they have the opportunity, even when they have just consumed substantial amounts of food. They tend to eat more and eat faster. While people of normal weight often lose their appetite when they become emotionally upset or aroused, fat people tend to eat more. Compulsive overeaters do not gorge themselves because they are hungry. Eating becomes a mechanism for coping with their feelings of inadequacy, despair, loneliness, stress, or any other disquieting sensation. Paul, a graduate student at Stanford, eats very sensibly during most of the semester. However, during periods of stress, just before exams, he rewards himself after periods of intensive study by "pigging out on junk foods." Although his weight is presently within the normal range, this method of mood control could insidiously creep, first into overweight and later into obesity.

Overweight people are especially attracted to foods that taste good or are pleasing to look at. Despite the fact that they are finicky eaters with gourmet tastes, likely to be turned-off by food that is not "just right," they still overeat. In a famous experiment at Columbia University, Stanley Schachter and Larry Gross rigged clocks to make subjects think that dinner was being served later than usual. Fat people ate more than their customary amount, although people of normal weight did not. Other studies have shown that fat people tend to react more voraciously to how the food looks, tastes, or smells. Findings such as these suggest that the obese are more responsive than others to external food cues.

Further investigations along these lines have shown that a large percentage of obese subjects had been dieting during their participation in food-responsiveness experiments. These studies have shown that people who are on a diet, and therefore hungry much of the time, pay more attention to food sensations—taste, appearance, aroma—than normal eaters. Whether thin, plump, or fat, when people are classified as "restrained" (dieting) or "unrestrained" (normal) eaters, those who are on a diet, even if they are thin, behave like typical obese research subjects. They tend to increase their food intake when under stress and are more likely to eat excessively when tempted by appealing food presentations.

A popular belief is that people become compulsive eaters because of unresolved childhood problems. Hilde Bruch explored this notion in her study of New York families during the Depression years. She observed that many mothers seemed to offer food to their children as a way of showing affection and devotion. Food became a means of appeasing the anxiety and guilt that these mothers felt about the material impoverishment that was imposed upon their children. The youngsters appeared to increase their demands for food as needs for gratification and security in other areas remained unfulfilled. Bruch later reported that obese patients suffered from "conceptual confusion," which she could trace to early childhood experiences. They seemed to have difficulty in perceiving and forming appropriate responses to their emotional needs. A desire to be with another person, for example, might be confused with a desire to eat with another person.

Christopher Rowland, Jr., a psychiatrist affiliated with Harvard Medical School, described his psychoanalytic treatment of a thirty-nine year-old obese woman whom we shall call Joan. She sought help for severe depression after the disintegration of her five-year marriage. Since childhood, Joan's eating disorder was characterized by bouts of yo-yo dieting. She experienced cycles of weight increase from twenty to fifty pounds, followed by lengthy periods of strenuous dieting, then losing control and regaining the lost weight. During her life she could truthfully say that she had lost hundreds of pounds.

Joan is a physician who married a physician during medical school. Her father was also a physician, obsessed with the fear that he would die, as his father did, from a weight-related disorder. He managed to contain his death-anxiety by placing himself and all other members of the family on a strict, low-cholesterol diet. Everyone became weight conscious and were fearful of his authority. He showed favoritism toward her young brother and often promised Joan rewards which were soon forgotten or somehow spoiled. On her graduation from college, for example, he gave Joan a sports car that wouldn't run. Her mother was unable to provide adequate emotional support to help Joan with her father's irrational and unfair behavior. In some ways, Joan's husband behaved as her father did; he was extremely critical at home and openly had affairs, blatantly violating Joan's understanding of the promise and commitment of marriage.

As a child, Joan sneaked forbidden foods as a way of mothering herself and rebelling against her tyrannical father. When she became fat, at least her father was interested enough to harass her about her appearance. He would offer her dollar rewards of so much per pound for losing weight. He also showed interest when she received good grades in school or accomplished projects at home. Beginning in the first grade, Joan compulsively reached for her father's approval through an endless stream of academic achievements. She used food as a means of rewarding herself for overwork, insuring her father's attention while continuously expressing her outrage toward his domination and control.

The breakup of Joan's marriage symbolized the loss of the battle for her father's attention and approval. Upon entering treatment she felt unable to control an overwhelming sadness that began when she and her husband first separated. After more than three years of psychoanalysis, Joan began to focus on her problems with weight and food intake. As she became aware of angry feelings toward her parents and husband, she became less obsessed with food. At the end of treatment, although her weight was still high, she appeared to be moving in a more self-assertive, independent direction. During the following year she lost forty pounds on her own incentive.

Psychotherapists report numerous case studies like Joan's, in which food is interpreted as a symbol of parental affection, a means of reducing internal conflict, or a passive expression of anger toward family members who are perceived as hostile and controlling. The obese person is trapped in a vicious circle: overeating originally relieves feelings of low self-regard, loneliness, and tension; however, the consequences of becoming fat are even more intense feelings of low self-esteem, anxiety, and lack of belonging; in response, the person eats even more and becomes even more overweight. Undoubtedly many people suffer from obesity as a consequence of psychological distress. Research studies, however, do not support blanket acceptance of this interpretation for the vast majority of corpulent people.

Actually, the backgrounds of most overweight people are no more psychologically disturbed than those of normal-weight people. Presently more evidence appears to be on the side of biological causes for obesity than psychological ones. Although fat people are often depressed, it may well be that their suffering is the result of overweight, rather than the cause

Richard Wurtman, a physician and neuroendocrinologist at Massachusetts Institute of Technology (MIT), has found what may be a biological link between depression and obesity. Wurtman was aware that some depressed people who are also obese have a low level of the neurotransmitter serotonin. It is known that serotonin is manufactured in the brain from its chemical precursor, tryptophan, an amino acid that is found as a component of many foods such as milk. Consumption of foods rich in carbohydrates favor the transport of tryptophan, over other amino acids, from the blood into the brain. Wurtman therefore theorized that some obese people might crave foods like spaghetti or cupcakes, rich in carbohydrates, in order to compensate for their brain serotonin deficiency. Since many carbohydrate snacks are high in calories and loaded with fat, obesity can easily result.

To test the serotonin deficiency theory, Wurtman and his wife Judith, an MIT nutritionist, studied a group of obese people who acknowledged a craving for carbohydrates. The Wurtmans discovered that at meals, these obese subjects consumed an average amount, about 1,900 calories per day with proteins and carbohydrates in balance. But for snacks, these carbohydrate junkies consumed an additional 1,000 calories per day in foods rich in carbohydrates. When asked to describe their mental state before eating, the subjects reported feeling anxious, tense, and unhappy. After snacking, they often reported feeling less tense and sometimes even relaxed. According to Wurtman, carbohydrates serve the same function for these people as antidepressant drugs: "They increase serotonin and thereby alleviate depression. They improve mood, diminish sensitivity to negative stimuli, ease the way to sleep." There is also the strong possibility that the act of eating releases endorphins, which further the sense of well-being and relaxation.

Another link between biology and overeating, "premenstrual gorging," has been reported by researchers at the University of Toronto. Many women have reported that they develop ravenous cravings, often for carbohydrates, as they approach their periods. A significant number of females were found to consume, at lunch, 20 percent more just before menstruation than they did just before ovulation. Once again the act of eating, especially foods rich in carbohydrates, would be expected to increase the amount of serotonin in the brain as well as cause the release of endorphins, both of which would be expected to decrease the negative moods often associated with premenstrual syndrome.

Another biological factor contributing to obesity is the number of fat cells within one's body. Normal adults have anywhere from 30 billion to 40 billion fat, or adipose, cells. These cells swell or shrink like sponges to accommodate the amount of fat that is stored inside them. Fat cells appear in early childhood, but more develop later, especially during adolescence. In overweight people, the cells expand to hold more fat. Extra fat cells have been found only when a person is at least 60 percent above the ideal weight for his or her height and age. In obese adults, the amount of adipose tissue is often three times greater than what is found in people of normal weight. If a fat person diets, the fat cells will shrink in size, but their total number remains unchanged. Indeed, some researchers speculate that this adipose albatross manages to fix a "set-point" for obesity. The brain's hypothalamus is thought to receive signals that urge further eating until shrunken fat cells are once again refilled. The person who manipulates his or her own weight to fall below the set-point may feel irritable or depressed as a consequence of unanswered brainsignals. The dieter often feels out of sorts until he or she regains every bit of missing cellular baggage. When a person uses an appetite-suppressant drug to lose weight, he or she may be artificially lowering the set-point and only momentarily suppressing appetite. Once the diet medication is stopped, the person usually gains weight rapidly because the brain is once again receiving set-point messages in accord with a permanent repository of adipose tissue. What has been jokingly referred to as "the rhythm method of girth control" may very well have an underlying biological substratum.

A related handicap for overweight people is their relatively low rate of energy expenditure. How the body uses food as energy depends on two interrelated factors: (1) physical activity and (2) basal metabolic rate, or the energy required to maintain minimal body functions. In people of normal weight, basal metabolism accounts for roughly two-thirds of their energy expenditure. Because the metabolic rate is lower in fat tissue than lean tissue, the obese person's basal metabolic rate decreases as lean tissue is replaced by fat. According to William James, a clinical nutritionist at Cambridge University: "It is not so much that these people get fat because they eat too much, but because they eat a normal amount." To make matters even worse, basal metabolic rate further decreases when a person starts to diet. These factors work against the efforts of an overweight person to reduce and also to maintain enduring weight loss. Some studies have reported that people can maintain a reduced level of body weight only if they consume about 25 percent fewer calories than people who are normally at that level. The "used-to-be-fat" may never be able to return to a "normal" eating pattern.

The obese smoker faces an even greater challenge than an obese nonsmoker. According to a recent study reported by a group of European researchers, when subjects smoked twenty-four cigarettes a day, they burned 10 percent more calories than when they abstained from smoking. The study indicates that people who quit smoking will have to eat less to maintain their current weight. The study did not suggest, however, that people continue as nicotine addicts in order to control their weight. George Bray of the University of Southern California Medical Center claims that "a person would have to be 50 or 60 lbs. heavier to have the same health risks from weight that you would get from being a normal weight smoker."

A low metabolic rate and tendency to store fat may be advantageous in times of famine. Obesity-prone individuals may have inherited these predispositions as an evolutionary safeguard for meager food production. The Pima Indians of Arizona, for example, have been a farming tribe for the past 2000 years. The majority are extremely obese and by the age of thirty-five nearly 50 percent have diabetes. Nature appears to have endowed the Pimas with the capacity to store extra calories in preparation for famine. In food-rich areas like the United States and Western Europe, however, biological readiness of this sort is neither necessary nor desired.

Genetics and early nutritional experiences are probably related to the number of fat cells a person carries throughout life, but the exact causal relationship is not yet clear. Some researchers believe that a person's fat-cell count is genetically fixed at birth. Others report that overfeeding during infancy stimulates the development of fat cells, which ever after remain constant in number. Recent data, however, rejects the notion that fat babies will necessarily become fat adults. A fifteen-year survey of 180 infants by researchers at the University of California, Berkeley, showed that babies who were obese at six months or one year of age were likely to be normal weight or thin by age nine. Most nutrition scientists agree, however, that obesity is not simply a random event that just happens out of the blue. Habitual patterns of hunger and feeding, which are regulated by biochemical messages between the body and brain, result in a remarkably consistent level of fat storage throughout life.

Claude Bouchard, director of the Physical Activity Science Laboratory at Quebec's Laval University, has extensively studied the relationship between heredity and body weight. He reports that adopted children are more similar to their biological than their adoptive parents in the amount and distribution of fat as well as in the size of their fat cells. Identical twins remain extremely close in weight until adolescence, when the environment seems to exert a stronger pull. According to Bouchard, heredity is particularly important in determining where the fat settles.

Obesity experts agree that overweight people generally can be grouped into two categories: "apples and pears." "Apples" are comprised mostly of men with beer bellies. For them the battle of the bulge occurs in the abdomen and chest. "Pears" are mostly women who carry their excess baggage below the waist, in chunky buns, love-handle hips, and saddlebag thighs. Compared to the beer belly, fat deposits in the buttocks and thighs are quite stable, and, to the dismay of many, more difficult to remove. However, while "pears" suffer mostly from cosmetic disadvantage, "apples" are the more endangered species in terms of health risk. Ahmed Kissebah of the Medical College of Wisconsin reports that men whose waists are bigger than their hips and women whose waists measure more than 85 percent of their hip size fall into the danger zone.

According to Albert Stunkard of the University of Pennsylvania School of Medicine, who studied hundreds of obese people in the late 1950s: "Most obese persons will not stay in treatment of obesity. Of those who stay in treatment, most will not lose weight and of those who do lose weight, most will regain it." In a January 1986 issue of *Time* magazine, endocrinologist John McCall is quoted as stating about obesity: "The statistics are horrible. It's like treating cancer." At least two-thirds of those who lose weight gain it all back within a few years. After seven years, only 2 percent are able to sustain their original dietary goals. According to obesity researcher Jules Hirsch of Rockefeller University in New York City: "Failure to lose is not a question of gluttony or immorality. . . . Losing weight permanently is an extraordinarily difficult thing to do."

If we acknowledge that biological influences are enormously important determinants of a person's weight, is there any recourse for the huge proportion of American adults who qualify as obese? In a 1982 article published in the *American Psychologist*, Stanley Schachter reported his finding that, in fact, a great number of obese people do lose a significant amount of weight on their own—and they manage to keep it off. Although it appears that a program for obesity may be written in childhood or adolescence, some people are able to overcome their historical inclinations through rational approaches to eating and activity.

People who desire to lose weight permanently while remaining healthy and productive must take a serious inventory of their behavioral budget. They must become converts to "thin-thinking" and be prepared for a degree of persistent discomfort from relentless dieting. They must first recognize that they eat too much and exercise too little. Crash dieting should be ruled out, as it results in nothing more than a setup for failure and lowered self-esteem. The diet is almost always broken and whatever weight has been lost is rapidly regained. As summarized by Marion Nestle, a nutritionist at the medical school at the University of California at San Francisco: "The best diets—losing no more than one pound a week—take a long time to do and occur with healthy eating, a reasonable amount of calories, a great deal of exercise and a program of behavior modification. It's got to be slow and long and for a lifetime."

Overweight people should be particularly on guard for excessive eating when they are emotionally aroused. Those who are serious about weight control must be willing to make enduring changes in their life-styles. They should set their sights on gradual weight loss, no more than 1 pound per week, over several months rather than a few weeks; enforce a continued policy of portion control; and value exercise, whether prearranged as in tennis or incidental as in choosing to climb a flight of stairs instead of using the elevator or walking to the store instead of riding in the car. The body may be considered a ruthless accountant; only a slight excess of calories will be converted into unwanted fat. Just a bit more than one hundred extra calories a day—a handful of peanuts or a glass of beer—and in one month the person has gained one pound of excess baggage. In a period of only one year it is possible to advance from petite to chubby, without ever appearing to lose control.

During the past two decades psychologists have developed several behavior-management programs that appear to be useful for achieving effective weight control. These programs are all based on the principle of keeping calorie consumption and physical activity in harmony. Physical activity, which accounts for only about one-third of a normal-weight individual's energy expenditure, plays a more critical role in the amount of energy spent by a fat person. When a person is characteristically sedentary, the metabolic mechanism operates improperly and the result is a lower basal metabolic rate. The fat person easily gets caught in a vicious circle; being overweight makes exercise more difficult and less enjoyable, and inactivity results in fewer calories being burned off, directly through lack of exercise and indirectly through a reduced basal metabolic rate.

Peter Miller, author of *The Change Your Metabolism Diet*, recommends that people who are serious about achieving permanent weight loss should plan twenty minutes of moderate exercise, two times each day, approximately twenty to thirty minutes after eating. He emphasizes that it is not necessary to increase your heart rate to a certain training level as in aerobic exercises. All that is required is to substantially increase body movement for twenty to thirty minutes, twice daily. To achieve the benefit of an increased metabolic rate, he recommends walking, bicycling, swimming, jumping, rowing, and dancing. While jogging burns about fifteen calories per minute, brisk walking uses about five. A person who is fitness-conscious can easily reduce his daily calorie account by 500, simply by skipping a 350-calorie milkshake and treating himself to a brisk 150-calorie walk, which takes about half an hour.

The typical American diet is partly to blame for the abundance of fatties in our society. People become predisposed to obesity because the kind of food they crave is often high in fat and sugar and low in nutrients and fiber. According to Miller, the best fuel for your metabolism is a proper combination of proteins, carbohydrates, and fats. Miller recommends the following proportions to achieve optimal metabolic efficiency: protein—15 percent; carbohydrates—55 percent; fats—30 percent (simple carbohydrates from candy and pies should make up no more than 10 percent of your daily calories).

As Anastasia Toufexis wrote in an article in *Time* (January 20, 1986):

> Dieters are taught to make useful substitutions—more chicken and fish in place of beef and pork, low-sugar cereals for breakfast in-

stead of butter-laden muffins or cheese-stuffed Danish, vegetables like cabbage and summer squash rather than lima beans and avocados. They are urged to use herbs and spices instead of salt for seasoning, lemon juice and vinegar in place of creamy salad dressing, to rely on low-fat milk, cottage cheese and yogurt instead of whole-milk products, and to drink seltzer and mineral water rather than cocktails and wine. People learn that some foods normally thought of as fattening, namely potatoes, pasta, rice and bread, are acceptable as long as they are not fried, or doused in butter or cream.

In the course of working with hundreds of overweight people, Michael and Kathryn Mahoney, authors of *Permanent Weight Control: A Total Solution to the Dieter's Dilemma,* have developed what they refer to as the SCIENCE program for permanent weight control, described in an article in *Psychology Today.* An adaptation of the SCIENCE program is as follows:

S—*Specify the problem.* Is it too much food (what kind?), too little exercise, or both?

C—*Collect data.* Keep a diary of your eating habits including what and where you eat, as well as how much. Also record your exercise habits—time walking, jogging, playing a sport, or doing calisthenics. Keep an honest account for one week without making any attempt to modify your behavior. Keep a record of your thoughts about food, making note of the circumstances under which your thoughts turn to food.

I—*Identify patterns.* After calculating your ideal weight, compute your daily calorie requirement and scrutinize your diary for where and when you are picking up unnecessary calories. Are you eating too much at meal time, or does your problem center on excess recreational snacking?

E—*Examine possible solutions.* Note several possible means of either reducing calorie intake or increasing exercise.

N—*Narrow options and experiment.* Select only the possible solutions that appear most realistic, in terms of your personality and daily routine. If you hate exercise, don't plan to become an avid jogger. Yet you might consider brisk walks in lieu of afternoon tea.

Table 2–2
SAMPLE FOOD/EXERCISE DIARY

Monday, April 1		Tuesday, April 2	
(Day 7 of data collection before behavior modification)		(First day of behavior modification)	
8:00 A.M.	Orange juice, 2 scrambled eggs, 2 pieces of toast, hash browns, 2 sausages, coffee.	8:00 A.M.	Orange juice, 2 scrambled eggs, *1 piece of toast*, hash browns, *1 sausage*, coffee.
8:30 A.M.	Bus to work	8:30 A.M.	*Walk to work (20 mins.)*
10:30 A.M.	Coffee and donut	10:30 A.M.	Coffee and donut
11:30 A.M.	Thinking about lunch	11:30 A.M.	Thinking about lunch
12:00	Hamburger, fries, malted milk.	12:00	Hamburger, fries, *coffee*
2:30 P.M.	Coke	2:30 P.M.	*Soda and lime*
3:45 P.M.	Chocolate bar	3:45 P.M.	*Oatmeal cookie*
5:00 P.M.	Catch ride with friend to home	5:00 P.M.	Catch ride with friend
6:00 P.M.	Watch news—thinking about dinner. martini	6:00 P.M.	Watch news—thinking about dinner. *wine cooler*
6:30 P.M.	Lasagne, dinner salad, 2 pieces of garlic bread, 2 beers.	6:30 P.M.	Spaghetti & meatballs (2) *1 piece of garlic bread, 1 beer.*
9:00 P.M.	Ice cream (2 scoops)	9:00 P.M.	*Soda and lime*
10:30 P.M.	3 cookies	10:30 P.M.	*Think about snack but resist*
11:00 P.M.	Bed	11:00 P.M.	Bed

Note: Italicized entries signify constructive behavior modifications.

C—*Compare current and past data.* Keep track of your patterns for at least four weeks and evaluate whether your plan is working.

E—*Extend, revise, or replace solutions.* If you appear to be making progress, carry on. If not, consider alternative means of exercise and calorie reduction.

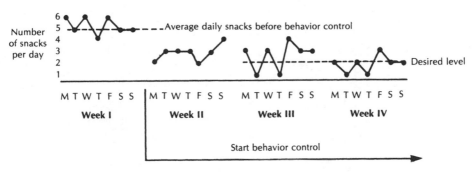

Figure 2–8. SAMPLE BEHAVIOR/TIME CHART

Given that the eataholic cannot survive without food, how can controlled consumption be achieved? Part of the answer lies in understanding the individual's unique pattern and causes of overeating. In many cases food provides the means to alter an unpleasant feeling or mood. Complete elimination of all edible commodities that relieve stress through satiation is doomed to failure. In many instances the price is too high, and addicts revert to predieting behavior. Understanding how satiation results from the process of digesting delicious food might well inaugurate a positive behavior change leading to weight loss and stress reduction. For example, it is unnecessary to eat two or three pieces of pie over a ten-minute period to achieve the desired "hit." A small piece consumed slowly over the same interval, coupled with a conscious effort to savor the taste of every bite, will lead to nearly identical mood modification without blowing one's calorie account out of the water. Over a period of time, the overeater recognizes that it is not quantity, but the enjoyment of savoring, that produces the desired satiation experience. At this point the all-important concept of portion control becomes an invaluable ally in the dieter's repertoire of coping skills.

3

The Joy of Fear

Security is mostly a superstition. It does not exist in nature, nor do the children of men as a whole experience it. Avoiding danger is no safer in the long run than outright exposure. Life is either a daring adventure or nothing.

— Helen Keller

DENVER, January 1, 1983. A week after the great snowstorm. The city is even quieter than usual as the traffic is still half paralyzed because of weather. It is an unusually bright, sunny, crystal clear day. Robin Heid and Brian Veatch ascend the 700-foot United Bank of Denver building, eager to jump off. Upon reaching the top, both men fastidiously check their parachutes, making sure that everything is correctly rigged. Robin's father, who accompanies the duo, comments, "I'll bet you boys are feeling some butterflies now." His son replies, "We were scared yesterday and the day before . . . we're just in the groove . . . we're ready to go for it."

Robin steps out on the end of a scaffold that is being used to finish the building's construction. He begins the countdown as he and Brian focus in on the momentary leap. "Okay—four . . . two . . . three." He turns to Brian and both begin to laugh. Robin continues, "Boy that was great, wasn't it?" Then he resumes concentration, makes the proper countdown, and delicately steps off the edge. Time seems to stand still as Robin savors a sense of weightlessness and the dual feelings of fragility and power in the same instant. Exhilarated by the experience of total control, his life seems at once supreme and valueless.

When the chute opens, he is pleased. He gracefully navigates his floating assemblage through a half circle, deliberately drifting to an

urban clearing, descending on a stunned pair of middle-aged pas-
sersby. Wide-eyed, smiling, and invigorated with curiosity, one ex-
citedly blurts out, "Jesus, what planet did you come from?" Robin's
nonchalant reply: "Oh, you liked it, huh?"

Brian jumps. As soon as he lands, the two hop in the getaway
car, driven by Robin's mother. The police arrive four minutes after
the daring fait accompli.

In the aftermath, Brian and Robin become intoxicated by the
wine of success. The pristine ecstasy of free-fall is replaced by group
celebration, euphoria, and bliss.

Stress-Hormone Highs

Psychologists have long known that people perform most effectively
when under some degree of stress. A moderate level of arousal tends
to produce alertness and enthusiasm for the task at hand. When emotional excitement exceeds an optimal point, however, whether the
evoked feelings are positive or negative, the result is progressive impairment of one's ability to function. Figure 3-1 shows the basic relationship between arousal and performance.

What is it about people like Robin and Brian that enables them
to remain composed while most of us would literally become scared
stiff under similarly arousing circumstances? As Lutfullah describes
in his autobiography (1857), when arousal becomes too intense,
adaptive coping is indeed no longer an option.

> It was about eleven o'clock at night . . . but I strolled on still with
> two people . . . Suddenly upon the left side of our road, a crackling
> was heard among the bushes; all of us were alarmed, and in an
> instant a tiger, rushing out of the jungle, pounced upon the one of
> the party that was foremost, and carried him off in the twinkling
> of an eye. The rush of the animal, and the crush of the poor vic-
> tim's bones in his mouth, and his last cry of distress, "Ho hai!"
> involuntarily re-echoed by all of us, was over in three seconds; and
> then I know not what happened till I returned to my senses, when
> I found myself and companions lying down on the ground as if
> prepared to be devoured by our enemy, the sovereign of the forest.
> I find my pen incapable of describing the terror of that dreadful
> moment. Our limbs stiffened, our power of speech ceased, and our
> hearts beat violently, and only a whisper of the same 'Ho hai!' was

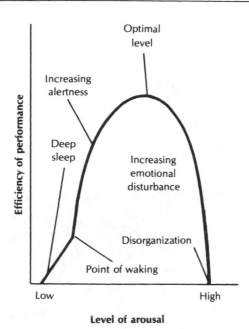

Figure 3–1. EMOTIONAL AROUSAL AND PERFORMANCE

The curve shows the hypothetical relationships between level of emotional arousal and efficiency of performance. The shape of the curve is probably somewhat different for different tasks or behaviors.

heard from us. In this state we crept on all fours for some distance back, and then ran for life with the speed of an Arab horse for about half an hour, and fortunately happened to come to a small village . . . After this every one of us was attacked with fever, attended with shivering, in which deplorable state we remained till morning.

Hans Selye introduced the concept of getting high on our own stress hormones. When we become excited, either through anger or fear, the brain signals hormone-producing glands to release chemicals that prepare us for fight or flight. The adrenal glands produce cortisol, a chemical that increases blood sugar and speeds up the body's metabolism. Other messages to the adrenal glands result in the release of the amphetamine-like stimulant epinephrine (adrena-

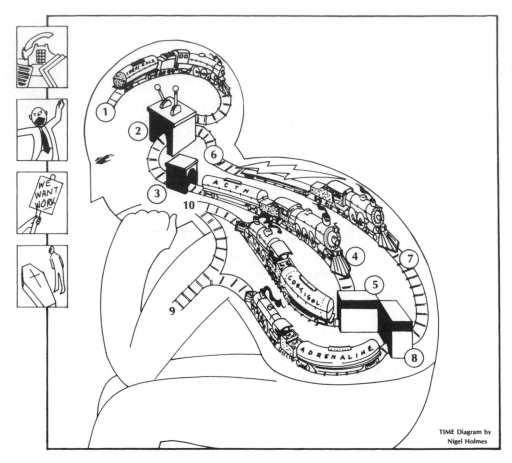

Figure 3–2. TRACKING THE CHEMISTRY OF STRESS

In response to causes of stress, ranging from overwork and quarreling to loss of a job or a
death in the family, chemical messages (1) are carried along neuron tracks in the outer
edge of the brain to the hypothalamus (2), stimulating the production of the chemical
CRF. Acting as a switching station, the hypothalamus sends the CRF and other chemical
messengers down two tracks. The first track goes to the pituitary (3), where the chemical
freight is changed again, this time into the hormone ACTH. It enters the bloodstream (4)
and travels on to the outer layer, or cortex, of the adrenal glands (5). Here ACTH
initiates the production of cortisol, a chemical that increases blood sugar and speeds up
the body's metabolism. On the second track, messengers leave the hypothalamus and
trigger electro-chemical impulses down the brain stem (6) and spinal cord (7), until the
signals reach the core of the adrenal glands (8). The result is a release of epinephrine
(adrenaline), which helps supply extra glucose to serve as fuel for the muscles (9) and
brain, and norepinephrine, which speeds up the heartbeat and raises blood pressure.
Both tracks feed back to the pituitary (10) to regulate further the stress response. (*Source:*
C. Wallis, "Stress: Can we cope?" *Time* [June 6, 1983]: 48–54.)

line), which helps supply glucose to the muscles and brain, and nor-epinephrine, which speeds up the heart rate and elevates blood pressure. Figure 3-2 illustrates the body's chemical response to stress.

The psychological by-products of a moderate biochemical emergency are noticeable increments in one's feelings of physical prowess and personal competence, often associated with strong sensations of pleasure. In many ways, the state of biological and psychological "readiness" produced by stress is mimicked by the effects of stimulant drugs. People may self-induce similar alterations of consciousness with amphetamine, cocaine, or caffeine (two and half cups of coffee will double the level of epinephrine in the blood); or by engaging in activities that appear to be life threatening. Positive experiences—falling in love, riding a roller coaster, or watching a great theatrical performance—can evoke the same stress hormones as more troublesome flirtations with danger or drugs. Selye, who is regarded by many as the grandfather of all modern stress research, has been acutely aware of the intoxicating correlates of fight or flight reactions. He points to stress-drunkenness as causing more overall harm to society than the universally acclaimed demon of demons, alcohol.

What is even more incredible than this seemingly outrageous claim by Selye is that much of the "stress-drunkenness" is deliberately self-induced. "Skydiving is the most fun you can have with your clothes on," proclaims Robin Heid, who dives not only from buildings but from smokestacks, mountain cliffs, airplanes, and bridges. "The greatest joy is being in such a dangerous situation that you nearly wet your pants," says a private detective who purposely seeks out dangerous assignments for thrills. Eric, a young man in his early twenties, goes to the most savage, bloodthirsty movies in town because he "loves to be scared." These seemingly outrageous utterances can be repeated many times over by "adrenaline junkies" who are addicted to a wide variety of risk-taking activities.

What is so attractive about risk taking and fear-inducing situations? In terms of brain chemistry, the symptomatic adventurer seeks the same mind-altering escape from depression, stress, or fear of nonbeing as the user of powerful stimulant drugs. Whether through skydiving, gambling, or cocaine, self-induced changes in neurotransmission may well lead to the familiar path of compulsion, loss of control, and continuation in spite of harmful consequences. In order to explain the biochemical progression of stress-hormone highs, we have adapted the enzyme expansion model for addiction, originally proposed by Avram Goldstein of Stanford University.

Figure 3-3 is a simplified representation of biochemical activity in the synaptic junction during neurotransmission. As previously discussed, the neurotransmitter is released from the presynaptic terminal, attaches to a receptor on the postsynaptic terminal, is released again and finally is reabsorbed into the presynaptic terminal.

As shown in figure 3-3, an enzyme known as adenylate cyclase is activated within the postsynaptic terminal, if it makes contact with a receptor site that is occupied by a neurotransmitter. This activated enzyme, which results from a three-way combination of the enzyme itself with the neurotransmitter and receptor, has the ability to convert an energy-rich molecule known as adenosine triphosphate (ATP) into another extremely important molecule, cyclic adenosine monophosphate (cAMP). Increasing the level of cAMP has the effect of increasing the sensitivity of the postsynaptic membrane, which in turn brings about an additional increase in neurotransmission. As we have seen earlier, an increase in neurotransmission results in an increase in a person's state of arousal and elevation of mood. Any activity that increases the number of three-way combinations of neurotransmitter, receptor, and adenylate cyclase will bring about an increase in the level of cAMP, with the resultant elevation of mood.

The most efficient way to accomplish this three-way combination is to increase the level of neurotransmitter in the synaptic junction. Therefore, any activity or drug that increases the number of excitatory neurotransmitter molecules (dopamine or norepinephrine) in the synapse will elevate a person's mood. For example, skydiving increases the release of excitatory neurotransmitter molecules from the presynaptic junction, while cocaine slows the reabsorption of these neurotransmitter molecules into the presynaptic junction. The effect is the same: an increase in the level of neurotransmitter molecules in the synaptic junction, resulting in more three-way combinations between neurotransmitter, receptor, and enzyme, followed by an increased production of cAMP, with an accompanying elevation of mood. Thus the sky diver elevates his mood by risk-taking activities and the cocaine user by substance use.

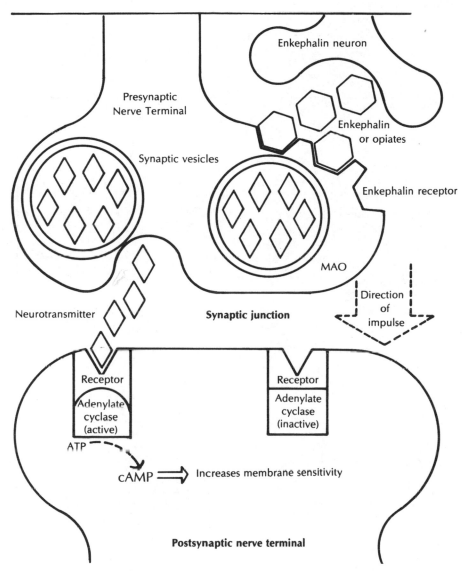

Figure 3–3. CHEMICAL TRANSMISSION OF A NERVE IMPULSE

Adapted from H. Milkman and S. Sunderwirth, Addictive processes, *Journal of Psychoactive Drugs* 14(3):177–192 (1982).

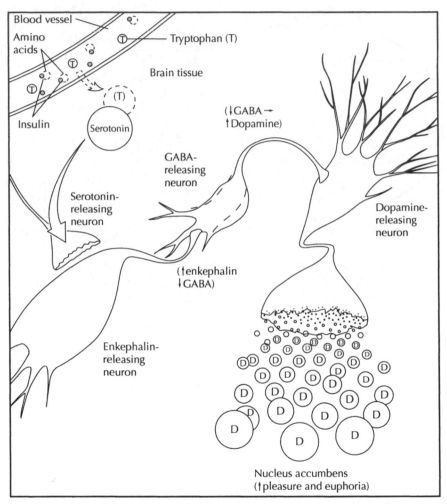

Figure 3–4. THE REWARD CASCADE.

Neurotransmission and Ecstasy

Now that we have seen how neurotransmission functions, let us consider its role in that most rewarding human experience, pleasure or, in extreme cases, ecstasy.

Scientists have known for decades that the brain possesses several pleasure or reward centers which when stimulated produce feelings of extreme well-being. In laboratory tests, rats will forego food in favor of stimulation to a brain reward center, thereby choosing ecstasy over survival. In 1989 Ken Blum at the University of Texas Health Science Center proposed that a cascade of chemical events in a reward center of the brain can result in an enhancement of positive feelings. The "feel good" chemical essential to Blum's model, which he calls the "Reward Cascade" (figure 3–4), is the neurotransmitter dopamine.

To produce feelings of well-being or pleasure, the activity, drug, or behavior must have the ability to increase dopamine in the nucleus accumbens, a major reward center. For example, Nora Volkow at the Brookhaven National Laboratory showed that the exhilarating rush caused by cocaine is due to dopamine. Whereas, Gaetano DiChiara at the University of Caliari in Italy showed that marijuana and heroin both increased dopamine transmission in the nucleus accumbens. Apparently, activities as different as skydiving, sex, and grandchild hugging; drugs as different as cocaine, marijuana, and heroin; and behavior as simple as eating milk and cookies can trigger the reward cascade. Grandmother gave us those milk and cookies to soothe us at bedtime, but as we explained, her tasty snack converted to serotonin in our brain chemistry. As shown in figure 3–4, serotonin is a trigger for the dopamine-producing reward cascade.

In our discussion of stress hormone highs, we explained that skydiving or your favorite excitatory activity increases neurotransmission and the level of dopamine. Quieter but very satisfying, the pleasure of grandchild hugging releases enkephalin, a kind of endorphin, also releasing dopamine. It may seem that there is some contradiction here. How can enkephalin (and heroin), which slows neurotransmission, and skydiving (and cocaine), which increases neurotransmission, both enhance dopamine?

Another major player in the drama of neurotransmission is gamma aminobutyric acid (GABA). This neuromodulator retards the release of excitatory neurotransmitters from the neuron with which it makes contact. The brain needs this inhibitory mechanism if it is to have an ability to maintain homeostasis. Otherwise we would find ourselves in a frantic state of constant excitation. As can be seen from figure 3–4, the GABA neurons impinge upon the dopamine-releasing neurons. Since GABA retards the release of dopamine, anything that slows the release of GABA will enhance the release of dopamine into the nucleus accumbens. Recall that heroin (and endorphins) retard the release of neurotransmitters including GABA whose function, as we have seen, is to regulate dopamine. So if GABA is reduced, dopamine is increased. On the other hand, cocaine prevents the reuptake of dopamine (figure 1–5), thereby increasing its availability in the reward center. We realize that a heroin or endorphin high is different than that of cocaine or amphetamine, which also increase neurotransmission in another reward center.

Although this explanation is a simplification of a very complex process, it serves as a model to explain the euphoric effect of both arousal and relaxation types of activities and drugs. It also serves to explain how a single chemical, dopamine, may be the key to addiction.

Addiction: The Curse of Ecstasy

Let us now turn our attention to the role that pleasure can play in the addictive process. Addiction is a by-product of the brain's ability to restore neurotransmission to a baseline level (homeostasis) following "self-induced changes." Consider the person who engages in either cocaine ingestion or a risk-taking behavior (skydiving). As the self-induced level of dopaminergic neurotransmission shifts into overdrive, the brain's homeostatic restoring mechanism prepares for action. Continued cocaine induced alteration of dopamine levels brings about changes in enzyme (adenylate cyclase) levels which decrease the effectiveness of dopamine neurotransmission by decreasing the number of three-way combinations of neurotransmitter, receptor, and enzyme (figure 3–3).

As the abuse continues, the brain begins to decrease production of both adenylate cyclase and dopamine. Because the dopamine remains in the synapse, there is no reason to make more. Adenylate cyclase decreases in order to restore baseline neurotransmission which is being upset by an increase in the three-way combination of dopamine, receptor, and adenylate cyclase. The abuser then experiences an escalating need for increased activity, drug, or behavior. At some point, the person becomes dependent on the activity or drug just to feel normal. The earlier dose of cocaine no longer excites. To experience an elevated mood, he must use more of the drug or an even more potent type of drug such as crack cocaine. Removal of the drug or cessation of the behavior produces a feeling of dysphoria from a deficiency of dopamine in the nucleus accumbens. This deficiency results from a decrease in the adenylate cyclase needed for neurotransmission as well as the dwindling supply of dopamine. Also, the number of dopamine receptors and their sensitivity have become altered during the time of substance abuse.

In a similar manner, the abuser of opiates experiences alterations in brain chemistry which have the potential for addiction. Interestingly, it is known that not everyone who uses drugs or engages in mood-altering behavior becomes addicted. It is believed that those who do become addicted may be attempting to compensate for a genetic or environmentally induced deficiency of dopamine in the nucleus accumbens. It is important to keep in mind that any drug or activity repeated specifically for pleasure has the potential to become addicting.

The Up and Down Game

Thousands, possibly millions, of pages have been written about human orgasm, which many would describe as the ultimate ecstasy, yet we are far from a complete understanding of the physiology of this most pleasurable and mood-altering human experience. However, it is becoming more evident that orgasm is not so much a function of the genitals as it is of the brain. As early as the sixteenth century it was known that opium ingestion decreased sexual activity and in some cases could cause impotence. As we mentioned earlier, opiates occupy endorphin receptor sites on the presynaptic terminals of neurons in the central nervous system. In this way opiates mimic the pain-killing and the euphoric effects of our own endorphins. The inference is obvious: endorphins (and the limbic system) must somehow be involved in the ecstasy of sexual activity and orgasm.

The relationship between endorphins and orgasms was demonstrated by a group of neuroscientists who showed that the level of endorphins in the blood of hamsters increased dramatically after several ejaculations. This finding would account for the well-known decrease of pain during and after sex. Interestingly enough, the excuse, "I have a headache," for avoiding sex would seem to be counterproductive in light of this discovery. The rush of endorphins into the central nervous system could also explain the euphoria usually experienced immediately following orgasm and loss of romantic interest just after sex.

Yet sexual pleasure cannot be reduced to the biochemical effects of pain-killing molecules. If orgasm and ecstasy were identical, humans would masturbate continuously, forever enjoying the blissful intoxication of autoerotic delight. Clearly, it is the novelty and risk of a romantic spree that ventilates the flame of nature's most impassioned experience. Without some element of danger or sacrifice most sexual encounters fade into the abyss of lackluster experience, tainted by an umbra of boredom and bruised feelings.

The repeated pairing of opposite emotional experiences, and their underlying physiological counterparts, may be the sustaining force behind all forms of human compulsion. According to University of Pennsylvania psychologist Richard Solomon, the same principle that produces alcoholics and dope fiends can be used to account for daredevils, coke addicts, and promiscuous sex junkies who cruise the bars or bathhouses in relentless search for Mr. or Ms. Goodbar.

According to Solomon's opponent-process theory of motivation, every event in life that exerts a potent effect on mood or feeling also triggers an oppositional biochemical process. When first attracted to a pleasurable experience induced through drugs or activities, people are motivated by the dominant sensations of euphoria or well-being. Mood-altering behavior is often sustained, however, because people seek to avoid the unpleasant effects that have been set in motion by the opponent process. In some addictions, for example, running, the initial experience of pain is followed by a highly pleasurable reaction, probably related to the release of pain-relieving endorphins. The addiction is maintained, at least in part, because runners develop a craving for the biochemical opposition to the primary activity. The opponent-process model may be used to explain the pleasure that some people apparently derive from inflicting pain on themselves or others, or from taking unnecessary risks through unsafe physical or sexual practices.

Figure 3–5 illustrates a predictable pattern of mood changes in a thrill-seeking adventurer who self-induces alternating sensations of arousal and satiation as a regular means of coping with stress. The peak of arousal intensity corresponds to the maximum state of biochemical excitement achieved during a risk-taking activity such as skydiving. The potent adrenaline rush, subjectively experienced as an ecstatic state, is followed by a period of adaptation in which the intensity of pleasure declines, although the person continues to enjoy the exciting sensations of free-fall. Shortly after landing the diver feels a satiation aftereffect, the quality of which is very different (opposing) from the primary hedonic state. It is a sense of blissful relaxation, often bolstered by group celebration and alcohol intoxication.

Afterstate changes may occur in minutes, hours, days, weeks, or even months following the primary life event. A prolonged experience of stress and physical immobility from a traumatic automobile accident, for example, may be followed by an extended rebound of invigoration and euphoria. The opponent process leads to a waving pattern of mood alterations, which varies between people in terms of frequency and intensity. Some people seem to exist on a constant roller coaster of mood change, while others remain emotionally bland with only minor ripples in how they feel.

Shopping, a seemingly benign arousal activity, may achieve the status of a mood-altering addiction, characterized by powerful mood swings from intense arousal to blissful satiation, often followed by depression and remorse. Karen, a Los Angeles based writer and single mother of two school-aged children, reminisces about her uncontrolled passion for clothes.

Sometimes I go for months without buying anything; however, I recently went through a major binge in which I bought a Dior suit (at half price, $130), a dress and suit ($268) and ski pants and a parka ($240). All in about one week. I had some extra money because my father sent me some, but I should have used it to pay off part of my credit card debt. So I started thinking about this behav-

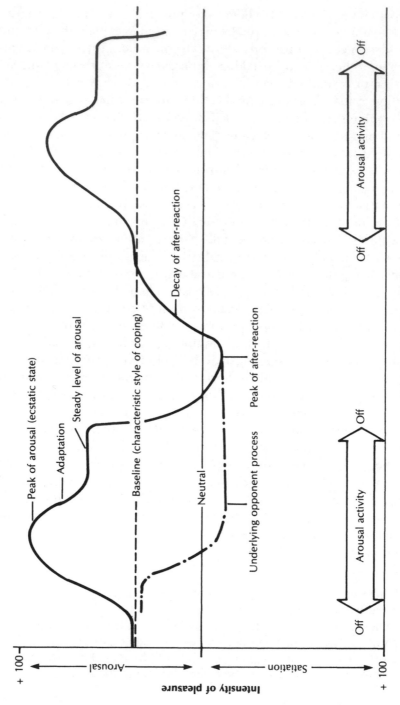

Behavioral mood oscillation

ior and my inability to control it. I know the experience—when I see something I like, and I try it on, and it looks good on me, I get a euphoria that I love. It's seeing myself in the mirror looking good; there's also an aspect of costume to it—wearing many different kinds of clothes is like playing lots of different roles, being different people. I began remembering my fascination with the images of women in comic books when I was 8–10 years old. There was a comic series about Katy Keene the Pinup Queen; these comics were full of pictures of clothes. I cut them out and filled two large scrapbooks with the pictures. When I woke up in the morning and it was time to get dressed, I would look in the scrapbook and try to put together an outfit from my own clothes that resembled something in the book. It usually meant wearing a red blouse to try to copy a red strapless evening gown. I wished I could have all those numberless outfits for every kind of fantasy occasion. And in fact, one of Katy's two boyfriends (the other was a tall, rich blond) was K. O. Kelly, a red-headed freckle-faced boxer who looked a lot like my last boyfriend, John.

For three years, a friend and I owned and ran a small dress shop. There I was able to buy clothes on a grand scale for the shop, and we had a rule that whenever we marked anything down, one of us could take it for herself if she wanted. Every Saturday when I worked in the shop, after I closed up, I pulled everything I liked off the sale rack and tried it on—everything I liked, I took home. I built an enormous wardrobe that way. When we sold the shop, for months afterward, I dreamed of being in the shop and being able to have all the clothes I wanted. And it was after we sold the shop that I started to go on clothes buying binges. Before having the shop, I had always been very frugal about buying clothes, as about everything.

Figure 3–5. RISK TAKING AND ALTERED STATES OF FEELING

Adapted from Solomon and Corbit's (1974) "standard pattern of affective dynamics." Baseline level shows the individual's characteristic style of coping with stress. Primary motivation toward the arousal state is associated with repetitive arousal-seeking activities, with each episode culminating in a peak of pleasurable sensation. Cessation of the preferred activity permits the manifest afterreaction, which, if isolated at a single point in time, may paradoxically appear as a change in motivational preference. The risk taker, for example, may take pleasure in using a satiation drug such as alcohol or opium.

The first time John and I broke up, I was devastated, I couldn't sleep properly for months, and for the first few weeks I went two nights out of three hardly sleeping at all, and then the third night I would fall into a sort of coma from sheer exhaustion. Getting through every day was a struggle, trying to keep my feelings under control and maintain an appropriate demeanor at work. One day, about four or five weeks after we broke up, I dropped the kids off to see a movie at a shopping center. I was going to kill time till the movie was over, browsing. I saw some wonderful clothes in a store window; I went in and started trying things on, and in twenty minutes I had picked out $500 worth of clothes and shoes. I put a deposit on them and came back the next day and paid for them all. After trying them all on and picking them out, I floated out of the store on a cloud. It was my first happy moment after breaking up with John, and it was a heady, euphoric high.

Unfortunately, the initial high experienced in connection with the newly acquired symbols of self-love soon fades into what has become known to psychologists as "buyer's remorse." Shopping euphoria turns to depression and feelings of unworthiness. After the binge, addicts confess that they didn't discriminate between purchases. They find that they bought clothes that are either all the same, or don't seem to match at all. In either case, they do not seem to use what they buy; sometimes they return all the purchases, only to go off on another binge. Some addicts fear embarrassment that they will be recognized by shopkeepers as binge-purge shoppers. They maintain their composure simply by keeping the items around, much as a young child clings to a security blanket.

In some patterns of behavioral excess, a person may continue an experience that is no longer pleasurable because of a growing aversion to the sensations brought about through stopping it. In the case of extended risk taking, for example, chronic thrill seekers may increasingly seek to avoid the unpleasant feelings associated with lowered levels of adenylate cyclase. In the case of continued opiate ingestion, drug-induced euphoria is soon replaced by the anticipation of suffering and pain from narcotics withdrawal. In other patterns, such as gambling or meditation, both the direct and opposing biochemical effects may contribute to the frequently observed pattern of compulsion, loss of control, and continuation in spite of adverse consequences.

Perhaps the most extreme and bizarre example of the relationship between opponent processes and human compulsion is drawn from a growing body of literature on autoerotic fatalities. Each year, an unknown yet substantial number of people, primarily males, accidentally die in the course of voluntary participation in dangerous sexual practices. According to Park Elliott Dietz, associate professor of law at the University of Virginia School of Law:

> For certain individuals the preferred or exclusive mode of producing sexual excitement is to be mechanically or chemically asphyxiated to or beyond the point at which consciousness or perception is altered by cerebral hypoxia (diminished availability of oxygen to the brain).
>
> Other individuals for whom these are not the preferred or exclusive mode of producing sexual excitement nonetheless repeatedly, intentionally induce their own cerebral hypoxia to or beyond the point at which consciousness or perception is altered in order to produce sexual excitement.

In a more or less typical case reported by Rosenblum and Faber in the *Journal of the American Academy of Child Psychiatry,* a fifteen-year-old boy was referred for psychiatric care after he told the police of his practice of suspending himself from a door and ejaculating while hanging. The boy would repeatedly hang himself from the clothes rod in his closet by lifting his feet from the ground and learned to place a towel around his neck, under the rope, to prevent marks or bruises. He reported that he would hang for one-half to two minutes and nearly always ejaculated while suspended. The frequency of self-hangings increased from one every two weeks to four times a week. The boy said that he repeatedly engaged in this bizarre practice because he wanted to anger his mother and because it relieved his depression and temporarily made him feel good.

In another report, a team of Los Angeles researchers interviewed nine men and three women who were identified by the study group as bondage practitioners. Of the nine men, six used hanging or strangulation in their sexual practices. To be sure, sexual excitement is clearly heightened for some people when they engage in sexual acts in which they might be caught breaking a social custom or religious taboo. Risk taking is more than simply spicing an already tasty dish, it can be the major component of the entire sexual act as in widely practiced sadomasochistic sex rituals, with or without the aid of mechanical props or psychoactive drugs. In a recent chapter on sex-related deaths, J. C. Rupp stated that, to date, no well-designed study of this phenomenon has been carried out. Rupp concluded: "Autoerotic asphyxia is carried on by thousands of individuals who arrive at this practice independently of one another."

It represents an as yet unexplored, almost unknown, aspect of human behavior.

Although there are obvious differences in withdrawal symptoms from the diverse array of pleasure-inducing activities, scientists at Columbia University in New York City have suggested that the same brain mechanism may account for the experience of craving, which is common to all addictions. Alexander Glassman, who directed the Columbia University study, found that whether people are trying to kick alcohol, cigarette, or opiate addiction, they experience similar changes in brain chemistry, which create craving for drug use. According to Glassman, all these addictions are characterized by an excess of norepinephrine, which is concentrated in a small area of the brain called the locus ceruleus. A person may subdue biochemical excitation in this area of the brain by using cigarettes, alcohol, or opiates. During withdrawal, however, the locus over-fires, producing too much norepinephrine, which results in the common experience of craving. The fact that stress elevates the level of norepinephrine in the brain may account for the increased craving and frequency of addiction relapse during periods of duress or conflict. The model may also help to explain the high frequency of dual addictions, as in the upper-downer cycle of cocaine-heroin dependence; and the various combinations or switches between risk taking, alcohol, cigarette, and opiate abuse.

Speed Demons

People vary considerably in how much arousal they can tolerate before their performance begins to disintegrate. Of people observed during natural catastrophes such as fires and floods, about 15 percent are able to function in an organized, effective manner. The majority, about 70 percent, show varying degrees of disorganization but manage to function somewhat effectively. The remaining 15 percent are so debilitated that their coping is completely ineffective; they may wander about aimlessly, screaming or exhibiting other forms of mal-adaptive behavior.

To be sure, a thrilling adventure such as skydiving, mountain-eering, or white-water rafting would elicit squeals of delight from some and shrieks of horror from others. When we consider that: (1) a mild to moderate level of arousal tends to help people perform at their maximum effectiveness; (2) people are aroused to different de-grees by the same stimuli; and (3) optimal performance is usually accompanied by enhanced self-esteem; then it becomes readily ap-parent that some people thrive on excitement while others become disoriented and emotionally disturbed by it. Indeed, it is not at all surprising that when John Delk of the Department of Psychiatry at the University of Arkansas studied the personalities of forty-one vol-unteer skydivers—who may represent a broad spectrum of high-risk adventurers—all forty-one agreed that "skydiving is the most enjoy-able sport imaginable." They unanimously agreed that the greatest feelings of excitement and pleasure were experienced during free-fall.

Consistent with this formulation, Frank Farley of the University of Wisconsin at Madison has identified a Type T or thrill-seeking personality. According to Farley, thrill seekers opt for excitement and stimulation whenever they can find it, through intense physical or mental activity, or both. Farley postulates that a combination of genetics, early childhood experience, and nutrition contribute to the development of a thrill-seeking disposition. Under positive environ-mental conditions a Type T might channel his or her propensity toward risk to the benefit of society, as exemplified by heroes such as Charles Lindberg or Martin Luther King. In the negative case, however, a Type T predisposition may lead to pointless self-destruction or even the bizarre criminal behavior of a mass killer like the infamous Ted Bundy.

In terms of general characteristics, Farley describes Type T peo-ple as creative, risk-taking extroverts who prefer more sexual variety than average. Their artistic preferences tend to be experimental; they are more likely to be juvenile delinquents and reckless drivers. In the mental arena, Type T's are creative thinkers who have a talent for transforming one type of mental representation into another. They may shift from abstract to concrete thinking and tend to form images to words more easily than other people.

Farley finds that biology is the major determinant of the Type T personality, but socialization decides whether the individual will become a preserver or destroyer. Underlying the constitutional predisposition for the thrill-seeking personality may be a low level of physiological arousability.

According to Marvin Zuckerman's research on the biological basis of sensation seeking, numerous studies point to low levels of monoamine oxidase (MAO) as a biochemical determinant of the risk taking personality. This enzyme plays a vital role in the regulation of excitatory neurotransmission in the brain. Perhaps sensation seekers require higher levels of external stimulation to evoke a substantial change in their already high rate of excitatory neurotransmission.

From 1969 to 1972 at Bellevue Psychiatric Hospital in New York City, Harvey Milkman and William Frosch conducted a study of the relationship between personality and drug preference. Subjects who preferred amphetamine as their drug of choice were similar in many respects to both Zuckerman's biologically based sensation seekers and Farley's Type T thrill seekers. When rated according to their responsiveness to external stimuli, which included noise, light, sound, and pain, amphetamine users appeared to be less responsive than normal and significantly less sensitive than those who preferred narcotics as their drug of choice. The "speed freaks" observed by Milkman and Frosch appeared to use stimulant drugs as a means of putting themselves in closer touch with environmental stimuli—stimuli that they would ordinarily find dull or uninteresting because of their "thick-skinned" reactions to sensory cues. In terms of personality characteristics, Milkman and Frosch found that amphetamine users fit Farley's description to a "T".

> The amphetamine user is characterized by active confrontation with his environment. While the heroin user feels overwhelmed by low self-esteem, the amphetamine user utilizes a variety of compensatory maneuvers. He reassures and arms himself against a world perceived as hostile and threatening via physical exhibition of alienated symbols of power and strength. Identification with radical political groups further serves the need for active expression of hostility. Promiscuity and prolonged sexual activity may be the behavioral expression of needs to demonstrate adequacy and potency. High level artistic and creative aspirations are usually unrealized self-expectations, bordering on delusional grandiosity.

Such beliefs often lead to compulsive and unproductive behavior. Active participation in hand crafts, music, drawing, or physical labor is striking in nearly all of the amphetamine users studied. To maintain his tenuous sense of self as a potentially productive individual, the amphetamine user deploys many defenses. Denial, projection, rationalization, and intellectualization are characteristically observed. Equilibrium is maintained at the cost of great expenditures of psychic and physical energy.

After more than a decade of clinical observations on the personality characteristics of cocaine users, it appears that they are much like their predecessors, the sensation-seeking amphetamine users of the late 60s and 70s. Each generation of speed demons seems to cope with underlying feelings of helplessness via the energizing effects of stimulant drugs. The arousing qualities of both amphetamine and cocaine serve the users' needs to feel active and potent in the face of an environment perceived as hostile and threatening. Massive expenditures of psychic and physical energy are geared to defend against underlying fears of vulnerability, passivity, and inadequacy.

The style of coping is reminiscent of a phase of early childhood development that culminates around the middle of the second year of life. During this stage, described by Margaret Mahler as the practicing period: "The freely walking toddler seems to feel at the height of his mood of elation. He appears to be at the peak of his belief in his own magical omnipotence which is still to a considerable extent derived from his sense of sharing in his mother's magic powers." The child seems to delight in flooding his or her senses while moving with reckless abandon through an environment fraught with diversity, difficulty, and danger. The fearless conduct is of course little more than a behavioral facade to compensate for continuous threats to a sense of self-importance or personal safety. As Annie Reich explains: "The need for narcissistic inflation arises from a striving to overcome threats to one's bodily intactness." If early traumatizations are too frequent, the primitive ego defends itself via magical denial. "It is not so, I am not helpless, bleeding, destroyed. On the contrary, I am bigger and better than anyone else."

Those who thrive on courting danger appear to have carried this primitive style of coping into the adult realm. They win admiration and approval from witnesses by appearing to be tougher and more daring than everyone else. As described by Tom Wolfe in *The Right*

Stuff, both heroes and psychopaths have the uncanny ability to tread on the brink of disaster while maintaining their calm; they can function with wit and poise even when confronted with gargantuan distress. Brigadier General Chuck Yeager, one of America's original astronauts, appears to fit Wolfe's criteria for a fearless person. He is said to have hidden the fact that he had broken several ribs during a reckless midnight horseback ride so that he could crawl into a tiny X-1 rocket and allow himself to be ejected from the belly of a B-29, flying at 26,000 feet to become the first man to travel faster than the speed of sound.

Other far less esteemed yet equally fearless members of our society attain the ignoble title of psychopath. As originally described in psychiatrist Hervey Cleckley's classic work, *The Mask of Sanity*, psychopaths are generally quite intelligent. Their charm is undoubtedly more compelling because they lack visible tension or anxiety. Yet they are basically incapable of genuine affection or love and have no respect for the truth. They are characteristically unreliable, taking senseless risks even after having been punished for similar acts. The psychopath does not seem to learn from unpleasant past experiences and lacks the capacity for genuine remorse or shame. He is usually male—in three cases out of four—and has great facility for blaming others for his inappropriate or criminal actions. He seems unable to appreciate or foresee how others will react to his behavior. Cleckley portrays the psychopath not as deeply vicious, but as unable to take seriously the threat of disaster or harm and respond accordingly.

According to David T. Lykken, professor of psychiatry and psychology at the University of Minnesota, psychopaths may be viewed as the black-sheep cousins of respectable adventurers. Both are cut from the same biological tree; they differ primarily in their early childhood experiences with parents and other socializing influences.

Detective Daril Cinquanta has been with the Denver Police Department for the past seventeen years. He has been involved in more than three thousand felon arrests without ever shooting a suspect. Detective Cinquanta is regarded by both criminals and responsible citizens as a law-enforcement hero and champion of justice. He attributes much of his success as a crimefighter to his ability to understand the mentality of the people that he arrests. Coming from a lower class background himself, Cinquanta is known among criminal adversaries for his cunning and fearlessness. He purposely cultivates the image of a maniacal daredevil to inspire as much fear as possible in his foes.

Cinquanta communicated the deep sense of pleasure and mental exhilaration that he derives from the excitement and risk of being a professional crimefighter:

We had a series of armed robberies in north Denver where somebody was robbing fast food restaurants with a sawed-off shotgun. We didn't have anything on this until one robbery when we got a surveillance photograph and it shows this Chicano male with a mask on. The only thing you can see is the shave line on his neck, that his wrists are hairy and his eyebrow . . . and he's got a sawed-off shotgun . . . One morning during this rash of robberies, a little girl gets killed at McDonalds at 38th and Irving . . . guy comes in, hits the place and shotguns this little girl—kills her in the robbery.

Well, I knew this guy. I just *had* to know him. I developed a suspect from his eyebrow. I went through my pictures and I figured out who it was . . . and then I directed an informant of mine who had done time with him—who was a friend of his—to make contact with him . . . and one day [the suspect] admitted to him that he killed the girl in McDonalds . . . So then my informant corroborates. He says, "God damned, he admitted it; said he shot her because she was ugly!" I go, "Jesus Christ!" He [informant] says he's [suspect] all strung out, doing dope and paranoid. So I figured the only way I'm going to do this guy is to follow him to his next robbery. I need to get some physical evidence; we need to make him surface that shotgun or the shoes he wore because we had a shoe print from the counter he jumped over at McDonalds . . . I convinced Command to let me follow this guy 24 hours a day and live with him.

And we did . . . On the 14th day he, guess what? He commits an armed robbery . . . Well, he tried to hit a Pizza Hut first, and we were moving in on him when he abandoned it because he saw a police car go by . . . he had the mask down and he was just getting ready to pull the gun and go in the back door . . . He went back to the car. So then he cruised around . . . This is after eight hours—we followed him eight hours the last day until he picked his target. So he picks this gas station and he got down by a dumpster, his partner parked about 100 feet away . . . and he pulled the mask down and got his gun out of his sock. He had a .25 and put the gloves on and then went around to the gas station.

As he was going around, I ordered that we move in. We had two teams coming around from opposite directions. Well, I was right behind him when they confronted him. He panicked . . . he had the gun . . . he turned around and I was going to do him and said "drop it!" He leaped between two fences, between a lumber yard and the back of the station . . . and he raised the gun . . . and one of the detectives shot him . . .

. . . it was exciting . . . it was wonderful . . . I loved it . . . it's just unbelievable . . . the exhilaration.

Some of the same qualities that distinguish Detective Cinquanta as a successful crimefighter have apparently gone astray in the people that he apprehends. Whether the game is Cops and Robbers or the computer sport Photon, children derive primal pleasure from both sides of the chase. The thrill of conquest or danger is undoubtedly connected with the excitement that one experiences when his or her senses become flooded by survival cues. Sensation seeking appears to be a trait common to the entire spectrum of adventurous personalities—cops, criminals, coke addicts, and Casanovas included. Marvin Zuckerman developed the Sensation Seeking Scale (SSS) to measure an individual's desire to engage in risky or adventurous activities, seek new kinds of sensory experiences, enjoy the excitement of social stimulation, and avoid boredom. Table 3–1 offers a sample of items from the SSS and a scoring procedure.

The people who score high on the SSS are more likely than others to enjoy risk in their work and play. High-sensation types are more probable candidates for variation and experimentation in their patterns of drug use and sexual practices; they tend to behave more fearlessly when confronted with such common phobic situations as heights, snakes, or darkness; they take more risks when gambling, and they report driving at higher speeds than low-sensation seekers. They are more likely to engage in such dangerous sports as parachuting, motorcycle riding, or scuba diving. Zuckerman and his colleagues have found that compatibility in sensation seeking is also a meaningful predictor of marital adjustment. According to one happily married team of underwater adventurers: "The couple that dives together, thrives together."

Table 3–1
AM I A SPEED DEMON?

Each item contains two choices. Choose the one that best describes your likes or feelings. If you do not like either choice, mark the choice you dislike the least. Do not leave any items blank.

1. A. I have no patience with dull or boring persons.
   B. I find something interesting in almost every person I talk to.

2. A. A good painting should shock or jolt the senses.
   B. A good painting should provide a feeling of peace and security.

3. A. People who ride motorcycles must have some kind of unconscious need to hurt themselves.
   B. I would like to drive or ride a motorcycle.

4. A. I would prefer living in an ideal society in which everyone is safe, secure, and happy.
   B. I would have preferred living in the unsettled days of history.

5. A. I sometimes like to do things that are a little frightening.
   B. A sensible person avoids dangerous activities.

6. A. I would not like to be hypnotized.
   B. I would like to be hypnotized.

7. A. The most important goal of life is to live to the fullest and experience as much as possible.
   B. The most important goal of life is to find peace and happiness.

8. A. I would like to try parachute jumping.
   B. I would never want to try jumping from a plane, with or without a parachute.

9. A. I enter cold water gradually, giving myself time to get used to it.
   B. I like to dive or jump right into the ocean or a cold pool.

10. A. When I go on a vacation, I prefer the comfort of a good room and bed.
    B. When I go on a vacation, I prefer the change of camping out.

11. A. I prefer people who are emotionally expressive even if they are a bit unstable.
    B. I prefer people who are calm and even-tempered.

TABLE 3–1 continued

12.   A.   I would prefer a job in one location.
       B.   I would like a job that requires traveling.

13.   A.   I can't wait to get indoors on a cold day.
       B.   I am invigorated by a brisk, cold day.

14.   A.   I get bored seeing the same faces.
       B.   I like the comfortable familiarity of everyday friends.

Scoring:

Count one point for each of the following items that you have circled: 1A, 2A, 3B, 4B, 5A, 6B, 7A, 8A, 9B, 10B, 11A, 12B, 13B, 14A. Add your total for sensation seeking and compare it with the norms below:

0–3	Very low	6–9	Average	12–14	Very high
4–5	Low	10–11	High		

Note: Adapted from Marvin Zuckerman's Sensation Seeking Scale (SSS). Reproduced with permission from Marvin Zuckerman.

Were it not for the motion and the colour play of the soul, man
would suffocate and rot away in his great passion, idleness.

— Carl G. Jung

4

Mental Excursions

Tell me where is Fancy bred,
Or in the heart or in the head?

— William Shakespeare

When I examine myself and my methods of thought, I come to
the conclusion that the gift of fantasy has meant more to me than
my talent for absorbing positive knowledge.

— Albert Einstein

Stuff of sleep and dreams, and yet my Reason at the Rudder.

— Samuel Taylor Coleridge

O UR ability to create mental events, which stand as intermediaries between biological impulse and instinctual reactions, may be the single most important difference between humans and all other life on earth. We not only forecast the weather and visualize tomorrow's clothing, but we can imagine our own death. The ability to project ourselves into future environments and to appreciate the likely consequences of intended actions has undoubtedly enabled the prolific survival of the human species. However bizarre, improbable, or grotesque, internal images usually reflect a response to psychological need. Fantasies are spoken about, privately savored, or preserved as forms of art.

Moderate use of imagination is necessary for adaptive living. Personality research with overeaters and drug abusers, for example, reveals their impoverished fantasy lives. These people often react as if they respond only to external stimulation. The outside world seems to cry out, "Taste me! Swallow me! Feed me! Hug me!" Similarly, children who do not partake of imaginative play tend more toward fighting, delinquency, and antisocial acts.

Images from our surroundings are the psychic nutrients for our fantasies. There is a constant interplay between a person's spontaneous production of thoughts and images and the incredible array of external stimuli to which we are exposed. To name but a few of these stimuli: advertising fantasies, pictures and stories in books and magazines, hopeful fairy tales, pessimistic myths, cartoon and comic books, record cover jackets and recordings, movies, video movies and games, tatoos, televised musicals, dramas, and horror shows. The content of each fantasy medium may range from easily understood pictures to highly abstract forms of modern expressionism, in which the artist's feelings supersede concentration on objective reality. As shown in figure 4–1, fantasy images exist on a continuum ranging from realistic to abstract. Themes may also vary from pleasant to horrible.

In addition, without actually forming images we may be engaged in the process of imagination when attending to other people's fantasy expressions. *Receptive* fantasy is the concentration on thoughts or pictures that have been produced by others, for example, watching television, reading a novel, or visiting a black-light poster display. *Active* fantasy is the production of images and thoughts that emerge spontaneously from one's own psyche. These may be highly representational and reality oriented, such as a person visualizing how to approach his or her employer, or they may be highly abstract and unrealistic, such as imagining the creation or destruction of the universe. To understand the interplay between receptive and active fantasy systems, it is necessary to clarify further the meaning and importance of imagination.

Jerome Singer of Yale University is renowned for his research and theorizing on the adaptive role of imagination. He proposes that fantasy may be described as: "The ability to reproduce faces of persons, snatches of dialogue or objects no longer immediately available to the primary senses and then to reshape further the memories of these experiences into new and complex forms."

The basic function of imagery is to explore our relationship to the world. We develop specific mental pictures of who we are, which become a kind of personal identity uniting our past experiences to our intended actions. By imagining, we can work through painful

Figure 4–1. CONTINUUM OF FANTASY IMAGES

I. Realistic . . .	*II. Surrealistic* . . .	*III. Unrealistic* . . .	*IV. Abstract*
Direct Sensory Experience	Incongruous Images Found in Real World	Other Worldly Images which Have Meaning	Unrecognizeable Forms; Intense Feelings

memories and sufferings or formulate models of enchantment through which we will soar to blissful heights with our lovers, family, or friends. The emergence of new ideas from the reshaping of a multiplicity of past events, in a sense, becomes a vast additional source of knowledge. Fantasy, the wellspring of creativity, may be thought of as a piece of God.

Whereas fairy tales provide fantasy guideposts for children to master the tasks of growing up, religion and myths provide ethical prescriptions for conduct in the adult world. The adaptive function of imagination, however, far exceeds that of helping to establish meaning, purpose, and patterns of conduct in an often confusing existence. Fantasy affords us an internal system for reducing stress. We can diminish tension through the imagined gratification of physical or psychological impulses. By creating alternative mental environments, we are temporarily released from internal conflict or from tension in the outside world. By virtue of these intense reward capabilities, we regularly rely on fantasy solutions to everyday problems in living.

When imagination is more satisfactory than direct action in the alleviation of perceived threat, we begin to tread on the road of harmful consequences. With each experience of pleasure or removal from pain, the probability of seeking out an imaginary solution increases. Indeed our work, love, and play may progressively falter as the result of an increasing reliance on imaginary pleasures. Hence, the compulsive fantasticator may suffer the same perils as his or her "rushing" or "laid back" counterparts: compulsion, loss of control, and continuation despite adverse consequences. Harmful effects may be overwhelming when an entire society relies on fantasy as a means of coping.

The Child's Use of Fantasy

The interplay of *receptive* and *active* forms of fantasy is best understood by examining imagination in one of its simplist forms; the child's experience with the fairy tale. In its pure form the fairy tale helps children to understand the inner pressures and concerns entailed in growing up. It offers both temporary and permanent solutions to pressing difficulties. Bruno Bettelheim, renowned for his expertise on the meaning and importance of fairy tales, offers profound insight regarding the child's benefit from enchanting stories:

> In order to master the psychological problems of growing up—
> overcoming narcissistic disappointments, oedipal dilemmas, sibling rivalries, becoming able to relinquish childhood dependencies, gaining a feeling of selfhood and self-worth, and a sense of moral

obligation—a child needs to understand what is going on within his conscious self so that he can also cope with that which goes on in his unconscious. He can achieve this understanding, and with it the ability to cope, not through rational comprehension of the nature and content of his unconscious but by becoming familiar with it through spinning out daydreams—ruminating, rearranging and fantasizing about suitable strong elements in response to unconscious pressures . . . Fairytales have unequaled value because they offer new dimensions to the child's imagination which would be impossible for him to discover as truly on his own. Even more important, the form and structure of a fairy tale suggests images to the child by which he can structure his daydreams and then give better direction to his life.

Examination of the tale of Peter Rabbit sheds light on youngsters' use of fairy tales to cope better with the fears and impulses of childhood. Beatrix Potter's now classic story begins:

> Once upon a time there were four little Rabbits and their names were Flopsy, Mopsy, Cottontail and Peter . . . "Now my dears," said old Mrs. Rabbit one morning, "you may go into the fields or down the lane, but don't go into Mr. McGregor's garden, your father had an accident there; he was put in a pie by Mrs. McGregor."
>
> Flopsy, Mopsy and Cottontail, who were good little bunnies, went down the lane to gather blackberries. But Peter, who was very naughty, ran straight away to Mr. McGregor's garden and squeezed under the gate!

Peter did not understand the value of portion control and was beginning to learn a lesson of giving carte blanche to wayward impulses.

> But round the end of a cucumber frame, who should he meet but Mr. McGregor! . . .
>
> Peter got frightened and ran but got caught by the large buttons on his jacket in a gooseberry net. . . . Peter gave himself up for lost, and shed big tears; but his sobs were overheard by some friendly sparrows who flew to him in great excitement and implored him to exert himself.

It was Freud's prescription that only by struggling courageously against what seems like overwhelming odds can one succeed in wringing meaning out of life. This may be an essential message of all fairy tales.

Peter had a very bad time running away from Mr. McGregor. He was frightened and cried, lost his clothes, and became wet and cold before he ran into a white cat who was staring at some goldfish. "Peter thought it best to go away without speaking to her; he had heard about cats from his cousin, Little Benjamin Bunny."

This is perhaps the cutest and most essential part of the story. Young Peter must learn to take the advice of others—vicarious learning—in order to avoid making similar mistakes. Recall his father who was turned into Rabbit pie.

Finally Peter slips by Mr. McGregor but not before he has a peek at what happened to his clothes: "Mr. McGregor hung up the little jacket and the shoes for a scare-crow to frighten the blackbirds." Perhaps this is a symbol of crucifixion and a last reminder that death may be a penalty for impulsive behaviors. "When Peter got home, he was not feeling well and his mother put him to bed and gave Peter a dose of camomile tea. One tablespoonful to be taken at bed time. But Flopsy, Mopsy, and Cottontail had bread and milk and black-berries for supper."

The good children were rewarded for their behavior and earned the fruit of their labor. Peter, on the other hand—whose nerves were undoubtedly shot—was mildly medicated and ordered to rest.

Religion and Myth

Be it Islam, Christianity, Buddhism, or Hinduism, modern religion provides allegorical counsel for *adult* questions about life and death. Throughout the world groups of people accept as truth ideas, concepts, or images that appear to violate the laws of nature. Beliefs in the supernatural are generally regarded as myths by outsiders. Often, these shared stories and legends become so ingrained that entire cultures are guided by their meaning.

The organization of beliefs, rituals, and images that collectively purport to explain the meaning of life for a specific group may be considered a religion. For example, a large segment of the people in

India share a set of beliefs, rich in imagery, depicting incredible supernatural events. To a Westerner the stories enveloped by the religion of Hinduism are understood as fascinating myths. To the Hindu, the causes of the fantastic events in these widely shared stories are attributed to gods.

Religion and myth, fairy tale and fable, folklore and legend collaborate to form intricate systems of informal social controls over human impulse and action. Whereas the law provides direct mandates for correct action, shared parables usually enhance survival within a culture by providing internalized roadmaps for correct action. In the well-known Judaic-Christian story of Abraham and Isaac, for example, Abraham must defer to powers that supersede individual will or self-love. Clearly the shared belief in the benefits of Abraham's willingness to sacrifice his only son promotes respect for a force mightier than personal volition. To be sure, survivability of the group is enhanced if its members can be guided by symbols that encourage group cohesiveness and allegiance to a shared set of values and leaders.

Hindu stories are probably the richest in imagery of all living religions. The Hindu religion has survived for thousands of years in spite of repeated conquests from foreign powers who brought with them different religious beliefs. According to Hindu faith, men are often unable to combat the powers of evil. In situations such as these, the Hindu god Vishnu temporarily returns to help the people on earth in their struggle against the evil person or situation. Thus the people are informally encouraged to struggle against influences that threaten survival.

One of Vishnu's more interesting reincarnations is as Narasinha, who comes to the earth to free the world from the powers of a demon king who had obtained a promise from the god Brahma. The promise consisted of an immunity that would prevent the demon king from being killed by man or beast, by day or by night, inside or outside his house, in heaven or on earth. Instead of using this incredible immunity from death to help the people, the demon king became so depraved that he forbade worship of all other gods and demanded the worship of himself in their place. He even attempted to kill his own son whom he found doing obeisance to Vishnu. The demon king finally created so much misery for the people on earth that

Vishnu returned in the form of Narasinha, the man-lion. He immediately attacked the demon king, took him to a doorway of a house at twilight, held him on his knees, and tore out his heart.

The myth of Narasinha illustrates the concept that good will triumph over evil in spite of all odds to the contrary, that is, if one continues a struggle success will follow (recall the sparrow's message to Peter Rabbit). Also, consider the power of visual imagery in this story. Narasinha is usually pictured as the half-man, half-lion hybrid holding the demon king on his knees. Combination creatures are found not only in other Avatars of Vishnu, but are fairly common in mythology throughout the world. The Olmec people who lived in the land occupied by present-day Veracruz in Mexico, for example, believed that they were descendants of a mating between a jaguar and a goddess. Much of the art of the Olmecs depicts people as were-jaguars, hybrids between men and jaguars. The centaur of ancient Greek mythology is a hybrid of a man and a horse, while the Roman griffin has the head and wings of an eagle and the body of a lion.

The psychological meaning of hybrid animals is elucidated by mer-people, who have been regarded for centuries as near-human inhabitants of the sea. The folklore of mermaids traverses time, culture, and continents. Although the exact traits and habitats of particular mer-people vary, we have come to associate some features with a generic mermaid. Most visualizations tend to merge women with fish near or below the waist, where the female torso starts to taper with seal-like grace to a fish's tail. Generally, mermaid bodies are designed for underwater seductions and quick getaways. The basic idea of literally pulling good men down is a constant theme of mermaid lore.

It is easily apparent that the mermaid fantasy is a persistent coping device of lonely men in frightening places. The wish for female pleasure and companionship is merged with the fear of aquatic demise. The last stanza of an English sea chanty, "Married to a Mermaid," supports this view:

> We lowered a boat to find him, we thought to see his corpse,
> When up to the top, he came with a shock, and said in a voice so
>   hoarse,

"My ship mates and my mess mates, oh, do not weep for me,
For I'm married to a mermaid at the bottom of the deep blue
sea."

The hybrid being represents a condensation of human wishes
and fear. As with Narasinha, the man-lion, mermaids symbolize the
lonely sailor's most profound expectations: That he may survive with
beautiful companionship (wish) the most horrendous nautical fiasco
(fear). Communal tales contain symbols, which are characters or objects of great psychological significance, with the power to influence
human life. In effect, symbols become the "sociotransmitters" of cultural impulse. Often, through the vehicles of entertainment or religion, some symbols such as national heroes, deities, or movie stars
become institutionalized as ongoing features of public life. We identify or put ourselves in the place of the darlings of our time and shape
our behavior through vicarious experience of their lives.

In some cases the fantasy of being *like* one's chosen idol uncon-
sciously insures the wish to be *liked* by that idol. It is not at all unusual for members of a social group to mimic the behavior of their
heroes. Certainly Marlon Brando, Elvis Presley, and Clint Eastwood
have had their share of look-alikes. John Hinkley's attempted murder
of President Reagan involved his fantasy identification with Robert
DeNiro's role as a psychotic assassin in the movie *Taxi*. Mark Chap-
man reasoned that he murdered John Lennon "because he loved
him." In a letter to the *New York Times* he wrote that the answer to
the murder could be found in J. D. Salinger's *Catcher in the Rye*.

Marked idolatry or compulsive overidentification with highly
visible members of a community is yet another vehicle for "patching
the self from without." The highly stylized dress patterns of "punks"
in contemporary society are another example of fantasy identification. Undoubtedly the bizarre costuming reflects rejection of the or-
derliness and sex role differentiation emphasized by the mainstream
of our society.

Electronic Bogeymen

In Western culture, the gods of science and technology have developed synthetic tools for our compulsions and rituals. As the home-

sick sailor repeats chants of mermaids and booze, and the forlorn Indian makes offerings to the Hindu god Shiva, Western youth become devoted to drugs and media. The compulsive use of video games and the current epidemic of cocaine abuse may be viewed in this context.

In the past decade journalists have reveled in the concept of electronic addictions. TV junkies have been described as mindlessly surrendering to electronic bogeymen. Meanwhile, market researchers have dichotomized pathological TV patrons into "zippers" and "zappers." The latter switches channels at any hint of an advertising break, while the former fast-forwards his or her prerecorded video show through commercial periods. The average U.S. television is said to lumber through 6.5 hours of use per day and U.S. Surgeon General C. Everett Koop commented (while admitting that he lacked scientific data) that video games are addictive and hazardous to the mental health of youngsters.

Perhaps the most comprehensive perspective on the dangers of compulsive TV viewing is offered by Jerry Mander in his 1978 publication, *Four Arguments for the Elimination of Television*. The sentiment of his work is conveyed in Fred Allen's quip: "Television is a triumph of equipment over people, and the minds that control it are so small that you could put them in a gnat's navel with room left over for two caraway seeds and an agent's heart."

Mander's first argument concerns the limitations of the knowledge that we get from the processing of TV information. The electronic milieu is an unnatural intervention between humans and direct personal experience. What we celebrate as an expansion of knowledge is merely a limited form of information gathering at the expense of the more vital forms of human experience.

Second, television should be understood as a political device used for psychic colonization and human domination. It should have been immediately obvious on January 7, 1927, when Philo T. Farnsworth applied for the patent on television that it could be used for social control. The enormous human capacity for identification and modeling of lifelike figures has been a means of steering human actions in every civilization. Certainly the values and behaviors reflected by television heroes have tremendous impact on the life-styles of their viewers. It is not surprising that the Soviet Union may have the best-equipped television broadcast system in the world. The Soviet satellite system spans ten time zones with international soccer and ice hockey as the only outside programs. High priority is given toward the broadcast of socialist achievement and the rhetoric of Soviet philosophy.

The third argument concerns the neurophysiological responses of human beings to the television signal. It is argued that the TV signal itself produces a hypnotic-addictive effect. Mander cites a 1975 study completed by a team of research psychologists, Merrelyn and Fred Emery at the Center for Continuing Education, Australian National University in Canberra. The report states: "The evidence is that television not only destroys the capacity of the viewer to attend, it also, by taking over a complex of direct and indirect neural pathways, decreases vigilance—the general state of arousal which prepares the organism for action should its attention be drawn to a specific stimulus." We have described the drug-like quality of television and related media in chapter 2.

Finally, Mander argues that television has only limited potential for improved programming and no potential for democratic use. Most information that would be genuinely useful to improve human understanding of the complexities of life cannot be conveyed by the medium. Information that is transmitted is lacking in subtlety and overly simplistic. The mentality that emerges nicely fits a simplified and commercialized life. Mander finds that television itself is not a benign device that may occasionally fall into the wrong hands, but that "there is ideology in the technology itself. To speak of television as neutral and therefore subject to change is as absurd as speaking in the report of a neutral technology such as guns."

The major objection to television from less radical factions centers on the extent of media-portrayed sex and violence. It may seem unlikely that watching cartoon characters flatten one another could cause children to behave aggressively, but a large body of research on the relationship between television viewing and aggression indicates that this in fact occurs.

In a 1982 report published in *The American Psychologist*, L. D. Eron described how and when TV violence begins to influence children. He found that around the age of eight children become more susceptible to what they see on the screen. The degree to which they are affected depends on how closely they identify with the program's characters and how realistic they believe the programs to be. Those children who watched violent TV were consistently rated as more aggressive by their peers.

Television networks often try to refute this kind of evidence by arguing that TV violence has a socially redeeming quality because the child learns the principle of good winning over evil. This point is strongly contested by a major report published in 1982 by the National Institute of Mental Health on the psychological effects of television on young viewers. The report argues that young children cannot yet understand the relationship between violent actions seen during the course of a show and punishments viewed at the end. Furthermore, children who watch a lot of TV tend to develop a distorted view of the world. Heavy viewers believe that more unpleasant and scary events take place than actually occur.

This type of data is particularly alarming when we consider that the average preschooler spends about four hours a day watching television, and viewing time increases as children get older. Overall, children spend more time watching television than they do attending school!

After hardly more than fifty years of electronic viewing, we find ourselves at yet another level of the neuro-electronic revolution. Television screens can now be scripted by viewers, who may interact with select computer data via software programs.

Robert Rossel, in his May 1983 discussion in *Psychology Today*, named video games as a new and more advanced stage in our addiction to media. Scripts are parallel to the basic dramatic themes of cartoons, westerns, space fantasies, or murder mysteries. However, whereas television requires passive observation with occasional lapses in concentration, video games require full attention and active participation. The games graphically play out fantasy confrontations with fundamental anxieties of life: conquest and defeat, pursuit and flight, heroic struggle, envelopment and escape. The participant can enjoy fantasy experiments with life-threatening situations, in a limited and safe way.

The problem with these newly evolved devices, however, is that they constrain imagination. Video games may be considered highly evolved forms of what have been described as "pre-scripted" toys. Creative fantasy is limited because the player is restricted by the play options that the toy has. Examples of these highly seductive yet creatively limiting playthings are omnipresent. Dolls are programmed to shoot, eat, cry, burp, or wet, making it difficult for the child to invent alternatives. The pre-scripting maneuver is beneficial for manufacturers. The initial appeal of the toy is high, but boredom and abandonment quickly set in. In a short time the youngster will look for a similar play object, only with a slightly modified script.

The alienating and dehumanizing capacity of video technology is perhaps best illustrated by a bizarre, yet true, clinical example. A thirty-year-old Los Angeles cocaine user reported that he was no longer satisfied having sexual intercourse with "biological units." A career musician, familiar with electronics, he was able to develop a biofeedback contrivance that could register changes in penile erection and transmit the information to an Apple computer. He would mechanically masturbate via an automatic vacuum device, developed to provide sexual stimulation for people who could not masturbate because of spinal injury. The biofeedback penile information would program the computer to project varying degrees and kinds of pornography footage, excerpted and stored from a database of four hundred pornographic video tapes. The whole experience was augmented by repeated and heavy use of cocaine.

Indeed, video toys (and creative variations thereof) provide fantasy reprieves from problems in living. The unhappy or confused adolescent may experience video interactions as islands of alienated comfort, much preferred to human intercourse. The mystique that attracts the user has several parts. One is the basic process of behavior modification known to even the most elementary psychology student as *operant conditioning*. Simply stated, this means that when behavior is followed by reward, the probability of that behavior recurring will increase. The video game provides a series of intermittent (variably timed) rewards, dependent upon proper behavior: if the joystick is correctly manipulated, degrees of success are registered via points, lights, noises, and free replays. This basic principle of increasing the probability of behavior through subsequent reward is central to most scientifically designed learning programs. Emotionally disturbed children, for example, are often helped by professionally trained staff to improve their functioning through carefully dispensed rewards that follow adaptive behaviors.

Video magic is bolstered by an even more compelling lure than the rewards associated with skill development and competitive success. The pre-scripted fantasy of conquering hostile or alien forces propels a segment of youthful users into flurries of compulsive excess. The fears associated with technology, space, and war may be diminished through video success. The fantasy fulfillment of a wish to survive electronic or nuclear holocaust may heavily contribute to a compulsion to improve one's skills. Consider the fantasy relief that a frightened youngster might glean from success at any of the popular video game scripts shown in table 4-1.

Aside from fantasies of mastering technology, video compulsion is augmented by what the newly acquired skill symbolizes to the youthful enthusiast. Just as the parents of computer whiz kids were obsessed with baseball cards, rock groups, innovative social or sexual practices, and psychoactive drugs, today's youngsters are taking charge of their own piece of cultural turf. We are now in the revolutionary era of the computer age, with 80s youth threatening to surpass the seemingly inexhaustible legacy of the 60s. It is no wonder that juvenescence so zealously embraces a symbol that distinguishes it from an era whose psychological, social, and sexual impact has dominated our culture for the past two decades.

Table 4–1
VIDEO SCRIPTS

Missile Command	*Space Invaders*	*SCRAM* *(A Nuclear Power Plant Simulation)*
Defend our civilization. Use your antiballistic missile (ABM) system to protect six major cities against incoming ballistic missiles (ICBM) armed with nuclear warheads. Guard against killer satellites, bombers, and "smart" bombs that dodge your ABM fire. Each wave of ICBMs becomes harder to destroy. The game lasts until all your cities have been destroyed.	Attack the aliens. Strange creatures from outer space threaten our moon base. Your mission is to destroy the aliens with your laser cannon before they reach the surface. When you think you have destroyed them all, a new army of invaders appears. But watch out! The aliens have weapons too.	Learn how a nuclear power plant operates. Let your home computer build a nuclear power plant, then you control its operation, even under adverse conditions. Lower the control rods, vent steam. Turn on the auxiliary feedwater pumps to cool the reactor vessel. Watch out for earthquakes. If they happen you send in workers to make repairs. But, above all try to prevent a meltdown! SCRAM is more than a game. It simulates the operation of a nuclear power plant that's modeled after real-life situations. Discover the basics of thermodynamics and plant operation.

Reprinted by permission of Atari Corporation, Sunnyville, California.

The futuristic computer sport Photon represents a breakthrough in the integration of computer technology and physical activity. The game, which originated in Dallas, is a space-age version of Capture the Flag. The playing field is a 10,000-square-foot indoor arena. An extraterrestrial atmosphere on planet Photon is suggested by low lighting, electronic noises, infusions of mist, and futuristic props. Towers and passageways are cover spots for hiding from fast-moving opponents. All players are "armed" with "phaser" weapons and encouraged to wear dark clothing for camouflage in the dim light. Players are divided before each match into two opposing teams—red and green. The object of the game is to register as many points as possible on a computerized scoring device by blasting your opponent with an electronic phaser gun. Hits are scored by making laser contact with the opponent's electronically sensitive vest or helmet. Photon "warriors" may have their scores recorded by the computer under such preferred code names as Nightwolf, Elf, Slime, or Pope.

Playing time is approximately six minutes at a cost of $3.50 per player for each game. A special discount is offered during "Zappy Hour," when players can purchase two tickets for $4.00. In addition to signing a release form that absolves the Photon Center from responsibility in case of accident, participants must obtain a Photon ID card before playing the game. Players with proper credentials may gain access to any of the 100 planned Photon Amusement Centers throughout the United States. So far ten operative Photon Centers exist nationwide, with more than 20,000 registered Photon players in the Denver center alone. Some young players—many still adolescents—have been spending more than $100 per week on this electrifying sport.

As with drugs or other excessive behaviors, it is not the video game that makes the addict but the impulse to use. A concerned parent or educator would be well advised to invest energy in discovering the hidden fears and fantasies that may underlie the child's compulsion toward video play. This seems a useful alternative to sponsoring a growing number of city ordinances that restrict access to video arcades. The resources that would be dissipated in bootleg electronic devices make the concept of video-game prohibition seem ridiculous.

In an important sense, video games have become the latest scapegoat for more basic problems in Western culture which center around the erosion and breakdown of interpersonal relationships within the family. Children's addiction to video games may be a compromised form of coping with a human environment that is not loving, attractive, or stimulating enough. This scenario, which has been the unhappy plight of some children since the beginning of time, has been even more prevalent in the past twenty years. In relation to the values and behavior patterns of the 60s, contemporary parents may be more likely to emotionally shortchange children in the name of pursuing personal happiness or self-development.

Some have likened the onset of the computer age to the early years of the Industrial Revolution. The portable home book was first made possible by the development of the printing press in 1456. Suddenly a universe of previously unavailable printed information became usable to a great number of people. Home computers serve a similar function. Data banks now available exponentially expand the information fund of any user. Futurists envision the dissolution of the conventional work office in favor of privately based, electronically connected, work alcoves. We are experiencing the first electronic-neurological generation in which knowledge of computer systems will increase the probability of fulfillment in life. Video fascination among youth, like the toy cars and guns of yesterday, simply reflect the profound drive toward survival and self-realization present in all humankind. Through identification, imitation, and observational learning, young people are gaining the skills to manage the technology of the future. In response to the criticism of the computer's limited interactional capabilities, "meta-mind" enthusiasts point toward the development of software with chance, paradox, ambiguity, and humor. Indeed, the video game is an important symbol of tomorrow. Understanding the fears and anxieties that are interwoven with our future will inevitably help us to unravel the mysteries of computer compulsions.

Imagination Colored by Drugs

Pharmaceutical compulsion may also be viewed as symbolic of cultural transition and human concern. Western preoccupation with hallucinogens and the present-day cocaine epidemic may be considered in this light. The images in figure 4-2 are derived from photographs of LSD in the 80s street market. Each segment represents a one-fourth inch square of paper with a drop of LSD infused on its

Figure 4–2. LSD IN THE 80s STREET MARKET

surface. As the user orally administers the chemical magic, he or she symbolically absorbs the images on the paper's surface. The pictures conjure up fantasies of Eastern spirituality and connote benefits from practices such as yoga and meditation. Specifically they suggest a Buddhist influence, based on the doctrine that inward extinction of the self and the senses culminates in a state of illumination and release from suffering. To be sure, there is a strong wave of youthful protest against the technocratic influences of our time. The reckless abandon of "Punkdom" and the quest for existence on a more spiritual plane are compensatory cultural expressions.

Cocaine has evolved as a symbol of adequacy, sexuality, and worldliness. According to recent estimates, more than twenty million U.S. citizens have experimented with the fine white powder. The figure becomes even more striking if one calculates that if the very young and very old are excluded as likely participants, in a country with a total population of more than 200 million, about one fifth of all the inhabitants have tried cocaine! Clearly the *meaning* of cocaine experimentation and use has exceeded its pharmacologic effect.

It is generally acknowledged that cocaine is among the most pleasure inducing of substances for animals or humans. Rats will take the drug to the exclusion of food, companionship, or sex. Yet aside from the primitive delight that we derive from middle-brain cocaine titillation, humans are even more motivated by rumor of the drug's power. The vast majority of those who experiment with cocaine find that they neither like the type of intoxication it produces nor have any compulsion to continue use. As Henry Miller wrote in *Tropic of Cancer*, "Paris (cocaine) is like a whore. From a distance she seems ravishing. You can't wait until you have her in your arms. And five minutes later you feel empty, disgusted with yourself. You feel tricked."

Yet, according to present calculations, cocaine use and abuse is on the rise. What street mythology underlies this often empty and desperate experience? B. F. Skinner once remarked that there is a greater probability of getting killed on the way to the polls than of changing the course of a national election. In the face of a world shadowed by corporate power, nuclear threat, and widely felt impotence, cocaine is rumored to bolster one's sense of personal power and well-being.

In the drug scene, cocaine is sometimes referred to as "the other woman." Sexually transmitted diseases have put a damper on the sexual wanderlust licensed by the 60s. For many, cocaine is thought to be a substitute for sexual adventure and an aphrodisiac as well. Imagine the sense of disappointment and confusion when a naive experimenter encounters sexual impotence related to the actual drug effect. What has become known as "shrivel dick" in street-wise inner circles remains undercover to the middle-class novice. In fact, the mystique of cocaine as an exotic delicacy has been bolstered by journalistic fascination and sensationalism. How many can resist media's false promise of "white-hot euphoria"?

In a culture that is clearly impressed with disciplined health enthusiasts and shimmering electronic calculating units, there is a gap in our daily commerce with "the foreign." This appears particularly true when our lives are increasingly monitored by computer tracking. Even the checkers in the supermarket are using electronic calculating and credit-checking devices. It is no wonder that the image of somehow being connected to a daring conglomerate of ancient South American tradition, exotic sensuality, and a space-age pirate Mafia is irresistible to some.

Mind Trips

Imagination is the staple of psychic nutrition, without which the human psyche would atrophy and perhaps perish. Like food, fantasy has a great potential for abuse because it is vital to survival. Adaptive in providing a solution or reprieve from conflict or stress, fantasy may also destroy by compromising one's ability to perceive and react effectively to objective reality. This outcome is most likely when, as with cocaine, imagination is colored by intoxication. Culturally influenced fantasy without drugs may be used as an adaptive coping mechanism. In excess, however, the process of mental excursion may provide endogenous intoxication and lead to drastic consequences for the individual, the society, or both.

A colleague's dream illustrates how imagination, influenced by society, can be an effective coping mechanism. Prior to the dream, Dr. X was engaged in a fierce bureaucratic struggle at work. He perceived institutional attempts to crush a professional goal that symbolized fifteen years of research and academic concentration. He was consciously considering abandoning his project and resigning from work. The dream began with the visualization of a theater marquee that featured the film *Holocaust from the Side of the Germans*. Dr. X awakened with full recollection of his dream and wrote the following verbatim report:

> Last night before I went to sleep I was feeling persecuted by a number of people, primarily faculty and other associates with whom I've recently had some rather unpleasant business dealings. I had a vivid dream of Nazi persecution billed as "The Holocaust From the Side of the Germans," shown in cinéma vérité.
>
> The dream was extremely lucid and showed huge German armies engulfing relatively small groups of Jews who were armed with primitive jousting instruments, i.e., long sticks with hatchets tied on the ends. The weapons were modifications of the stickball bats I used as a child in the Bronx. In my adolescent bursts of power I revelled in the thrill of hitting a rubber ball a distance of more than three sewers.
>
> I recall the feeling of becoming so irate about having to defend my right to exist as a free human being that I, along with hundreds of others, lunged into ferocious battle with the German tormentors. My whole being screeched in terror as I maimed and killed German soldiers, helter-skelter; all the time feeling that I would most probably die.
>
> Miraculously, I survived the episode and was amazed at how nicely the Germans behaved toward the Jews. Suddenly the Jewish people were walking in peace among Nazis albeit a temporary

state of tranquility. I awakened with a distinct feeling of exhilaration along with the conscious thought that I had acted heroically. I was true to myself and my people by successfully opposing the sadistic tormentors. As soon as I woke up, I pondered how I could create this wonderful dream again.

Clearly the dream fantasy was a symbolic representation of what the dreamer was experiencing in waking life. He was of Jewish descent and felt exposed to a hatred similar to what he experienced as a child from neighborhood kids. Upon waking he reported a sense of increased vigor, optimism, and heightened commitment to pursue his academic goals. The tension of the past week had suddenly dissipated. The vivid dream fantasy served to channel an aggressive impulse that might otherwise have been expressed through self-punishment or self-defeating hostility towards his employers.

Daydreams or night dreams are augmented by fantasy objects in our midst. In *The Movies on Your Mind* (1975), psychoanalyst Harvey R. Greenberg shows how cinema preferences may be used as diagnostic interviews, much like the Rorschach test. Greenberg discovered in analyzing his patients that most were at least "moderately addicted" to the cinema and that movie associations were an effective route to the unconscious. A patient's ruminations about a particular movie may give invaluable insight into his or her previous Oedipal struggles, troubled present, or anxious premonitions about the future. Greenberg cites the example of an adolescent with school-phobia who reported that this favorite film was *King of Kings*.

> He especially enjoyed the part where the Roman soldiers pounded the nails into Jesus' hands. I discovered that his cranium was jammed with homosexual and masochistic fantasies: he avoided school because of a tremendous fear—and hidden wish—that a gang of local bullies would beat and rape him. In his daydreams, he would show a Christ-like forbearance and pity for his tormentors, so that they would give up their evil ways and worship, rather than despise him.

Certainly, *King of Kings* helped this young man to validate his persecutory beliefs and to organize his most underlying fears and wishes. Greenberg finds that those most prone to movie mania are rigid, inhibited types who characteristically avoid any close inter-personal contact. Individuals such as these become intolerably anx-ious when faced with the spontaneity of a personal encounter and only feel alive as vicarious participants in adventures of their movie heroes.

Compulsive Fantastication

Fantasy excess does not always remain a private enterprise. Often it becomes integrated with the lives of those around us and forms a symbiotic system in which the parties involved reap mutual benefit from a shared alteration of reality. Data from the life history of a thirty-year-old male homosexual prostitute, referred to as Bill, illus-trates this point.

Bill's clientele includes mostly middle-aged homosexual men who contract his services for acting out various sexual fantasies. Most of the staged scenarios involve some form of make-believe dom-ination of the client. Below is Bill's verbatim description of his rela-tionship with his primary repeat client, followed by his overall per-spective on the type of relationships he has had with other customers.

> The primary repeat client with whom I deal has a very interesting fantasy in which he is symbolically powerful and powerless, super-stud and super-slut, lady of great refinement and common slut. The evening starts out with him in a supra-masculine, Nazi, black leather motorcycle type outfit. He is a physically imposing and very handsome man and one would expect him to be quite domi-nant in sex (inserter) or play (master, whipper, etc.) However, this is only a preliminary posturing . . . when he makes contact, visual, verbal or physical, with a potential playmate, he immediately switches to a very feminine role. He becomes a refined lady who wants to be used and abused; to be whipped on his "pussy" (his asshole) . . . to have clamps put on his shaved "titties." Frequently he has this done while being restrained in stocks or slings in front of a large public audience (30–100 people) or at an S & M bar. In the privacy of my bedroom he likes to change into full female un-dergarments and beg me to fuck his "pussy." I find myself unable to be aroused by either his fantasy or his submission and so I talk dirty, make up fantasies for him and bring him to a climax with

my hand on his "clitoris" (penis) and a vibrator in his anus.

Other typical fantasies center around sexual domination also. The clients almost always (90% +) want to feel as though I want to "use" them to get off; (climax or not, but I have to be apparently desirous of the contact and the "use" of them). They may want me to be the hot young stud in which case I "talk high school" and dominate or they may want me to be 25–30, in which case I develop scenes with older men for them to visualize while I dominate them sexually. In these cases "domination" is limited to the fact that I am fucking them aggressively or verbally forcing them to suck me with commands like "suck my dick—yeah—suck my big cock—you like my dick?—yeah—make my dick happy—suck it." Heavily stressing "dick"and "cock" usually elicits groans of excitement from the tricks. They become so excited that they are pleasing me that they usually come almost spontaneously—if they don't come within 10 minutes I will touch or suck them and that never takes more than 1–2 minutes. Some also want me to be the helpless boy-stud that they take advantage of. So they are the oppressor; but even when they are the aggressor and nominally dominant, they give me the control almost always because the whole point for them is to succeed in giving *me* pleasure.

In addition to prostitution, Bill conducts a lucrative "phone sex" business where he receives credit card payments of $35 for sexual fantasies dispensed over the telephone. This is a growing enterprise in most urban locations, with major daily newspapers carrying access telephone numbers in their classified sections. Listings include such mnemonic ploys as FRED HOT and EAR FULL. Some phone-sex entrepreneurs have managed to clear more than $1,000 per week, hiring groups of operators to manage the lines on a twenty-four-hour basis. A typical heterosexually oriented ad reads:

Rochelle's Phone Sex
I love to talk Dirty
Don't do it alone
Get off over the Phone!
Whether you're in bed, in your office, or even at a phone booth, satisfy yourself and Rochelle or one of her delicious friends now.

Bill and a growing number of phone-sex dealers service a burgeoning consumer market. In much the same manner as the drug merchant caters to the pharmaceutical needs and whims of a steady drug-using clientele, phone-sex dealers dispense fantasy. Interestingly, the phone commodity for Bill and other operators is usually a run of sexy verbiage with a general theme of the caller being dominated. One man, for example, enjoys having his operator describe a scenario where he is diapered and repeatedly spanked. Like drugs, phone sex can provide temporary relief from loneliness, anxiety, and fear.

The fantasy of being punished for one's wrongdoing, while at the same time being attended to and sexually desired, is wish fulfilling for the consumer. For Bill, the short-term psychological payoff of acting out his own sexual and interpersonal wishes, while earning money for self-maintenance, outweighs considerations of personal risk or legal culpability.

Those compelled by interactive fantasy are not limited to sexually explicit scenarios. *Dungeons and Dragons* is the most popular of the recent deluge of fantasy role-playing games in general practice. The game involves two or more players involved in exploring new worlds and having imaginary adventures. The players consist of a Dungeon Master and one or more role players who take on a fantasy identity throughout the game. The Dungeon Master is the narrator or commander of the ever-changing story. He or she describes the current predicaments of the role players and answers questions (purportedly within reason) about their situation. The Dungeon Master describes and creates dungeons, lands, planets, galaxies, planes of existence, or anything else one might imagine. These may emerge from an already published "module" or something of the Master's own creation. Maps, illustrations, charts, and so on may be used to help define the adventure or quest. Finally, the Dungeon Master explains the outcome of every decision, action, or move a role player makes. The competent Master preferably has had a long apprenticeship as role player in past games. He or she is ideally perceived by the other players as intelligent, creative, and having the skills necessary to communicate effectively with the others.

A description of the psychological attraction of the game is offered by a former *Dungeons and Dragons* enthusiast:

Imagination is a wonderful escape from the real world and all its problems. It allows you to daydream of seeing and experiencing things that may not otherwise be possible. It is also a very personal experience, uniquely tailored to your personality. That is why a book is often better than its movie; we individually interpret the book using our imagination, something the movie could never replicate. Imagination and escape from reality are therefore major attractions to fantasy games. Another attraction to *D & D* is the whole concept of role playing. When reading a book you may associate yourself with a major character, but you are only observing and experiencing what is happening in the story. In *D & D* you make active decisions in what is happening, using your own knowledge, intuition, and personality. In reality we make decisions every second of our days, but when we imagine, it's usually a scene, image, object, concept, idea, story, etc. Rarely do we go through the decision-making process that we are so accustomed to in our every day lives. In *D & D* you are responding to another person's imagination, forcing you to make imaginative decisions in a fantasy world. This opens a new door to imagining and fantasizing. Finally, role playing allows you to be someone else. It allows you to be stronger, more powerful, more daring, more attractive; anything you want to be. And it allows you to experience things never before possible in the "real world." That alone is a strong attraction.

There is currently much debate regarding the question of whether an unstable youth might lose his or her tenuous equilibrium and fail to emerge from a role-playing fantasy. In William Dear's (1984) nonfiction account of *The Dungeon Master* he describes the 1979 disappearance of James Dallas Egbert, who is reported to have been a sixteen-year-old computer genius. Egbert is described as a shy, homosexual youth with a history of drug abuse. He is said to have been given to writing odd poems about trapped insects and was reportedly "addicted" to *Dungeons and Dragons*. Egbert suddenly vanished in the maze of heating tunnels under the campus of Michigan State University, where he was a student in a University-sponsored children's program. He left a clue to his whereabouts via a stick-pin map of his route in *Dungeons and Dragons*. Egbert surfaced a month later in Louisiana and committed suicide about a year after returning to his Ohio home.

In a more recent November 1984 tragedy, sixteen-year-old David Erwin and his twelve-year-old brother Stephen were found shot to death in an apparent murder-suicide. Local Colorado police linked the deaths to the boys' fascination with *Dungeons and Dragons*. According to the police investigation, David had been obsessed by the game for several years and near the time of the killings he had just finished devising a variation with "new characters and armaments." The boys were said to have died in a macabre murder-suicide effort to journey together into a mysterious "third dimension." After interviewing the victims' ten-year-old brother and reading three notes the boys left for their parents, police inferred that their "fantasy-world game became a suicide pact." Investigating Police Chief Larry Stallcup reported at a press conference shortly after the tragedy that there was indication that the boys believed that the intertwining of their legs in a certain way, at the time of death, would permit them to go into a third dimension together. This bizarre posturing was intended to keep them together in the new dimension for mutual protection. The boys' bodies were found at their favorite hideout, under a railroad trestle, on November 2, 1984. Their legs were intertwined. The coroner for the case concluded that Stephen shot his older brother in the head and then shot himself in the head with a .22 caliber revolver taken from their home.

Reports such as these have prompted some concerned citizens to lobby for removal of the game from school and local libraries. One Colorado Christian group referred to the game as "satanic" after the suicide of a teenage player in Virginia. The death occurred after a "curse" was placed on him during a game. In February 1983, the Alamogordo, New Mexico, school district decided not to allow the game to be played as part of an afterschool education program, following protests from some parents.

Efforts to outlaw *Dungeons and Dragons* and similar role-playing games belong in the same camp as the legal prohibition of video games. The game takes on the role of simplified scapegoat, and public attention is diverted from more complex and frightening factors that underlie the disturbing phenomenon of teenage suicide. Opponents to the game argue that the only way of resolving a fantasy role is through death, and that this is the underlying cause of many fatalities. On counterpoint, advocates claim that, just as in real life, characters can be retired from active play to live comfortably on a country villa and sightsee around their fantasy world. The concerned parent or friend of an adolescent who seems dangerously involved in a fantasy role would be best advised to seek competent psychological guidance. The idea of outlawing a game that can be played without any board or paraphernalia other than an adventurous and creative mind makes about as much sense as eliminating buildings in fear that people might jump off.

Unreal Worlds

When a person's belief system challenges mainstream cultural precepts, he or she is often called crazy or mentally ill. It is not uncommon for "schizophrenics" to hear voices from other worlds or to believe that they are Napoleon or Christ. To be sure, schizophrenics are among the most fantasy-oriented people in our midst. Yet the syndrome is so prevalent that nearly one in every hundred U.S. citizens will bear the stigma at some time in their lives.

Thomas Szasz argues that the entire concept of schizophrenia as a disease is erroneous. In *The Myth of Mental Illness* he reasons that without definitive evidence of organic dysfunction, people should not be labelled as sick because of their beliefs. Actually, people frequently experience problems in living, and they may develop eccentric beliefs as highly personal and specialized coping devices. Clearly, drug toxicity or internal biochemical imbalances are involved in much of the personality disorganization that we describe as emotional disturbance. Yet the ability of many who have psychotic thoughts to function with great rationality stimulates a fascinating question. Are some "crazy" people compulsively dependent on fantasy, as drug addicts may be to heroin or alcohol? Certainly there are some intriguing parallels, as the following list of schizophrenics' characteristics reveals:

Denial. Schizophrenics often deny that there is anything wrong with them or that their perceptions are inaccurate.

Compulsion. Schizophrenics often will choose not to take antipsychotic medicines, which when properly administered serve to reduce fantasy productions.

Loss of Control. Schizophrenics may suffer great damage to social, economic and health functions in relation to their uncompromising belief in the importance and authenticity of their delusions or hallucinations.

Relapse Rates. For schizophrenics, drug addicts, and alcoholics, recidivism is roughly the same; about 60-80 percent after six to twelve months of "abstinence."

In Robert Lindner's now-classic psychiatric tale, "The Jet-Propelled Couch," Lindner takes the position that Kirk Allen's psychosis, which involves his belief that he can transport himself back and forth to different galaxies, is actually an addiction to fantasy.

Kirk was brought up by a series of governesses as the only white child on a remote island. One of the governesses, whom he called Sterile Sally, imbued him with a dread of contamination from his surroundings. She considered the native children "filthy niggers," and forbade Kirk to converse with his friends.

> As a consequence of this added isolation, his fantasy life—until then of a fashion and degree usual among lonely children—increased sharply. Daydreaming now came to occupy much of his time, and there appeared those lavish, imaginative reconstructions of the world which were to be so significant for him and so characteristic of his life up to the day we met. The details of the initial fantasy that Kirk toyed with during Sterile Sally's residence and for some while thereafter need not concern us here. It was a childish hodge-podge, constructed from odd remnants of reading. He identified himself with characters from the Oz books, for example, and mentally played out a cordial existence in a friendlier, more exciting world. This primary experience unfolded the imaginative facility and the technique of mental detachment which he developed to astonishing proportions in adulthood.

Beverly Delores Dark is the pen name of a forty-three-year-old woman who was first diagnosed as paranoid schizophrenic at the age of twenty-one. Her self-proclaimed identity is "the writer." Prior to her first psychiatric diagnosis and subsequent hospitalization, she was an aspiring college student engaged in the study of English literature. *Pierre Blake* is one of her early writings, exemplary of her creativity, logic, and humor.

Pierre Blake

There once lived a man, Pierre Blake
Who constantly craved milk and cake
His baker named Glum
One day couldn't come
Said Blake, "My own cake I shall bake."

Quite often he'd watched how Glum fussed
So he started right off but got mussed
Though he used enough dough
And the flame wasn't low
'Stead of cake he got stuck with the crust

Pierre Blake though was quite a shrewd guy
"Throw it out!" he exclaimed, "No, not I!"
Fruit filling he found
Shaped it out to be round
And short for Pierre
Called it "pie."

After a series of late-adolescent disillusionments with friends, teachers, and writing, Beverly became absorbed in the idea that her destiny was to bring a universal language to earth. She began to "see" movies of her life projected on her bedroom wall. Shortly after the onset of these bizarre experiences, at the age of twenty-one, Beverly was diagnosed as paranoid schizophrenic. She was given shock treatment, and drug therapy, and began a prolonged series of psychiatric hospitalizations.

Episodically Beverly returned to college, where she completed a baccalaureate degree in English literature. In her junior year, she began to develop the notion that Shakespeare had written much of his poetry about herself and her college friends. She increasingly believed that Shakespeare had used his famed sonnets as a secret device to communicate his inner feelings about their relationship. The fact that their physical lives were chronologically quite separate had nothing to do with their communication and romance on a spiritual plane.

The comparative writing samples shown in Table 4-2 are excerpted from one of Beverly's academic papers entitled "Six Sic Son-

Table 4–2
SIX SIC SONNETS

My thesis cites that, at least on one level, Shakespeare—in his sonnets—sees himself as a beautiful, sensitive, young, bi-sexual poet reincarnated in the 20th Century; and that he is writing about three women with whom this young Poet is involved: The Dr., Elaine, who graduated from College in '61; the Psychologist, Arlene, in '62; and the Artist, Beverly (Beverly Delores Dark) in '63. Sonnet 61 is a companionpiece to Sonnet 16, because upon graduation the woman involved (rival Elaine) is like a 16 yr. old girl; Sonnet 62 is a companionpiece to Sonnet 26 because after graduation, the woman involved (rival Arlene) marries a 26 year old young man is therefore parallel to him chronologically (as is later to be revealed in the 26th Sonnet); and Sonnet 63 is a love-sonnet which is to be coupled with Sonnet 36—because the Dark Lady (Who is always addressed as one with the Homosexual Friend) possesses the faculties of a 36 yr. old woman upon termination of her early education.

Decomposition

(using each letter once only and re-arranging the order)

SONNET SIXTY DASH ONE BEVERLY DOLORES DARK

N.Y. Broken Dr. Elaine tt (tooties) (to
tease) loves hard sex. Dos(e)s Yo(u) (her)
           (e)   (u)
       knee   u

SONNET SIXTEEN BEVERLY DOLORES DARK

RT Elaine loves sex . . . body reeks
N-O n(u)t(s)
          (u)   (s)

SONNET SIXTY DASH TWO BEVERLY DELORES DARK

   vd   hr   sub dodo ns
(vide-French) (whore) (substitute) (anus)
Arlene seeks trix to lay you
      (tricks)

SONNET TWENTY DASH SIX BEVERLY DOLORES DARK

iu   tt   Arlene looks bad here . .
Dry sex u donut
    (a "dough" nut)

SONNET SIXTY DASH THREE BEVERLY DOLORES DARK

Rx:
Love her dark say   yy   notes.
        (too wise)
N-O sleet bed . . . H(u)rts
        (u)

SONNET THIRTY DASH SIX BEVERLY DOLORES DARK

Dislikes hard sex. Lover her rays
Don't toy . . . B(u)rnt   (u)
 (u)   (us)   (e)   (uu)

You   use'd e to   use
a   U.S.   e   to use
     (knee)

nets." In the left panel she describes Shakespeare's "hidden motive" for composing his poetry. The discussion centers on her belief that Shakespeare is actually a sensitive, young, bisexual poet, reincarnated in the twentieth century. His love sonnets contain cryptic messages about his relationships with Beverly and two of her close friends. According to Beverly, only she can decipher the secret sonnet code.

The right panel shows how "decomposition" unveils the "true meaning" of the sonnets. The "writer's" pen name, Beverly Delores Dark, is combined with a particular sonnet number, for example, Sonnet Sixteen Beverly Delores Dark. Then "using each letter once only and rearranging the order," Beverly reveals the secret meaning.

According to Beverly, she and Shakespeare are carrying on a love affair through the sonnets. She is Shakespeare's mistress (or Dark Lady) and her friends are jealous of the relationship. Shakespeare's outrage at his lover's friends is revealed when the sonnets are "decomposed." The writing samples included represent only a small segment of "Six Sic Sonnets," which is a thesis of approximately thirty pages in length. Another paper by the same author is entitled "Space Travel During the Renaissance." In recent years the "writer" has concluded that she is "The Messiah of all the Messiahs."

Obviously, Beverly's unusual thought process involves more than simply a chemical imbalance, resulting in mental illness. She shows a tenacious clinging to her highly personalized relationship with Shakespeare and lives a fantasy identity as Shakespeare's mistress. At present we can only speculate that the development of such an imaginary self represents an extreme case of addiction to fantasy. As stated by R.D. Laing: "The self, in order to develop and sustain its identity and autonomy, and in order to be safe from the persistent threat and danger from the world, has cut itself off from direct relatedness with others and has endeavored to become its own object (of interest): to become, in fact, related directly only to itself. Its cardinal functions become fantasy and observation."

Laing, who founded Kingsley Hall in England, believes that the "returned schizophrenic" is the most effective therapist since only such a person can fully comprehend the dimensions of another's schizophrenic experience. This model has long been appreciated in the treatment of addictive disorders. In the end, there is no benefit in forming negative judgments about those who are compelled to seek out the fantasy state. "If we cease to degrade those who may truly 'see' the world in a grain of sand . . . and eternity in an hour, they may stop responding with confusion and fear to their perceptions."

Internal Hallucinogens

Over the years a number of abnormalities have been proposed as the biological basis of schizophrenia. One of the more prominent theories is that schizophrenia is the result of too rapid neurotransmission in the dopaminergic pathways (pathways in the central nervous system that use dopamine as the neurotransmitter). In fact, schizophrenics show a number of metabolic differences that are characterized by an excess of either dopamine or dopamine receptors, or both. Any one or a combination of these two abnormalities would lead to hyperactivity in the dopaminergic pathways. The hyperactivity may be related not only to schizophrenia but to other cerebral aberrations.

It is of great significance that dopaminergic pathways are concentrated in the prefrontal or neocortex, and as might be expected, an exceptionally large concentration of dopamine is in this area. Patricia Goldman-Rakic of Yale University School of Medicine believes that there is a high possibility that the prefrontal cortex is the site of the dopamine imbalance responsible for the distorted thinking characteristic of schizophrenics. As might be expected in a disorder characterized by a chemical imbalance, a large body of evidence suggests that there is a genetic predisposition to schizophrenia. This genetic propensity could be manifested by a number of metabolic abnormalities that would result in an increase in dopamine. One such abnormality observed recently in schizophrenics is a deficiency of the enzyme dopamine B-hydroxylase, which would result in a decrease in the rate at which dopamine is converted to the next normal metabolite, norepinephrine. This decreased rate of conversion would then be manifested by an increase in the level of dopamine in the central nervous system.

It is not a coincidence that the frontal lobes of the cerebral cortex are also the site of dream imagery, as is illustrated by the activation of this portion of the brain during REM sleep, which is undoubtedly the height of fantasy experience. Since many of the pathways in the frontal lobes (or neocortex) use dopamine as the neurotransmitter, the bizarre dreams experienced in REM sleep may be biologically related to the rapid neurotransmission present in hallucinating schizophrenics. These pathways are very susceptible to excitation, either from external stimuli or from self-excitation, as occurs in the case of fantasy. In REM sleep, it is clear that the bizarre images are created without external stimuli. This is also true in the case of the schizophrenic hallucination. Thus, we begin to see a relationship between fantasy, at least as expressed in REM sleep, and the hallucinations present in some forms of schizophrenia.

Related to rapid dopaminergic neurotransmission in the neocortex and REM sleep is the phenomenon of nightmares. Nightmares are represented by vivid imagery—often in color—and occur during the REM portion of the sleep cycle. Ernest Hartman of Tufts University School of Medicine has shown that people who frequently experience nightmares tend to have more than the statistically expected number of schizophrenic relatives. He also reports that nightmare-prone individuals themselves are more at risk for schizophrenia than the general population. This is not surprising in view of the belief that rapid neurotransmission in the dopaminergic pathways in the neocortex is related to schizophrenic symptoms, dream images, and fantasy.

Although the mechanisms by which the brain stores memory are far from being completely understood, several theories have enabled scientists to propose models that are useful in understanding this very complex function (memory) of the most complex entity in the universe (the brain). Although the brain is composed of billions of interconnecting neurons, not all of these neurons are uniformly wired in all cerebral processes. It is believed that within the brain small networks of interconnecting neocortical neurons act as a storage bunk for certain images, including those associated with fantasy. In 1958 Donald H. Hebb, a Canadian psychologist, proposed that these networks, which are called "cell assemblies," are strengthened by repetition of stimuli that trigger retrieval of the stored images. The idea that memory of events, names, numbers, and places is strengthened by repetition is not exactly earthshaking news to anyone. However, by using this concept, Francis Crick and Graham Mitchison were able to develop a model in which cell assemblies are represented by artificial electronic networks. Not unlike similar situations in our real brains, Crick and Mitchison found that it is possible to overload these systems by attempting to store too many associations (units of information) in a given period of time, resulting in "bizarre associations," a characteristic of fantasy. They also report that overloading may cause the networks to produce a limited set of "memories" (electronic outputs) regardless of the stimulation received by the network. This may be translated into a real-life situation where nearly any stimulus results in the production of the same image, as in the case of repetitious schizophrenic hallucinations and delusions. The overloaded network may also respond to a mock stimulus that ordinarily would not cause a response by printing out a bizarre image analogous to a hallucination. Thus, we begin to see the implication of this model for schizophrenia as well as for excessive reliance on fantasy. An important point is that dopamine pathways in the neocortex are so readily stimulated or excited that it is relatively easy to overload the cell assemblies present there. In schizophrenia, these cell assemblies seem to be constantly overloaded because of the genetic predisposition to produce more than the normal amount of dopamine. This results in a super-excitable neuronal pathway readily capable of producing hallucinations.

Compulsive reliance on fantasy involves overloading image-storing cell assemblies by self-stimulation. Repeated stimulation of these networks results in more robust synaptic connections, which facilitate the reproduction of particular tension-reducing images. It becomes increasingly probable that a bizarre thought or fantasy will reoccur or will be remembered more easily. Psychiatrists have referred to this neuronal predisposition as "scratch a schizophrenic", that is, he or she will bleed (fantasize profusely) with minimal provocation. For example, Jim, a schizophrenic living in Denver, responds to almost any verbal stimulation by repeating his contention that Trans World Airlines has initiated a "nuclear plot" to beam deadly rays at him in order to destroy his brain. Also, repeated and intense participation in *Dungeons and Dragons* requires a considerable amount of imagination. Compulsive involvement in the game would result in a strengthening of the cell assemblies in the frontal cortex to the point where the distinction between real-life situations and those present in the game could become blurred in susceptible players (those with overactive dopaminergic pathways). The tragic incident of the two brothers described earlier may be related to the brain's adaptation to repeated fantasy episodes, which diminished the ability to distinguish between internal and external imagery.

Some forms of schizophrenia may well be viewed in the context of biochemical addiction to fantasy. Beverly Dolores Dark's delusion that Shakespeare is talking to her through his sonnets might be related to overactive dopaminergic pathways in the prefrontal cortex. Although it is a temptation to label her writings as "thought disorder," in actual fact considerable organizational skill is required to "decompose" the sonnets as she has done. It is obvious that her fantasies are very important to her self-image and possibly even to her sense of survival. Clearly there is an element of "self-induced changes in neurotransmission" contributing to Beverly's problem behaviors. Beverly seems to use Shakespeare as the alcoholic relies on drink. Although her options are limited, she can cook meals, entertain guests, and teach elementary school on a part-time basis. She seems to "turn on" Shakespeare when she has the luxury of doing so.

Self-stimulation of the neocortex in order to produce altered states of consciousness must somehow be rewarded by a desired feeling, or else there would be little reason for reproducing such imagery. The center of positive and negative emotion is the limbic system, which has neuronal connections that extend into the neocortex. Self-induced imagery in the neocortex is translated into the desired emotional state through neuronal pathways to the limbic system. As we explained in chapter 1, self-induced activities or experiences can bring about the release of endogenous chemicals (norepinephrine, if the desirable experience is arousal; or endorphins, if the desired experience is satiation). The release of these endogenous substances creates an imbalance as a result of the accompanying change in neurotransmission, which is then countered by enzymatic changes in the brain. Thus, the individual must engage in more frequent and more intense episodes of self-stimulated fantasy in order to achieve the desired level of fantasy reward.

In this manner, various fantasy addictions may be associated with arousal or satiation states, depending on the type of limbic stimulation desired. For example, Bill, by using phone sex, is able to arouse his clients through verbal imagery alone. These susceptible individuals may be thought of as having vivid imaginations possibly aided by abnormally active dopaminergic pathways in the prefrontal cortex. They can achieve preferred levels of arousal by using Bill to stimulate cortical images, which result in desired excitement of arousal neurons in the middle brain.

Just as the arousal-prone person's preferred drug group is stimulants, and the satiation-prone person chooses opiates, those prone to fantasy also have a drug of choice. They often select hallucinogenic drugs, which facilitate overloading neocortical cell assemblies to produce desired fantasy experiences. Considered in the light of the discussion in this section, the distinction between compulsive fantasy and schizophrenia begins to fade. Fantasy, like other addictions, may lead to compulsion, loss of control, and continuation in spite of adverse consequences.

Armageddon: The Ultimate Fantasy

The tumultuous and sometimes tragic experiences of individual fantasy addicts usually concern only a small circle of friends. Associates sympathize with the torment of being compulsively involved in imaginary happenings, but only rarely accept the delusional beliefs as "true." Occasionally, however, a completely irrational precept is embraced as gospel by a powerful constituency of society. In cases such as this, the adverse consequences of fantasy addiction may reach catastrophic proportions.

The history of the ancient Nahua people of Mexico reveals the destruction of an entire civilization because of a bizarre and destructive belief. One of the Nahua gods was said to have voluntarily sacrificed himself in a fire to give life to the sun. This myth later gave rise to the Aztec belief that the sun needed to be nourished by human hearts. The Aztecs felt compelled to feed the sun with thousands upon thousands of human hearts ripped from the bodies of sacrificial victims. What started as a well-contained ritual sacrifice degenerated into compulsive genocide when 75,000 humans were sacrificed in a fifteenth-century ceremony at El Templo Mayor. The necessity of purging neighboring cultures in order to obtain sacrificial victims led to a state of war with victimized groups. When Cortez began the conquest of Mexico, surrounding civilizations were eager to join him in the destruction of the Aztec capitol.

Unfortunately, a fundamentalist belief within our own culture has the earmarks of a devastating social intoxicant. The theology of Armageddon is described in Revelation, the last book in the New

Testament, traditionally attributed to John. According to contemporary fundamentalist interpretations, Revelation predicts that before Christ returns to earth to establish His Second Kingdom, a last great battle between the forces of good and evil will occur. As told in Revelation 9:2–6:

> He opened the shaft of the bottomless pit, and from the shaft rose smoke like the smoke of a great furnace, and the sun and the air were darkened with the smoke from the shaft.
> Then from the smoke came locusts on the earth, and they were given power like the power of scorpions on the earth;
> They were told not to harm the grass of the earth or any green growth or any tree, but only those of mankind who have not the seal of God upon their foreheads; they were allowed to torture them for five months, but not to kill them, and their torture was like the torture of a scorpion, when it stings a man.
> And in those days men will seek death and will not find it; they will long to die, and death will fly from them.

Armageddon, the worst time on earth, will be preceded by an exceedingly troubled period referred to as the Tribulation. Believers explain current world unrest as evidence that we have entered this period. Those who have accepted Christ into their hearts "in the wink of an eye" will experience Rapture. During Rapture, those who are aligned with the forces of good, namely fundamentalist Christians, will be brought to heaven and protected from the destruction below. Some fundamentalist bumper stickers read: "Caution, in case of Rapture this vehicle will be unmanned." Armageddon theology is explained in a book by Hal Lindsey, *The Late Great Planet Earth* (1976), reported to have sold more than ten million copies.

The prophesy of Armageddon is viewed by some as a forecast of nuclear war. In an interview published in the December 26–January 2, 1984, issue of *People* magazine, President Reagan was asked: "In the Jerusalem Post you were quoted as saying that this generation may see Armageddon, that a lot of biblical prophecies are being played out today. Do you really believe that?"

Reagan's reply: "I've never said that publicly. I've talked here with my own people because theologians, quite a while ago, were telling me that never before has there been a time when so many prophecies were coming together. There have been times in the past when we thought the end of the world was coming, but never anything like this."

Some have used Armageddon theology as a defense for the use of nuclear weapons. They believe that the Bible identifies the Soviet Union with the anti-Christ or Evil Empire and the precipitator of the final battle between good and evil—Armageddon. Of course, those who are on the side of good need not fear a nuclear holocaust (Armageddon) because it is God's will that the Evil Empire be destroyed.

One of the signs of the imminence of Armageddon is that people will wear the "mark of the beast," which is said to be number 666. Revelation 13:16–17 explains: "Also it causes all, both small and great, both rich and poor, both free and slave, to be marked on the right hand or the forehead, so that no one can buy or sell unless he has the mark, that is the name of the beast or the number of its name." The "mark of the beast" is interpreted by some as the symbolic representation of our credit-card culture. When the anti-Christ gains control of the earth, no one will be able to participate in any commerce without the "mark" on his or her American Express, Carte Blanche, Master Charge, or other "beastly" credit-charging device.

The apocalyptic fantasy in which "nuclear winter" is attributed to the will of God may be psychologically construed as a denial of nuclear addiction. Like the hopeless alcohol addict who insists that he can control his drinking, militant leaders insist that we can control the world's most devastating intoxicant. Part of the report rushed to President Truman in 1945, after the earliest nuclear test explosion, reads as follows: "It lighted every peak, crevasse and ridge of the nearby mountain range with a clarity and beauty that cannot be described but must be seen to be imagined. It was the beauty the great poets dream about but described most poorly and inadequately . . . Then came the strong, sustained, awesome roar which warned of doomsday and made us feel that we puny things were blasphemous to dare tamper with the forces heretofore reserved to the Almighty."

Heretofore reserved to the Almighty and today reserved for Ronald Reagan, Mikhail Gorbachev, and Muammar Gaddafi? No wonder there is so much inclination to attribute this awesome power to a superior being. Yet the fantasy that it is God's plan to arrange for Armageddon permits a mystical rationalization for the continued development of nuclear armaments. Armageddon theology serves as a denial mechanism for those who will not take responsibility for the fact that, like lemmings, we are rushing headlong toward the precipice of world destruction. Indeed we have far exceeded the thresholds of compulsion and loss of control when a war between the Soviet Union and the United States could mean a Second World War every second.

The compulsive militants of planet Earth would be well advised to take their cue from the wisdom of Alcoholics Anonymous: Stop Arming! Go to Meetings! Get a Sponsor! Ask for Help!

"Loose joints . . . blow . . . what you need . . . crack it up?
— 1986 Street Pusher

5

Journey to Oblivion

What are the conditions of a trip to oblivion?
The voyage is destined for hardship and suffering.
It can begin anywhere in time and space.
The universe abounds with capsules for transport.
One blurs the senses with lightning velocity.
Another creeps slowly leaving trails of combustion.
The passenger sleeps through much of the way,
while observers mark progress via symbols of change.
A robot pilot is strong at the helm.
Only mutiny can adjust the ship's scattered course.
A guard must be posted or the android returns.
The traveler remains altered by this sojourn in hell.

The Voyage of Hardship

Of particular concern is the effect of the drug epidemic on youth.
The only group in our society that has shown an increase in mortality rate in the past two decades has been those sixteen to twenty-four years old. Alcohol, drug-related accidents, homicides, and suicides are major factors in the accelerated death toll. At the time of this writing, crack—a widely available form of smokable cocaine—has taken the lead as the most devastating street drug on the market. Fast food of the drug scene, crack reaches the brain within ten seconds and produces an intense euphoria, which is followed in minutes by a crushing low. It can be purchased in most large U.S. cities in the form of chips that sell for as little as $10 each—yet within just a few weeks a rapidly evolving crack habit may escalate to a cost of more than $100 per day. In New York City, where crack is the most urgent law-enforcement problem, an 18-percent increase in robberies is believed to be directly related to crack.

Indeed, the metaphor of a hyped-up journey to nowhere that produces incomprehensible hardship and suffering seems to describe the suicidal experience of addiction:

> He [the addict] had momentary visions as his mind floated in a sea of befogged escape. He felt a soothing warmth that expanded to fill the cavities of his shrinking torso . . . he was a maestro, a commander—invulnerable to the blades and knuckle-busters of a hostile and frightening world. He felt complete . . . needed nothing. He dreamed that he was a hero; that he would be honored at majestic kingdoms on his route.
>
> Despite these reveries, he went nowhere. His ship was captained by an android—programmed to mindlessly rotate through one drab circle after another. Slowly, the warmth that he once felt began to fade as his torso was besieged by dampness and chill. Shivering, he sold his last bit of freedom for a moment of peace.

The concept of addiction as a progressively incapacitating disease originates from a series of lectures presented by E. M. Jellinek at the Yale Summer School of Alcohol Studies in July 1951 and July 1952. On the basis of a questionnaire study of more than 2,000 male alcoholics, Jellinek formulated his four-phase concept of alcohol addiction. He distinguished between two categories of alcoholics: "alcohol addicts" and "habitual symptomatic excessive drinkers." The disease concept applies only to alcohol addicts who, after a variable period of problem drinking, lose control over their alcohol intake. Excessive drinkers, on the other hand, may pathologically use alcohol to relieve conflict for many years, yet the phenomenon of loss of control never becomes part of their drinking history.

In the first phase of alcohol addiction, which Jellinek called the "pre-alcoholic symptomatic phase," the prospective alcoholic begins to experience an inordinate amount of tension reduction through drinking and drinking-related activities. Generally, within a period of six months to two years, Jellinek's typical subject begins to use alcohol nearly every day to relieve stress. Although his tolerance for alcohol exceeds that of his peers, that is, he can drink a good deal more than they before reaching a desired level of intoxication, his excessive drinking remains relatively inconspicuous and undetected.

The sudden emergence of alcohol-related blackouts marks the second, prodromal stage of alcohol addiction. A blackout may be understood as a period of intermediate memory loss, whereby a person who imbibes as few as two ounces of absolute alcohol may carry on a reasonable conversation or complex pattern of activity without a trace of memory the following day. The blackout period is indeed intermediate in that the drinker experiences normal memory functions before and after the lost interval.

Soon after the onset of blackouts, the drinker begins to understand, in some very vague manner, that his pattern of drinking is different from that of others. He begins to sneak drinks at social gatherings and becomes preoccupied with when and how to get high. At this point, the prodromal drinker may be observed to gulp drinks, while increasing guilt leads to more obvious signs of covering up. The incipient alcohol addict may, for example, conspicuously avoid any reference to alcohol, pro or con, during conversation. Depending on the drinker's physical and psychological condition, as well as the nature of the social network, the prodromal period may persist for anywhere from six months to four or five years.

The next stage of alcohol addiction, which Jellinek referred to as the crucial phase, is marked by loss-of-control drinking. The addict appears to lose the faculty of making rational choices about how much to consume. Any level of consumption, even the taste of one drink, seems to trigger an irresistible demand for alcohol that continues until he is either too drunk or too ill to consume any more.

Loss of control comes into play only when people respond to conflict or stress by succumbing to drink. Before drinking, the alcoholic may appear sensible, affable, and emotionally intact. During this phase he begins to rationalize his unseemly drinking by creating easily detected alibis, attempting to convince himself that he has good reason to become intoxicated. He minimizes the extent of his disturbance by drawing attention to irresponsible actions among friends and associates.

At this point alcoholism begins to bring about warnings and reprovals from family, friends, and business associates. The drinker, now thoroughly entrenched in the crucial phase of alcohol addiction, progressively withdraws from his usual social environment. He becomes noticeably more aggressive, with more frequent and penetrating feelings of desperation and remorse. He loses contact with most of his "straight" friends. Flurries of overcontrol (going on the wagon) alternate with episodes of alcoholic debauchery. The addict attempts to regain control by altering specific aspects of his behavior; he may change the times, beverages, or locations that have characterized his past drinking. His entire behavioral repertoire becomes markedly alcohol centered as drinking becomes his most salient need. Support from family and friends dwindles to a pittance, while sexual drive and nutritional prudence are negligible when compared to alcohol. The drinker may now experience the first of a series of alcohol-related hospitalizations resulting from accidents or physical illness.

The crucial phase begins to terminate when the addict becomes so demoralized and confused by the conflict between outside pressures, inner needs, and his growing dependence on alcohol that he begins each day by steadying himself with a drink. Intoxication, however, usually remains restricted to the evening hours. The crucial-phase alcoholic may succeed in retaining his employment through many years of compulsive, loss-of-control drinking, although family life usually deteriorates dramatically.

The final, or chronic, phase that Jellinek identified is marked by prolonged periods of intoxication, colloquially referred to as binges. At this stage the alcohol addict may drink with characters who are morally and intellectually inferior to his customary clique. His thinking and physical functioning begin to show dramatic signs of impairment. A relatively small percentage (approximately 10 percent of alcoholics experience full-blown psychotic symptoms, such as hallucinations, delusions, or both. Tolerance for alcohol is diminished (half the amount previously required may be sufficient for intoxication and stupor), while undefinable fears and physical tremors begin to emerge. These symptoms of withdrawal appear as soon as alcohol is no longer present in the body. Consequently the drinker "controls" them through continuous consumption.

Finally, the need for alcohol looms so large that the addict can no longer maintain any pretense that he has control over his drinking. According to Jellinek, many alcohol addicts (approximately 60 percent) develop vague spiritual desires as they begin to call upon a higher power to rescue them from the alcoholic abyss. At this point the addict has spontaneously become amenable to treatment for the disease.

Since Jellinek's early formulation, the disease model for alcoholism has been embraced by Alcoholics Anonymous, the National Council on Alcoholism, the National Institute on Alcohol Abuse and Alcoholism, and the American Medical Association. According to

George Vaillant, regarded by many as the nation's leading authority on alcoholism: "Alcoholism becomes a disease when loss of voluntary control over alcohol consumption becomes a necessary and sufficient cause for much of an individual's social, psychological and physical morbidity." In short, an alcoholic may be thought of as a person who cannot always control when he or she starts or stops drinking. His or her life becomes unmanageable, with or without the bottle.

Capsules for Transport

In the past decade the disease concept of alcoholism has been enlarged by treatment practitioners to include gambling and the currently popular stimulant, cocaine. David Smith, founder and director of the Haight-Ashbury Free Medical Clinic of San Francisco, where thousands of addicts have been treated, finds that the disease model accurately describes addiction to a broad spectrum of mind-affecting drugs. Like cancer, addiction is viewed as a potentially fatal disease that may be triggered by a variety of causes. Among the many substances that Smith associates with addictive disease are: (1) alcohol; (2) the sedative hypnotics, including the barbiturates (for example, seconal and tuinal) and the benzodiazepines (for example, valium and librium); (3) the opiates and opioids (for example, heroin, morphine, codeine, percodan, demerol, and methadone); (4) the central nervous system stimulants, including amphetamine and cocaine; and (5) the hallucinogens, including LSD, PCP, and marijuana. Addictive substances may be used separately or in various combinations. As in other disease processes, a person may have a genetic predisposition for a particular disorder, yet may circumvent most of its complications by avoiding the substances or activities that trigger its symptoms. For example, a person who has a genetic predisposition to skin cancer can dodge most of its harmful consequences by avoiding undue exposure to the sun. Table 5-1 describes some of the emotional, behavioral, and physical consequences associated with a wide spectrum of contemporary drugs.

Michael's escalating struggle with cocaine exemplifies how the disease model for alcoholism may be applied to millions of cocaine addicts in the United States today. According to Michael, he began to enjoy "recreational" use of cocaine nearly four years ago. Although he seemed to enjoy coke somewhat more than his friends, he limited

Table 5–1
CONTEMPORARY DRUGS OF ABUSE

	Street Names	Possible Effects	Withdrawal Symptoms	Adverse/Overdose Reactions
Narcotics				
Heroin	H, hombre, junk, smack, dope, horse, crap	Apathy, difficulty in concentration, slowed speech, decreased physical activity, drooling, itching, euphoria, nausea	Anxiety, vomiting, sneezing, diarrhea, lower back pain, watery eyes, runny nose, yawning, irritability, tremors, panic, chills and sweating, cramps	Depressed levels of consciousness, low blood pressure, rapid heart rate, shallow breathing, convulsions, coma, possible death
Morphine	Drugstore dope, cube, first line, mud			
Codeine				
Percodan	Perks			
Demerol				
Methadone	Meth			
Sedative Hypnotics				
Nembutal	Yellow jackets, yellows	Impulsiveness, dramatic mood swings, bizarre thoughts, suicidal behavior, slurred speech, disorientation, slowed mental and physical functioning, limited attention span	Weakness, restlessness, nausea and vomiting, headache, nightmares, irritability, depression, acute anxiety, hallucinations, seizures, possible death	Confusion, decreased response to pain, shallow respiration, dilated pupils, weak and rapid pulse, coma, possible death
Seconal	Reds			
Tuinal	Tueys			
Phenobarbital				
Quaaludes	Ludes, 714s			
Valium	Vs			
Librium				
Equanil				

Stimulants

Drug	Slang	Effects	Withdrawal	Overdose
Alcohol	Juice, booze, sauce			
Benzedrine	Speed	Increased confidence, mood elevation, sense of energy and alertness, decreased appetite, anxiety, irritability, insomnia, transient drowsiness, delayed orgasm	Apathy, general fatigue, prolonged sleep, depression, disorientation, suicidal thoughts, agitated motor activity, irritability, bizarre dreams	Elevated blood pressure, increase in body temperature, face-picking, suspiciousness, bizarre and repetitious behavior, vivid hallucinations, convulsions, possible death
Dexedrine	Speed			
Desoxyn	Speed, crystal methedrine			
Biphetamine	Black beauties, speed			
Ritalin				
Preludin				
Cocaine	Coke, blow, crack, toot, snow, lady			

Caffeine

Drug	Slang	Effects	Withdrawal	Overdose
	Coffee, tea, colas, Java mud, brew, cocoa	Rapid heart rate, elevated blood pressure especially during stress, increased urination, interference with sleep, enhanced endurance, mildly increased energy, decreased boredom	Fatigue, tremulousness, severe headache, irritability	Headache, jitteryness, nervousness, chronic insomnia, persistent anxiety, depression, stomach upset, mental confusion (prolonged use of more than 8 cups per day)

Nicotine

Drug	Slang	Effects	Withdrawal	Overdose
Cigarettes	Weeds, fags, butts, tobacco	Increased heart rate and blood, pressure, drop in skin temperature, increased respiration, sense of relaxation	Craving, erratic emotions, nervousness and agitation, dullness and drowsiness, G-I disturbances, headache, impaired concentration, judgment, and physical skills	Diarrhea and vomiting, heart and lung problems

Table 5–1 *continued*

	Street Names	Possible Effects	Withdrawal Symptoms	Adverse/Overdose Reactions
Hallucinogens				
LSD	Electricity, acid, quasey, blotter acid, microdot, white lightning, purple barrels	Fascination with ordinary objects, heightened esthetic responses to color, texture, spatial arrangements, contours, music; vision and depth distortion; hear colors, see music; slowing of time; heightened sensitivity to faces, gestures; magnified feelings of love, lust, hate, joy, anger, pain, terror, despair, etc.; paranoia, panic, euphoria, bliss, impairment of short-term memory, projection of self into dream-like images	Not reported	Nausea, chills; increased pulse, temperature, and blood pressure; slow deep breathing; loss of appetite; insomnia; longer, more intense "trips"; bizarre, dangerous behavior possibly leading to injury or death
Mescaline	Peyote buttons (natural form)	Similar to LSD but more sensual and perceptual; fewer changes in thought, mood, and sense of self; vomiting	Not reported	Resemble LSD, but more bodily sensations, vomiting
Psilocybin	Mushrooms, shrooms, rooms	Similar to LSD but more visual and less intense; more euphoria, fewer panic reactions	Not reported	Resemble LSD but less severe
Cannabis				
Marijuana Hashish Nash oil	Bhang, kif, ganja, dope, grass, pot, smoke, hemp, joint, weed, bone, Mary Jane, herb, tea	Euphoria, relaxed inhibitions, increased appetite, disoriented behavior	Hyperactivity, insomnia, decreased appetite, anxiety	Severe reactions are rare, but include: panic, paranoia, fatigue, bizarre and dangerous behavior

| PCP | Angel dust, hog, rocket fuel, superweed, peace pill, elephant tranquilizer, dust, bad pizza | Increased blood pressure and heart rate; sweating, nausea, numbness, floating sensation, slowed reflexes, altered body image; altered perception of time and space; impaired immediate and recent memory; decreased concentration; paranoid thoughts and delusions | Not reported | Highly variable and possibly dose-related; disorientation, loss of recent memory; lethargy/stupor; bizarre and violent behavior, rigidity, and immobility; mutism, staring, hallucinations and delusions, coma |

Note: Adapted from J. Kaufman, H. Shaffer, and M. E. Burglass, The clinical assessment and diagnosis of addiction II. The biological basics—drugs and their effects. In *Current treatment of substance abuse and alcoholism*, edited by T. Bratter and G. Forrest. (New York: MacMillan, 1983).

his use to parties and what he considered to be weekend treats. After several years, he began to rely on cocaine as a source of energy for business and school obligations. About two years ago he found himself working on three separate, yet highly demanding projects: completing course requirements for a college degree in creative writing; editing the advertising section of a commercial newsletter; and devising a business plan to open and operate a video store with several of his friends. He rationalized that he needed cocaine daily in order to muster sufficient energy to complete each task. Michael realized that his drug problem was becoming severe when he found that he was using more cocaine even after his school obligations were completed. In what may be described as the prodromal phase of cocaine addiction, he began to make up excuses for why he needed to get high. Each time there was any sort of business or advertising deadline he would rationalize that he needed cocaine to help him get through.

Michael agreed with his therapist that he was in the loss-of-control or crucial phase of cocaine addiction when he spent $10,000 in three months solely to purchase the drug. He repeatedly experienced an irresistible urge to buy just a moderate amount, allegedly to help him cope with some temporary business stress. When the coke was gone, he would purchase more and more, until he either ran out of money or could find no more coke. Like the crucial-phase alcoholic, Michael would alternate between flurries of complete abstinence and cocaine debauchery.

After a moment of reflection it becomes obvious that any stress-reducing activity—whether cleansing the body, ingesting a psychoactive substance, or praying for forgiveness—may be subject to compulsive overuse and the escalating consequences of loss of control. We propose that the disease concept may be applied to the entire spectrum of compulsive problem behaviors. As we have shown throughout this book, the distinction between internally or externally induced alterations of mood, thought, or behavior is arbitrary and misleading. Activities that evoke sensations of arousal, satiation, or fantasy bring about alterations in brain chemistry and patterns of compulsive behavior that are similar to the symptoms traditionally associated with psychoactive substances. Arousal, satiation, and fantasy may be regarded as psychological organ systems that are vulnerable to attack by multiple agents of addiction. As in viral and bacterial infections, the specific disease carriers may differ widely in origin and structure, and yet the consequences of foreign invasion may be virtually identical in terms of symptoms, prognosis, and treatment. Each of the behaviors shown in the following list may become an agent of addiction, subject to compulsion, loss of control, and continuation despite harmful consequences.

Drug ingestion. Includes major psychoactive drugs; and marijuana, alcohol, and nicotine.

Eating. Includes overuse of particular foods, for example, sugar.

Sex. Includes autoeroticism, pornography, and varieties of sadomasochistic activity.

Gambling. Includes numbers, horses, dogs, cards, and roulette.

Activity. Includes work, exercise, and sports.

Pursuit of power. Includes spiritual, physical, and material power.

Media fascination. Includes TV, movies, and music.

Isolation. Includes sleep, fantasy, and dreams.

Risk taking. Includes excitement related to danger.

Cults. Includes groups using brainwashing or other techniques of psychological restructuring.

Crime and violence. Includes crimes against people and property.

Bonding-socializing. Includes excessive dependence on relationships or social gatherings.

Institutionalization. Includes excessive need for environmental structure, such as prisons, mental hospitals, and religious sanctuaries, and institutional use of psychoactive medication.

Figure 5-1 shows degrees of probable risk between various agents of addictive disease. Five levels of risk are distinguished, with multiple agents (capsules for transport) within each level. Crime and drugs, for example, are viewed as very risky addictions because they usually bring about great harm to the individual and society. Institutionalization, which is the compulsion to subject oneself to the del-

Figure 5–1. LEVELS OF ADDICTION

This impressionistic chart depicts levels of probable risk (loss of adaptive social functioning) between groups of problem behaviors. Five levels are distinguished with no discrimination of relative danger within each level. Religion transverses all levels and may be used to short-circuit the usual course of an addictive process. Dotted lines indicate the potential for overlap, substitution and flux between addictions. In the case of any given individual, a statistically low risk behavior, *e.g.*, "activity," may actually occupy a space on the threshold of suicidal vortex.

Source: H. Milkman, Addictive processes: An introductory formulation, *The Street Pharmacologist* 2(4):3 (1979).

eterious effects of confinement in prisons, psychiatric hospitals, or other social-service facilities, is also considered a high-risk addictive behavior.

The dimension of religion and cults transverses all levels and may be used to short-circuit the usual course of an addictive process. We have observed a multitude of recovering addicts who seem to strengthen their resolve by leaning on the pillars of religion. Members of AA, for example, usually proclaim a renewed faith in a higher power, who aids them in maintaining sobriety. Yet religion, as signified by the opposing arrows on figure 5-1, may be a double-edged sword. In the tragic example of Jonestown, blind devotion to a religious cult burned a path straight to the suicidal vortex.

Eldridge Cleaver is an example of a person who was able to extricate himself from addiction through religious conversion. Cleaver may have combined several addictive behaviors (power, crime, and drugs) during his years as a political activist and accused criminal. He eventually found himself on the threshold of suicide with a loaded gun pointed to his head. Looking at the full moon, he saw the faces of his heroes, Marx and Engels, gradually fade into the countenance of Christ. He renounced his former life-style and commenced a spiritual journey, zealously preaching the Gospel and love of God.

The dotted lines in figure 5-1 indicate the potential for substitution between the agents of addiction, and fluctuations in the relative danger of a given problem dependency. In any particular case, a behavior that is usually low risk, for example, activity, may occupy a space close to the suicidal center. The addict may eventually risk life and limb as he attempts to recapture the ecstatic moments of arousal that he once experienced through participation in a sport such as skiing. It has been frequently observed that compulsive drug users often switch intoxicants only to find that the symptoms of their addiction resurface through another capsule for transport. Cocaine users often switch to heroin, while some heroin addicts abandon narcotics only to find themselves hopelessly dependent on alcohol.

The Passenger Sleeps

When children are asked if they would like to be addicts when they grow up, invariably they respond with a combination of disdain and perplexity. There is no way that they want to be hooked on anything, and besides, how could you have ever come up with such a goofy question? Yet statistically, 5–10 percent of all grade school children will become addicted to alcohol or drugs; if we include food and other behavioral compulsions such as gambling or sex, the figure easily exceeds 20 percent. Nobody wants to be dependent on anything, yet the number of people who develop pathological habits is huge. How do people reconcile the difference between what they value in the morning of their life and what they actually do in the afternoon and twilight hours?

The key word is denial. Addicts insulate themselves from the glaring discrepancy between their natural inclination toward well-mindedness and the depraved life-style of addiction. As if they have fallen into a deep sleep, space trippers become oblivious to a multitude of observers imploring them to take heed of their compulsion and loss of control. In the face of massive evidence to the contrary, they continue to believe in their independence and self-determination. Reverend Joseph L. Kellerman describes alcoholism as "a merry-go-round named denial," on which the alcoholic, together with a regular cast of supporting actors, enacts a predictable scenario: the group unintentionally protects the addict from the harsh reality of his or her desperate plight. Whatever the vehicle for transport, the addict's support system usually includes three unwitting contributors to the avalanching predicament: an Enabler, a Victim, and a Provocatice.

The Enabler is a character who is available to bail the addicted darling out of any crisis that might ensue from the demanding journey. This supporting actor might be a professional, such as a physician or counselor, who helps the addict to "get by" with irresponsible behavior. He or she may also be a friend who fills in, on the job or at home, when the journey to oblivion takes a wild turn.

The part of Victim is played by the boss, employer, or supervisor who saves the addict's job when he or she cannot perform the expected duties. The Victim picks up the tab for irresponsible conduct because love or concern for the addict prevents the Victim from initiating proper disciplinary action at the work place.

Finally, the Provocatice—usually the girlfriend or wife of a male addict—is the person who dutifully compensates for everything that goes wrong within the home or the marriage. She alternates between the roles of counselor, physician, mother, and wife as the addict vacillates between needing to be forgiven, taken care of, and reprimanded, on a cyclical basis. Although the Provocatice is deeply troubled by the addict's life-style, she is always there to compensate for any action that might threaten to dissolve the tenuous family unit.

According to Reverend Kellerman, if recovery from addiction is to occur, it must start with the people who have unwittingly maintained the addict's system of denial. The Victim and Enabler should find a source of information and insight if they are to change their characteristic roles. The Provocatice should enter some form of ongoing group program, possibly Al-Anon, to receive the support that she will need to make a substantial change in her life. Finally, parents are asked to consider that they may be unintentionally playing support roles on the "merry-go-round of denial" for addictive teenagers. According to Carla Lowe, a spokesperson for the Parents Movement, an organization of concerned parents that has gained momentum and status worldwide, "denial is the teething biscuit of the Parents' Movement."

Symbols of Change

It is virtually impossible for a friend or family member to accurately gauge the extent to which an addict depends on a neurochemical prop. After tolerance has developed, the addict may appear completely normal during an extended voyage in his or her capsule for transport. By far the most reliable indication of continuing addiction is the person's apparent inability to integrate his or her goals and behaviors. The allegedly recovering addict is exposed by an obvious inability to coordinate stated objectives and actual performance. He or she may miss appointments with intimate friends or fail to appear for critical work assignments. These inconsistencies, which might be dismissed among nonaddicts as faux pas, are the telltale signs of a flourishing addiction.

Figure 5-2 shows the deterioration of a person's values as the journey to oblivion progresses over time. The values closest to the center represent guiding principles in the addict's life. In the preaddiction (symptomatic) phase, a person's behavior may reflect the entire spectrum of moral precepts that he or she has internalized from well-minded people in society. However, as addiction progresses through prodromal, crucial, and chronic phases, the addict's ability to function in accord with his or her own values dwindles to near zero.

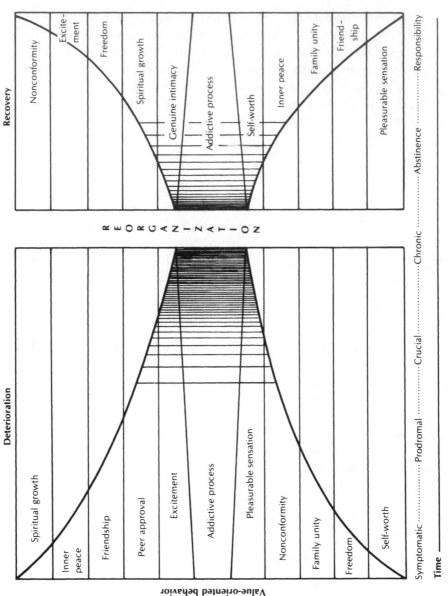

Deterioration

Spiritual growth

Inner peace

Friendship

Peer approval

Excitement

Addictive process

Pleasurable sensation

Nonconformity

Family unity

Freedom

Self-worth

Value-oriented behavior

Recovery

Nonconformity

Excitement

Freedom

Spiritual growth

Genuine intimacy

Addictive process

Self-worth

Inner peace

Family unity

Friendship

Pleasurable sensation

REORGANIZATION

Symptomatic .... Prodromal .... Crucial .... Chronic .... Abstinence .... Responsibility

Time

Figure 5–2. ADDICTION AND VALUES

With the onset of recovery, the principles that guide one's behavior may become reorganized. Those which formerly occupied positions of highest priority, such as the experience of excitement, may become peripheral and of minimal importance during the recovery phase of an addict's career. When a person assumes the commitment to get well, the preliminary and in a sense most superficial aspect of the task is to stop the self-defeating behavior, whatever that may be. The greater challenge, which may take years of self-discipline and support from treatment personnel, is to regain the full capacity to operate in accord with the values that one has chosen as guiding principles for his or her life.

The Robot Pilot

If you have never been enslaved by an irresistible impulse, it is difficult to appreciate a person's apparent inability to captain his own ship. Whatever the seductive agent—substances, services, or sweets—addicts repeat time and time again: "Whenever it's right there in front of me, I have no choice. I've never been able to turn down a . . . " This subordination of rational thought and value-based decision making to the lure of momentary pleasure is at once the most mystifying and destructive aspect of the addictive process. In order to understand the compulsion to be at craving's beck and call, we must again consider the multifactorial basis of addiction.

From the standpoint of biology, our formulation rests on the position that we can become physically dependent on the experiences of arousal, satiation, or fantasy, independent of whether the capsule for transport is a substance or an activity. Behavior in each sphere may be related to a particular kind of neurotransmission, possibly involving specific neural pathways and neurotransmitter combinations. Arousal dependence may be compared to biochemical alterations related to excessive amphetamine use, while satiation effects may be compared to those related to opiate use. Fantasy behaviors can be related to such neurotransmitters as dopamine, norepinephrine, or serotonin, all of which are chemically similar to the main psychedelic drugs, LSD, mescaline, or psilocybin. Repetition of each type of activity sets up a compensatory biochemical reaction that restores neurochemical balance in the central nervous system. The individual must increase the level of addictive behavior, for example, risk taking, to continue to achieve a subjective experience of pleasure. Addicts are also motivated by increasing discomfort from withdrawal effects when they stop or reduce the need-satisfying activity. The tendency toward reinstatement (doing it again) is encouraged by a substratum of neurochemical instability.

Alan Marlatt of the University of Washington in Seattle has studied the compulsion to repeat destructive behaviors from a combined psychological and social perspective. According to Marlatt, the irresistible urge to reenter the drab circle of progressive impairment is based on pressure from the following sources:

The addict's expectation that some positive effects might be experienced through a brief interlude with the seductive agent.

The initial rush of pleasure produced by the object of craving.

Social pressures to be one of the group.

The seasoned addict engages in a fierce battle for control over the object of his or her craving. Episodes of abstinence typically alternate with nearly complete submission and loss of control. The likelihood that an addict will repeat the characteristic pattern of excess and moral depravity is increased by an identified series of psychological reactions. According to Marlatt, the combined influence from a predictable set of internal messages convinces the addict to abandon control.

This process begins just after the addict first tastes the forbidden fruit. When a person who tries to be straight, sober, controlled, or clean experiences a slip, that person becomes confused in self-concept: "I thought I had control over . . . but now it appears that I don't." Most often, the individual attributes his or her failure or slip to personal weakness. These two psychological factors—identity conflict and self-blame—are cumulative in effect. The internal discord produced by the discrepant self-concept of "I am in control" versus "I have failed" results in a regressive shift in self-image from responsible person to addict. By attributing the slip to personal weakness, the addict unwittingly creates the expectation for continued failure in the future. The cumulative effect of role confusion and loss of confidence makes submission to the robot pilot an easier posture to maintain than abstinence or self-regulation. The intensity of this reaction depends on several factors:

The degree of personal commitment to maintain abstinence.

The period of sustained abstinence—the longer the duration, the greater the effect.

The importance of the behavior to the individual involved.

The Mutiny

The course of addiction is remarkably resistant to change. Approximately 75 percent of all those who attempt abstinence from heroin, alcohol, or cigarettes resume their habits between three and six months after beginning a program for recovery. The statistics for attempted weight control are even more appalling. Recidivism rates for juvenile and adult criminals range from 70 to 80 percent, depending on how recidivism is defined. Relapse rates for schizophrenia are reported to be as high as 92 percent. Indeed, the entire range of emotional-behavioral disorders appears to be unyielding in repetition and progression.

In consideration of the powerful influences from biological, psychological, and social sources, a continuing pattern of struggle and failure seems inevitable. To be sure, the traveler who survives must organize a powerful mutiny to overthrow the tyrannical Captain Addiction. The rebellious survival force must battle a sluc of weapons, massively deployed by a malevolent robot whose sophisticated armament includes habitual psychological responses, biochemically based emotional and physical disturbances, intense social pressure, and the random stress of unavoidable negative circumstance. A successful rebellion must effectively counteract all of these forces. Each mutiny must be tailor-made to fit the special requirements of each journey.

In the realm of substance abuse, for example, the initial tactics for recovery are determined by the specific needs of the user and the unique qualities of his or her drug. Withdrawal from a single drug, drugs from the same group, or a combination of drugs from different groups requires diverse detoxification procedures. Withdrawal from opiate dependence, for example, produces a well-defined abstinence syndrome, characterized by gastrointestinal distress, muscle aches, anxiety, insomnia, and narcotics hunger—none of which are life threatening. In contrast, withdrawal from barbiturates, or a bariturate-alcohol combination, may produce potentially fatal seizures, requiring vigorous medical intervention, often hospital-based care.

Stopping cocaine or amphetamine use usually involves only depression and lethargy. For these drugs, the symptoms of high-dose intoxication may become life threatening. Cocaine toxicity may result in brain seizures, heart failure, delusions, hallucinations, and potentially violent behavior. Additionally, mixed addiction may result from the alternating use of antagonistic substances as observed in the upper-downer cycle. Some addicts use high doses of stimulants such as amphetamines or cocaine and then use a secondary drug such as alcohol, a short-acting barbiturate, or an opiate to calm the side effects of excessive stimulation. Occasionally dependence and tolerance may develop to the secondary depressant drug as well. During detoxification such an addict may experience a complex of symptoms associated with the withdrawal from drugs of different classes.

For nonsubstance addictions, the primary strategy for recovery usually involves either completely stopping the compulsive activity (as in gambling) or dramatically reducing the pattern of abuse (as in eating disorders). Although addicts take the first steps to recovery for a variety of reasons, including family pressure, the threat of being fired, health, or legal problems, the ensuing battle for control is always decided according to one fundamental principle: The addict must discover alternative means to satisfy the needs that were previously resolved through the addictive activity.

An innovative client, whom we shall refer to as Max, developed a set of nonchemical alternatives that he successfully used to overcome his dependence on alcohol. With assistance from his therapist, Max realized that he used alcohol to cope with an identifiable set of psychological and physical needs. He and his therapist devised a program of behavioral alternatives, specifically designed to cope with the emotions and conflicts previously managed through the lure of alcohol. The program involved the use of sensory isolation, video movies, massage, and weekly psychotherapy sessions. After one year, Max was able to successfully terminate psychotherapy and continue to enjoy a comfortable and responsible life without using drugs or alcohol. Table 5-2 outlines the cognitive (insights gained from psychotherapy) and behavioral (alternative behavior) techniques that Max used to regain control over his own life.

A Guard Must be Posted

The recovering addict must gain the upper hand over negative social or peer influences, internal and external states of conflict, and sometimes excruciating physical discomfort. Often the challenge is too great, and the mindless robot returns. Those who avoid subjugation to the addictive process need to develop a mature set of emotional, intellectual, and behavioral skills that promote attainment of pleasure through internal rewards and life-enhancing activities. This may be accomplished through a variety of psychotherapy approaches, many of which we will discuss in the next chapter.

The vast majority of recovery programs—with the obvious exception of those designed for eating disorders—stress the need for complete abstinence. George Vaillant has summarized the effective ingredients of programs for the treatment of alcohol dependence. The same principles apply to the broad range of addictive behaviors:

Offer the client or patient a nonharmful substitute dependency for the addictive agent.

Remind him or her ritually that even one encounter with the addictive agent can lead to pain and relapse.

Repair the social and medical damage that has already occurred.

Restore self-esteem.

Depending on the personality and situation of the client, a recovery-oriented self-help group, such as AA or an AA derivative such as Narcotics Anonymous or Sexaholics Anonymous, is often required for successful treatment. The relief effect from participating in a group that offers empathy and belonging while continuously rewarding sobriety may be essential to the recovery process. In many cases group support can be bolstered by individual counseling. In other cases the only form of treatment that the addict will accept is one-to-one psychotherapy. Whether individual or group, effective treatment requires a readiness on both sides (client and therapist) for intensive work.

Table 5–2
DRUG-LIKE ALTERNATIVES TO ALCOHOL DEPENDENCE

	Isolation Tank	*Massage*	*Fantasy*	*Psychotherapy*
Device	Float in water to alleviate the effects of gravity. As much as possible eliminate all temperature difference while shutting out light and sound.	Soothing sensations to the skin and musculature are delivered by a qualified practitioner.	Video movies are selected from the complete range of fantasy productions available in the contemporary retail video market.	Individual psychotherapy is delivered by a qualified professional with a cognitive-behavioral orientation.
Rationale	Reduce external stimulation to trigger fantasies of power and immortality. Results in altered state of consciousness.	Reduce tension through internal chemicals released by touch. Diminish unresolved dependency needs.	Movies allow for passive means to achieve relaxation without the unwanted effects of intoxication and hangovers.	Therapist helps client understand the emotional, sensory, and intellectual needs that were previously met through alcohol.
Goals	Fantasies of power help to compensate for feelings of helplessness and lack of self-worth. These are examined during psychotherapy and replaced by self-actualizing behaviors.	Vigorous massage is used to dampen anxiety and aggressive drive. The client gradually learns to subdue emotional discomfort through positive interpersonal relationships.	Provide gratification for aesthetic, intellectual, and emotional needs that have been mismanaged at home or at the bar. Gain insight into origins of anxiety and fear.	The client learns to separate himself from infantile needs previously resolved in a self-destructive fashion. Through a safe, caring, insight-oriented relationship, client enlarges the scope of his coping skills.

Although recovery-oriented treatment has helped millions of addicts to reclaim their freedom, by far the most humane solution to addiction problems would be to prevent the life-corroding process from gaining even a foothold in the human psyche. As evidenced time and time again by the failure of our legal system to effectively bind the crippling hands of addiction, education—not legislation— is the key to preserving our cherished values of life, liberty, and the pursuit of happiness. Parents-as-educators are obliged to insure that their children are successfully inoculated against the false promise of external charms.

The strategy that we suggest is based on flexible use of a three-phase, addiction-inoculation approach that involves:

Mental preparation

Skill development

Rehearsal

The procedure can be modified to accommodate the specific needs of children, students, patients, or other high-risk community groups. The technique is based on Michenbaum's cognitive-behavioral method for managing anxiety, depression, and pain. It has been successfully used by Howard Shaffer of Harvard Medical School to prevent the onset of smoking. A similar technique has been suggested by Alan Marlatt of the University of Washington in Seattle to prevent relapse in alcoholics, smokers, and heroin addicts.

Mental Preparation

In the mental-preparation phase, high-risk people are taught basic principles that explain addiction in terms of biochemistry, psychology, and sociology. In terms of biochemistry, students learn the neurological and physiological origins and consequences of suicidal pleasure seeking. When a child vividly understands the deleterious effects of tampering with his own brain chemistry, he or she is less likely to be duped by claims such as, "LSD brings you closer to God," or "Cocaine will make you a better lover." Psychologically, children are helped to form positive values, sound judgment, and clear thinking. We communicate our expectation that they will grow up as caring people who will make special contributions to a great society. Subjects learn how unconscious perceptions of low self-esteem can lead to increasing personal failure and reliance on the "quick fix." On the sociological plane, children learn to appreciate how society itself may promote a deviant career: from a child who enjoys little self-worth, to a marked or stigmatized adolescent, then finally to a person who loses all self-respect as a sorrowful, depraved, and incapacitated adult. Young people are taught the effects of peer influence, parental role models, and learning through observation. Children are imbued with a firm understanding of how advertising and street rumor may entice youngsters to experiment with short-term pleasure and long-term harm. As parents, educators, and community members we can insist on responsible advertising while we develop our own slogans and symbols in the war against compulsive pleasure seeking.

Skill Development

The process of skill acquisition involves learning to cope adaptively with stress, through behaviors that provide internal satisfaction through heightened perceptions of self-worth. On the interpersonal level, children learn to experience a sense of well-being when they master the ability to withstand negative peer pressure. This can be accomplished through programmatic exposure to positive role models. The National Institute on Drug Abuse, for example, has developed a variety of drug-prevention videotapes in which an attractive role model, such as Brooke Shields or Mr. T., demonstrates assertiveness and sensibility in the face of drug temptation. Other media productions show a familiar-looking youngster who demonstrates the enormous personal value of being able to "just say no." At the level of emotional control, subjects are taught how to use relaxation techniques to gain mastery over their own internal states. Muscle relaxation, guided fantasy, and breathing exercises have all been shown to reduce tension and promote feelings of well-being. An exemplary program would accommodate individual differences in the attainment of pleasure through the channels of arousal, satiation, or fantasy. Ideally, students could develop a large repertoire of coping skills, including wholesome activities from each plane of pleasurable experience—arousal, relaxation, or fantasy.

Rehearsal

In the rehearsal phase, which can overlap with mental preparation and skill development, the learner is encouraged to role play appropriate verbal and behavioral responses to potentially harmful seductions. Simulated encounters with addictive agents are created in family, classroom, or group-counseling situations. All phases of the inoculation procedure should be conducted by addiction-free adults who command respect and admiration from the student population. The effective inoculator not only has the intellectual and emotional ability to cope with masochism and denial from the preaddict, but communicates a sense that he or she can "walk the talk" of an addiction-free life-style. The rehearsal stage should signify to every parent, therapist, and educator that one talk, one picture, or one story about addiction is not enough. We must go over and over this message in a variety of ways to overcome the enormous wall of denial and get through to our kids.

Finally, through the family, the school, and the culture, children should be inoculated to develop a healthy resistance to the seduction of a plastic paradise. To achieve this outcome, we must successfully promote the values of commitment, control, and challenge. These three C's may be thought of as the antidote for the three C's of compulsion, loss of control and continuation despite harmful consequences. We must demonstrate *commitment* to self, family and community; believe in our individual strengths and abilities to exert a significant measure of *control* over personal destiny; and view life as a *challenge*, a grand adventure, a mystery to be explored with the benefit of our full mental capacity, rather than as a riddle to be solved through artificial means.

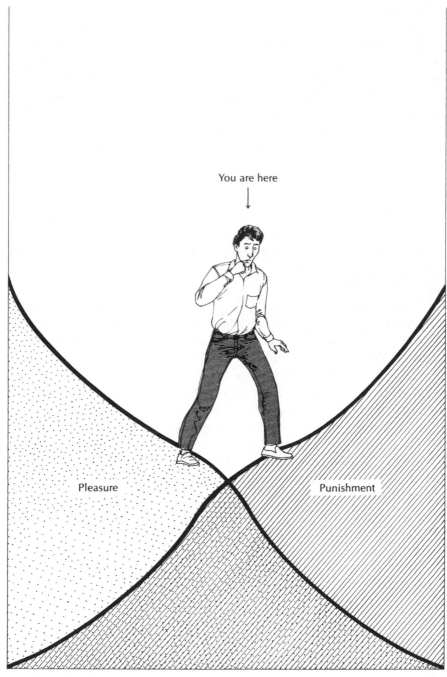

6

Finding the Right Substitutes

Let us assume that you or someone that you care about suffers from addiction. This chapter is intended as a consumer's guide to sound and appropriate treatment.

If you have an addiction, the first step toward recovery is admitting that your present substitutes aren't working. Granted, they have many alluring features—the soothing gush of cigarette smoke as it passes through your trachea; ice cream's anesthetic sweetness as it oozes down your esophagus; the dose of alcohol that loosens your libido; or the drug that finally affords sleep. But after all is said and done, you're really not up for suicide—in slow motion, as with tobacco and food; or at high speed, as with alcohol or heroin.

It is critical that you recognize the long-term consequences of compulsive pleasure seeking. As illustrated, initial experiences with the object or experience of your cravings have been extremely satisfying. In the course of time, however, rewards diminish and suffering begins to surface. Perhaps you have become unattractively overweight, developed a cigarette cough, or find that excessive drinking has caused a schism in your love relationship. Red flags may be distinctly visible. You can clearly see that present difficulties are minor in comparison with the dire consequences that lie ahead. Creeping obesity may be an overture to heart disease; a mild cigarette cough might well develop into emphysema or lung cancer; alcohol-induced blackouts may be a signal of deteriorating memory, defective judgment, and decreased ability to learn.

Acknowledge that your greatest source of pleasure has evolved into a crippling habit. Your brush with ecstasy should be remembered with humility and respect, yet the days of unmitigated pleasure are long gone. Continuing the present course will probably destroy the remaining quality of your life. Be thankful that you still have a chance. Reentering the world of sanity requires the development of alternative means of gratification. Restructuring ideas about the object of your craving is another positive move toward changing a negative life-style. Replacing self-defeating thoughts like, "I can't cope without . . . (for example, cigarettes)," with positive statements such as, "I care about maximizing my experience of life," represents a seminal shift in your self-image from loser to a person worthy of success. You might experiment with saying something like this to yourself: "I love . . . (perhaps, the feeling of being intoxicated—especially with my friends), but I value my health and the quality of my experience more."

If you earnestly believe that the importance of sound health and well-mindedness far exceeds temporary sustenance through sinking vessels of short-term pleasure, you have taken the most crucial stride toward genuine self-repair. When the values of comfortable and responsible living emerge as pillars of your new existence, you are ready for the next step toward finding the right substitutes—deciding whether you can manage your problem alone. Be open to the possibility that you cannot.

Most people who experience habitual problem dependencies have wasted years of their lives trying to convince themselves and everyone around them that they were actually in control of their addiction. In reality, this was not the case. A humorous but tragic example of a young cocaine addict's futile attempts at controlled use exemplifies the difficulty of exclusive self-reliance. The man worked as a traveling salesman in the San Francisco Bay area. He could easily purchase cocaine at a number of locations on his daily route. In repeated attempts to regulate his level of use, he would snort a few lines, then place the supply in a self-addressed letter and mail the leftover quantity to himself. By the time he reached the next destination, he came down from the previous dose and was out of cocaine. He would then make another purchase and repeat the entire process of snorting and mailing all over again.

An important indication of your own ability to control a substance or behavior is to face squarely the question of whether you can cease the activity, even for a brief period of time. Can you go without a drink for a month? For a week? Can you eliminate snacks from your diet, even for a day? What is the longest period you have endured without a cigarette? Addiction is very difficult to admit—sometimes it takes years before an addict will acknowledge the existence of a problem. The enormous wall of denial is, by far, the greatest obstacle to recovery. Many people die without ever having confessed, even to themselves, that they were unable to control crucial segments of their behavior. It is neither a sin nor a weakness to seek help, particularly when your future happiness and health are at stake.

Some are especially good at assisting the wounded; others profit from their suffering. Beware of miracle cures. It took far more than several days or weeks to arrive at your present condition, and it is highly unlikely that a treatment angel will suddenly materialize and fix you up in just a few days. The vast majority of people who arrive in therapy for overeating, drug abuse, alcoholism, or smoking relapse within twelve months. The longer they remain in treatment, however, the better is their chance of recovery. When you have reached the junction of seriously seeking help, you are especially vulnerable to charlatans. Those who proclaim fantastic success rates, in a short period of time, with minimal suffering or effort, are likely to be corrupt merchants of health. You have waited this long; don't compromise your chances by jumping into a program that is fundamentally unsound. By grasping for a miracle cure you merely prolong self-deception. When it fails, it may take years before you build up the courage to try again, and you'll have only yourself to blame.

Fortunately, many effective recovery programs exist, run by practitioners who have a genuine concern for your well-being. You may wonder, of course, how to choose from a multitude of possibilities a treatment approach that is best suited to your personality and needs. Ideally, your selection should be based on a synthesis of four vital sources of data:

1. Your personal philosophy of what causes self-destructive behavior.
2. Your belief about what forms of psychotherapy are most effective.
3. An awareness of the types of treatment program available in your community.
4. Recommendation of a suitable treatment program from a qualified individual.

Before reading further, please complete the Counseling Interest Inventory in table 6-1. This will help you to identify the psychotherapy systems that are most likely to be compatible with your philosophy and beliefs. Treatment effectiveness has been shown to increase dramatically when clients feel comfortable and compatible with the methods and beliefs of their therapists. The Counseling Interest Inventory is designed to orient you to counseling and psychotherapy systems that are consistent with your attitudes, biases, and beliefs.

Table 6–1
COUNSELING INTEREST INVENTORY

Read each of the statements that follow. Mark the box next to the concept that best represents your point of view. If you are unsure or feel equally strong about both extremes, reread the question and try to choose the phrase that is most appealing. Ignore the letters below each box, as they are for scoring purposes only. Take your time and remember that there are no correct or incorrect answers.

Example: I prefer to discuss family problems:

   ☐   With all members of   ☒   With one family
   F   my family present.   I   member at a time.

1. A person is most likely to bring constructive change to his or her life by:

   ☐   Setting goals and making positive   ☐   First understanding, then
   B,C decisions.   D   resolving, internal conflicts.

2. To alter a negative pattern an individual should:

   ☐   Change his or her self-defeating   ☐   Become aware of his or her
   C   beliefs.   E,D emotions.

3. When involved in a project or task, I prefer to:

   ☐   Work alone or with one other   ☐   Work with several others.
   I   person.   F

4. Which phrase best describes your view of humanity?

   ☐   Humans are basically rational and   ☐   Humans are often irrational and
   E,G fundamentally good.   D   basically programmed for their
                                                    own survival.

5. A person may alter a maladaptive quality of his or her life by:

   ☐   Modifying his or her behavior   ☐   Modifying his or her beliefs and
   B   C   expectations.

Table 6–1 *continued*

6. I feel most comfortable when engaged in conversation with:

☐ One person at a time.
I

☐ Several people at a time.
F

7. The most important cause of human suffering may be attributed to:

☐ Spiritual disharmony and
E,G confusion about the meaning of life.

☐ Environmental stress that triggers
A,D chemical imbalance resulting in mental illness.

8. To help a person who is experiencing emotional problems, it is most important to:

☐ Understand how he or she has
D been influenced by the past.

☐ Focus on the behavior that is
B causing current problems.

9. People are best able to experience more fulfillment in life when they:

☐ Change their thoughts and
C,E feelings about themselves.

☐ Change the behaviors that are
B causing problems.

10. My life seems most fulfilled when:

☐ I follow my religious convictions.
G

☐ I am able to live according to my
E,C personal values and innermost feelings.

11. The people who have been most able to help me with personal problems:

☐ Spoke at length about my
C,D,E thoughts and feelings.

☐ Prescribed medicine or suggested
A,B activities to overcome the problem.

12. When I'm with a group of people, I usually pay most attention to:

☐ The person I'm talking to at the
I moment.

☐ All people in the room including
F the person I'm talking to.

13. The majority of people with moderate to severe emotional problems are most effectively helped by:

☐ A form of individual counseling or
I psychotherapy that does not require medication.

☐ A combination of effective
A counseling and an appropriate level of prescribed medication.

14. Most psychological problems originate from:

☐ Absence of purpose and fear of
E,G nonbeing.

☐ Learned habits that have negative
B consequences.

Table 6–1 *continued*

15. An effective psychotherapist will focus most intensively on:

☐ The client's behavior and belief
B,C,I system.

☐ The client's relationship and
D,F feelings within his or her family or social group.

16. When something is wrong, I would be most likely to seek the advice of:

☐ My personal physician or a
A,I psychiatrist.

☐ A group of people who
G,F understand my spiritual or religious values.

17. With regard to problems in living, the people most equipped to be of help are:

☐ Physicians or other scientists who
A have studied the origins and treatment of mental disorder.

☐ People who have experienced
G similar problems and have discovered the spiritual meaning of their lives.

18. The opinions and ideas that seem to influence me the most are:

☐ Highly confidential
I communications from my most intimate associates.

☐ Observations about my behavior
F which are substantiated by group consensus.

19. All things being equal, I would tend to seek help from:

☐ My personal physician.
A

☐ A person qualified to offer
G spiritual guidance.

20. When I have been most anxious or upset the cause seems to have been:

☐ A physical problem.
A

☐ Disharmony in my family.
F

Scoring:
Count the numbers of As, Bs, etc., that correspond to the answers you have given. Record the letters that occur four or more times in the adjacent box: ☐ These letters correspond to the counseling and psychotherapy approaches listed below:

A—biomedical   B—behavioral   C—cognitive
D—psychodynamic   E—existential/humanistic F—family/group
G—spiritual   I—individual

The letters that appear most frequently are likely to represent counseling and psychotherapy approaches that are compatible with your personal philosophy and beliefs.

You may now wish to discover some of the fundamental ideas that are associated with the styles of intervention that seem most attractive to you. Brief descriptions of the basic philosophy that underlies each major psychotherapy system is provided in the rest of this chapter. Some guidelines for selecting group, family, or spiritually oriented approaches are discussed. Readers are encouraged to explore their interests further by obtaining relevant readings or contacting relevant organizations listed in the appendix, "Suggested Reading and Information Resources." A number of selections have been chosen on the basis of their superior quality and suitability for a nonprofessional readership. Addresses of treatment and information organizations are provided.

Treatment Philosophies

The Biomedical Approach

Those who advocate the biomedical model treat addiction as a physician would treat a disease: first identifying the syndrome (recognizing patterns of diverse symptoms that tend to occur together); then searching for the cause of the syndrome; and finally deciding on appropriate treatment for the illness. The symptoms of addiction are those of any psychiatric syndrome, for which three physical causes can be considered: germs, genes, and biochemistry. In the case of addiction, it is unlikely that the disorder is linked to either bacterial or viral invaders. Allan Collins of the Institute for Behavioral Genetics at the University of Colorado has shown that for most behavioral disorders, alcoholism and cigarette smoking in particular, genetic factors are highly relevant. Stanley Sunderwirth has shown the relationship between self-induced alterations in neurotransmission and the broad spectrum of possible problem behaviors that may result from these biochemical modifications.

Treatment specialists conduct careful review of the patient's family records to discover if the disorder has heritable components. If there is a positive family history for substance abuse, the patient is considered to be of considerably higher risk for addictive disease. David Smith, director of the Haight-Ashbury Free Medical Clinic of San Francisco, is a renowned advocate of this perspective. A promising new field of research focuses on biochemical predispositions toward addiction. Robert Freedman of the University of Colorado Health Sciences Center examines the addict's biochemistry and anatomy for possible irregularities. Analysis of blood and urine samples may suggest biochemical links between certain addictive behaviors and malfunctioning neurotransmission. Richard Wurtman of MIT has discovered a possible link between low levels of serotonin and carbohydrate craving. When biochemical irregularities are discovered, the patient's symptoms may be treated through prescribed abstinence, as well as appropriate dietary changes, exercise schedules, or medication—ideally combined with effective psychotherapy.

The Behavioral Approach

Behavior therapists, irrespective of their specific approaches to treatment, agree on the importance of scientific methods in research, assessment, and clinical practice. Behaviorists assume that addictive behaviors are to a considerable degree acquired through learning, and therefore they can be modified through additional learning. Therapy is delivered with the assumption that specific problem behaviors, for example, gambling, can be targeted for change without fear that unconscious causes will result in the substitution of new and equally severe symptoms.

Clients procure the services of behavior therapists with the clear understanding that the focus of treatment will be on reducing or eliminating undesirable behaviors. Neither exploration of early childhood experiences nor analysis of one's feelings toward his or her parents is required for successful treatment outcomes. The duration of treatment is usually considerably shorter than other forms of psychotherapeutic intervention. Behavioral therapies for the entire range of addictive disorders—from workaholism to heroin addiction—are very common among medical and nonmedical practitioners in the contemporary psychotherapy market. Howard Shaffer of the Department of Psychiatry, Harvard Medical School, at the Cambridge Hospital has recently reviewed current trends in the use of behavioral psychology in treating addiction.

Thomas Crowley, executive director of the University of Colorado's Addiction, Research and Treatment Services (ARTS), is a renowned medical advocate for a behavioral approach to the treatment of addictive disorders. Through a carefully managed program of randomly conducted urine analysis, clients receive swift and effective social punishment for continued drug use. Crowley uses a behavior management technique known as contingency contracting. An addicted physician, for example, agrees to write a letter to the state medical licensing board, admitting that he is addicted and offering to surrender his license. The letter is given to Crowley, and a contract is devised instructing Crowley to mail the letter if the patient returns to the use of drugs. In the ARTS treatment milieu, drug-incompatible behavior is modeled by therapists and former addicts, then promptly rewarded as it becomes mirrored in the client population.

Whereas unconditional abstinence is the usual goal of most treatments for addiction, some behavior therapists may work with some clients toward learning the skills necessary for controlled use. Alan Marlatt of the University of Washington in Seattle, who has done extensive research on alcoholism-relapse prevention, has eloquently articulated the tremendous controversy, yet considerable promise, of a controlled-use approach to problem drinking.

The Cognitive Approach

As opposed to strict behaviorists, cognitive theorists believe that thoughts and expectations have great influence on human behavior. The major tenet of the cognitive perspective is that maladaptive thinking causes psychological distress. Such negative mental constructs as self-devaluation, a negative view of life, and a pessimistic view of the future are viewed as irrational cognitions that lead to depression. Unnecessary clinging to false expectations or nonproductive beliefs, memories, and so on is perceived as the psychological underpinning of self-defeating behavior.

The therapist's job is to help clients first to express their negative distortions of reality, and then to confront and accept evidence to the contrary. For example, a man who relies excessively on sexual conquest to bolster his self-esteem may become aware of a deep-seated, counterproductive belief that, in order to be successful, he must have several love affairs going on simultaneously. His therapist might well confront him with his nonsensical expectation that his work, creativity, and health will falter and perhaps disintegrate without novel sexual encounters. Rational-emotive psychotherapy, developed by Albert Ellis, is certainly the most popular and probably among the most effective of the cognitive approaches.

A promising development in the efforts toward addiction prevention and treatment has been the recent synthesis of cognitive and behavioral approaches. Chad Emrick, past president of the Society of Psychologists in Addictive Behavior and current director of Abstinence Alternatives in Denver, extensively explores clients' beliefs and expectations about substance use, in conjunction with behavior-modification techniques. Howard Shaffer has successfully used a three-component cognitive-behavioral strategy to reduce the frequency of onset and the extent of cigarette smoking among teenage students.

The Psychodynamic Approach

Psychodynamic treatment focuses on early childhood experiences. This therapeutic technique places great emphasis on how the client copes with internal and external conflict. Personality is viewed as a changeable system that represents an individual's unique reaction to psychological, biochemical, and environmental events. Anxiety is produced because biological impulses have been blocked from their natural expression. Excessive or addictive behaviors are perceived as necessary psychological props for the short-term management of inner distress. Edward Khantzian of the Department of Psychiatry, Harvard Medical School, at the Cambridge Hospital has conducted extensive clinical research on the considerable number of drug addicts who appear to be using illicit substances as a form of self-medication to cope with their underlying feelings of anger and depression, often rooted in early childhood frustrations and traumas.

The development of inner resources for effectively coping with misguided impulses is viewed as a vital aspect of successful therapy. Through candid and uncensored discussion with the psychotherapist, early conflicts with parents and intimate associates are discovered and explored. Forbidden wishes and fantasies become conscious, thereby freeing energy that was formerly blocked from constructive use. Psychodynamic therapy aims at the attainment of adult coping skills by encouraging the reexperiencing of old fantasies that now distort current reality. Clients are assisted in separating previously important infantile needs and wishes from their current life situations. They develop internal means to effectively tolerate the inevitable frustrations of a more mature adult state. As coping strategies shift from dependence on drugs or other external supports, clients become more adept at work, love, and play.

An Elementary Textbook of Psychoanalysis, by Charles Brenner, provides an excellent overview of the enormous scope of psychodynamic thought. *The Psychodynamics of Drug Dependence*, published by the National Institute on Drug Abuse, is a valuable collection of articles on the theory and management of drug addiction by major proponents of the psychodynamic school. An important limitation in applying a traditional psychodynamic approach to addiction is that treatment is short-circuited by intoxication. Even the most orthodox practitioners agree that they must first focus on stopping substance abuse before any meaningful exploration of inner fantasies and wishes can occur.

The Humanistic/Existential Approach

The hallmark of the humanistic/existential perspective is the view that what characterizes humans most is our freedom to make responsible choices and to anticipate the consequences of our actions. Humanistic thinkers have great respect for the fundamental goodness of humankind, and they believe that we are responsible for our own behavior. Although some aspects of our experience are undoubtedly determined by genetic, social, and cultural influences, in many important situations people are the primary actors in determining their fate. Humans, more than any other species of life, form images, engage in reflective thought, use symbols, and create novel solutions to problems in their midst. Most significant perhaps is the human ability to conceive of infinity and death. These unique abilities and sensitivities allow people to choose between alternative courses of action rather than simply forming thoughtless responses to uncontrollable stimuli.

The humanistic/existential camp maintains that human experience is characterized by reciprocal determinism: we interpret our environment and plan our responses accordingly; we affect the world just as much as it affects us. When people believe that they do not have the freedom of self-determination, they react by becoming alienated and depressed. Addiction becomes a means of coping with feelings of futility and unworthiness. The diverse array of human-istic/existential approaches to psychotherapy share three philosoph-ical beliefs: (1) They actively seek to explore the client's inner expe-riences with primary emphasis on the here and now; (2) They stress personal responsibility and freedom of choice and will, in regard to both psychotherapeutic growth and fulfillment during everyday life; (3) They believe that humanistic/existential therapists should be ac-tive participants in the treatment process.

On Becoming a Person, by Carl Rogers, the most renowned spokes-man for the humanistic/existential camp, is a particularly important and easily read work in this area. Fredrick Perls, founder of Gestalt therapy, and Victor Frankl, who developed Logotherapy, have also made major contributions to humanistic/existential theory and practice.

Styles of Delivery

Group Approaches

Group therapy has its origins in the all-day dramas that were staged in ancient Greece, more than 2500 years ago. Greek citizens wit-nessed theatrical performances of what we now regard as classic hu-man tragedies. In the drama of Oedipus, for example, a young war-rior named Oedipus kills Laius, the king of Thebes, and marries the queen, Jocasta. Oedipus later discovers that the king was his father, and that he therefore married his mother. Horrified by the knowl-edge of his unintentional crime, Oedipus gouges his eyes out. Hundreds of bemoaning onlookers are presumed to have derived great therapeutic benefits from the emotional release triggered by dramatizations such as these.

Before the Middle Ages, Christianity is said to have achieved widespread popularity through open confession, whereby partici-pants would publicly admit their sins and ask forgiveness amidst scores of entranced devotees. In the modern world, religious insti-tutions form the backbone of informal psychological services. In temples, mosques, and churches, members receive group support, moral guidance, and encouragement to express their most profound fears about life and death, unmarred by the stigma of mental illness.

J. L. Moreno was the first to recognize that psychotherapy could be effectively delivered to groups of emotionally disturbed patients.

Impressed by the therapeutic benefits that could be derived from theatrical dramatizations, he attempted to integrate role playing—the inclination and ability to make believe we are someone else—with the deeper possibilities of spontaneous acting. From this he founded the theory and practice of psychodrama, which was introduced in the United States in 1925. Moreno discovered when people are encouraged to play the roles of important people in their lives, they are likely to experience powerful emotions that are associated with these characters. He theorized that spontaneous release of feeling was the first step toward improved psychological functioning.

Since Moreno's pioneer efforts, the style of delivering psychotherapy en masse has become widely used in the treatment of addictive disorders. Most current systems of individual psychotherapy, including behavioral and psychodynamic approaches, can be offered to clients in a group format. The most prominent group approaches are based on Transactional Analysis and Gestalt therapy.

Despite the diversity of techniques that are associated with various group treatments, several basic commonalities exist between them. Treatment groups usually consist of five to ten members, who meet with the same therapist, at least once a week, for ninety-minute to two-hour sessions. Group members are often seated in a circular pattern so that everyone can see and react to everyone else. Members may share similar problems, such as obesity or alcoholism, in ho mogeneous groups; or they may have a diverse array of identified problems in heterogeneous groups. Participants receive advice and guidance from other group members as well as from the primary therapist. Hope is instilled early in treatment, as beginning clients observe others who have successfully grappled with problems similar to their own. Group members experience relief in simply knowing that they are not alone. Feelings of self-worth are enhanced as participants discover that they can be of value to other members of the group. Watching and listening to others often leads to improved interpersonal relationships and heightened social skills. As the group begins to operate as a cohesive family unit, members discover the opportunity to resolve and explore problems related to their own families. The negative effects of childhood deprivation and stress can be dissolved by learning adaptive coping mechanisms in the current, growth-oriented family setting.

Group therapy for substance abusers has become known for the powerful interpersonal confrontations that are promoted during the treatment process. Most current group treatments for substance abusers are modeled after the Synanon Game, which was developed to help recovering drug addicts to remain abstinent. The Game is a type of group encounter in which the open and direct expression of hostility and anger is quite prominent. Neither physical threats nor violence of any kind are allowed, and mind-altering drugs are not permitted. Group leaders are usually nonprofessional, recovering addicts who have earned high status among fellow members of the treatment community.

Each meeting lasts about three hours, and participants are encouraged to go at each other in an uninhibited fashion. Screaming and yelling are common as individual participants are successively made the center of a series of verbal attacks. Group members are expected to be totally honest, as the conventions and restrictions of normal interpersonal relationships are cast aside. The use of ridicule, sarcasm, and hostility is intended to rip away the defensive shields that have been used by addicts to avoid genuine human contact. It is assumed that the healthy release of anger creates a bond of mutual caring among group members. At the end of each Game, confrontation and anger transform into warmth, support, and concern among participants. For many drug abusers, particularly heroin addicts, the Game is an important vehicle for personal growth. The vernacular and toughness of the street are preserved as vital aspects of the therapeutic encounter, where addicts can use their considerable verbal and manipulative skills toward positive ends. Most contemporary substance-abuse treatments use some variation of the Synanon Game as an integral part of the treatment process.

Family Therapy

Family therapists perceive addicted individuals as "identified patients," who are usually enmeshed in a network of disturbed family members. Addiction is viewed as a symptom of an overall family problem; drug dependence or other behavior disorders serve definite functions within the addict's family. If the addicted family member should improve or abstain, other family members may act to undermine or derail the success, returning the disturbed family to the prior state of equilibrium. Most authors who address this topic have noted the enormous difficulty of bringing family members of addicted individuals into treatment. Parents and siblings typically displace responsibility for the addict's problem to friends, schools, and neighborhood, or other external systems, allegedly beyond the influence or control of the family.

Family therapists have discovered that when relatives can be coaxed into entering family therapy, the probabilities for treatment success are greatly improved. When therapy is geared toward forming an alliance of family members who are mutually engaged in the treatment process, family influences can be modified from factors that maintain addiction to forces that overcome problem dependencies. Virginia Satir, author of *Conjoint Family Therapy*, is the most well-known advocate for the family therapy approach. She views disturbed functioning by a family member as symptomatic of violations of love and trust within the family. Addiction is viewed as a primitive survival mechanism in a family that has somehow communicated a need for mistrust and defensiveness to the disturbed family member. Claudia Black has achieved impressive results using family therapy with children who have alcoholic parents. Duncan Stanton, director of the Addicts and Families Project at the Philadelphia Child Guidance Clinic, has extensively written on the subject of family therapy for heroin addiction and other compulsive problem behaviors.

Spiritual Orientation

There is widespread belief among both therapists and addicts that craving and addiction reflect a state of spiritual disharmony. By placing their faith in a "higher power" addicts may be released from the influence of the substances or behaviors over which they have lost control. Since the founding of Alcoholics Anonymous in 1935 the membership of recovering alcoholics in this spiritually oriented treatment approach may exceed one million people. Alcoholics are helped to stay sober through mutual support, self-examination, and spiritual guidance. Alcoholics Anonymous groups exist throughout most of the world and are regarded by some renowned behavioral and social scientists as the most effective method for the treatment of alcoholism. In the past decade the AA model has needed only slight modification to address effectively the needs of people who suffer from the entire range of addictive disturbances.

Many contemporary addicts are simultaneously addicted to more than one substance or behavior. Cocaine addicts, for example, often become dependent on a variety of "downers," including alcohol, sedatives, tranquilizers, or heroin, in order to cope with the jitteriness and irritability that coke induces. Most contemporary alcoholics are said to mix drugs and booze. The AA membership has accordingly shifted from a nearly exclusive focus on alcohol addiction to an increasing percentage of polydrug abusers. Irrespective of their chosen drugs, AA members take comfort from what has become known throughout the world as the AA prayer:

GOD grant me the SERENITY
to accept the things I cannot change,
COURAGE to change the things I can
and WISDOM to know the difference.

Appendix
Suggested Reading and Information Resources

The following resources are suggested for further understanding of treatment for compulsive behavior and addiction. References marked with asterisks are suggested for nonprofessional readers.

Treatment Philosophies

Biomedical Approaches

Collins, A. C. (1985). Inheriting addictions: A genetic perspective with emphasis on alcohol and nicotine. In *Addictions: Multidisciplinary perspectives and treatments*. edited by H. Milkman and H. Shaffer. Lexington, Mass.: Lexington Books, 3–10.

Freedman, R. (1985). Biopharmacologic factors in drug abuse. In *Addictions: Multidisciplinary perspectives and treatments*, edited by H. Milkman and H. Shaffer. Lexington, Mass.: Lexington Books, 21–28.

*Smith, D., Milkman, H., and Sunderwirth, S. (1985). Addictive disease: Concept and controversy. In *Addictions: Multidisciplinary perspectives and treatments*, edited by H. Milkman and H. Shaffer. Lexington, Mass.: Lexington Books, 145–160.

Sunderwirth, S. (1985). Biological mechanisms: Neurotransmission and addiction. In *Addictions: Multidisciplinary perspectives and treatments*, edited by H. Milkman and H. Shaffer. Lexington, Mass.: Lexington Books, 11–20.

*Wurtman, R. (May 1985). Cited in Mind nutrients, by D. Kagan. *Omni*, 36–40.

Behavioral Approaches

*Crowley, T. J. (1985). A biobehavioral approach to the origins and treatment of substance abuse. In *Addictions: Multidisciplinary perspectives and treatments*, edited by H. Milkman and H. Shaffer. Lexington, Mass.: Lexington Books, 105–110.

Marlatt, G. A. (1983). The controlled drinking controversy: A commentary. *American Psychologist* 38: 1097–1110.

Shaffer, H., Beck, J., and Boothroyd, P. (1983). The primary prevention of smoking onset: An inoculation approach. *Journal of Psychoactive Drugs* 5: 177–184.
Shaffer, H. (1985). Trends in behavioral psychology and addictions. In *Addictions: Multidisciplinary perspectives and treatments*, edited by H. Milkman and H. Shaffer. Lexington, Mass.: Lexington Books, 36–56.

Cognitive Approaches

*Ellis, A. (1962). *Reason and emotion in psychotherapy*. New York: L. Stuart.
*Ellis, A., and Harper, R. A. (1975). *A new guide to rational living*. Englewood Cliffs, N.J.: Prentice-Hall.
Emrick, C. D., Hansen, J., and Maytag, J. (1985). Cognitive behavioral treatment of problem drinking. In *Addictions: Multidisciplinary perspectives and treatments*, edited by H. Milkman and H. Shaffer. Lexington, Mass.: Lexington Books, 161–179.

Psychodynamic Approaches

Blaine, J., and Julius, D., eds. (1977). *Psychodynamics of drug dependence*. NIDA Research Monograph no. 12. Washington D.C.: U.S. Government Printing Office.
Brenner, C. (1973). *An elementary textbook of psychoanalysis*. Garden City, N.Y.: Anchor Books.

Humanistic/Existential Approaches

Frankl, V. F. (1975). *Paradoxical intention and dereflection. Psychotherapy: Theory, Research and Practice* 12:226–237.
*Perls, F. S. (1969). *Gestalt therapy verbatim*. Lafayette, Calif.: Real People Press.
*Perls, F. S. (1970). *Gestalt therapy now*. Palo Alto, Calif.: Science and Behavior Books.
*Rogers, C. (1961). *On becoming a person: A psychotherapist's view on psychotherapy*. Boston: Houghton-Mifflin.
*Truax, C. B., and Carkhuff, R. R. (1967). *Toward effective counseling and psychotherapy: training and practice*. Chicago: Aldine.

Style of Delivery

Family Approaches

*Black, C. (1982). *It will never happen to me*. Denver, Colo.: M.A.C. Printing and Publication.
*Black, C. (1985). *Repeat after me*. Denver, Colo.: M.A.C. Printing and Publication.
Satir, V. (1967). *Conjoint family therapy: A guide to theory and technique*. 2nd. rev. ed. Palo Alto, Calif.: Science and Behavior Books.

Stanton, M. D. (1975). Psychology and family therapy. *Professional Psychology* 6: 45–49.

*Wegscheider, S. (1981). *Another chance: Hope and health for the alcoholic family.* Palo Alto, Calif.: Science and Behavior Books.

Group Approaches

*Berne, E. (1961). *Transactional analysis in psychotherapy.* New York: Grove Press.
*Berne, E. (1964). *Games people play.* New York: Grove Press.
Casriel, D. (1963). *So fair a house.* Englewood Cliffs, N.J.: Prentice-Hall.
Casriel, D. (1971). The dynamics of Synanon. In *Sensitivity training and group encounter: An introduction,* edited by R. W. Siroka, E. K. Siroka, and G. A. Schloss. New York: Grosset and Dunlap.
Frye, R., ed. (1984). Therapeutic community movement: Process and research. *Journal of Psychoactive Drugs* 16(1): 1 99.

Treatment and Information Organizations

The following organizations are suggested for treatment and information on various addictions. Alcoholics Anonymous and Narcotics Anonymous have a spiritual orientation.

Alcohol Addiction

Alcohol 24 Hour Line
1-800-242-6465

Alcoholics Anonymous
P.O. Box 459
Grand Central Station
New York, NY 10017

Al-Anon Family Groups
115 East 23rd Street
New York, NY 10010

National Clearing House for
    Alcohol Information
Box 2345
Rockville, MD 20852

National Council on Alcoholism
733 Third Ave.
New York, NY 10017

Women for Sobriety
P.O. Box 618
Quakertown, PA 18951
(215) 536-8026

Drug Addiction

Cocaine Hotline
1-800-COCAINE

Haight-Ashbury Drug Detox
529 Clayton Street
San Francisco, CA 94117
(415) 621-2014

Narcotics Anonymous
World Service Office
16155 Wyandotte Street
Van Nuys, CA 91406
(818) 780-3951

National Institute on Drug Abuse
Prevention Branch, 5600
Fishers Lane, Room 10A–30
Rockville, MD 20857
1-800-662-HELP

Sexual Addiction

Sex Addicts Anonymous
Twin Cities S.A.A.
P.O. Box 3038
Minneapolis, MN 55403

Gambling Addiction

Gamblers Anonymous
National Service Office
P.O. Box 17173
Los Angeles, CA 90017
(213) 386-8789

Food Addiction

Overeaters Anonymous
P.O. Box 92870
Los Angeles, CA 90009
(213) 320-7941

Spending Addiction

Spender Menders
P.O. Box 15000–156
San Francisco, CA 94115
(415) 773-9754

Training Health Care Providers
(public interest encouraged)

Center for Addiction Studies
Department of Psychiatry
Harvard Medical School and the Cambridge Hospital
1493 Cambridge Street
Cambridge, MA 02139
(617) 498-1148

References and Notes

Introduction

References

Hughes, J., Smith, T.W., Kosterlitz, H.W., Fothergill, L.A., Morgan, B.A., and Morris, H.R. (1975). Identification of two related pentapeptides from the brain with potent opiate agonist activity. *Nature* 258(5536): 577–579.

Jellinek, E. M. (1952). Phases of alcohol addiction. *Quarterly Journal of Studies of Alcohol* 13: 673–684.

Jellinek, E. M. (1960). *The disease concept of alcohol.* New Brunswick, N.J.: Hillhouse Press.

Reagan undergoes surgery. (July 22, 1985). *Time,* 6–15.

Zinberg, N. (Oct. 29, 1983). Personal communication with the author.

Notes

Figures on the extent of America's drug problem are cited from: Bartecchi, C. E., MacKenzie, T. D., and Schrier, R. W. (May 1995). The global tobacco epidemic. *Scientific American,* 44–51; Alcohol in perspective. (Feb. 1993). *University of California at Berkeley Wellness Letter,* 4–6; Guttman, M. (Feb. 16–18, 1996). The new pot culture. *USA Weekend,* 4–7; Johnston, L. D., O'Malley, P. M., and Bachman, J. G. (1994). National survey results on drug use. *Monitoring the future study,* vol. 2, 11–25.

Chapter 1

References

Chien, I., Gerard, D. L., Lee, R. S., and Rosenfeld, E. (1981). *The road to H: Narcotics, delinquency and social policy.* In *Classic contributions in the addictions,* edited by H. Shaffer and M. Burglass. New York: Brunner/Mazel, 95–116.

Collins, A. (1985). Inheriting addictions: A genetic perspective with emphasis on alcohol and nicotine. In *Addictions: Multidisciplinary perspectives and treatments*, edited by H. Milkman and H. Shaffer. Lexington, Mass.: Lexington Books, 3–9.

Donegan, N., Rodin, T., O'Brien, C., and Solomon, R. (1983). A learning theory approach to commonalities. In *Commonalities in substance abuse and habitual behavior*, edited by P. Levinson, D. Gerstein, and D. Maloff. Lexington, Mass.: Lexington Books, 111–156.

Goffman, E. (1963). *Stigma: Notes on the management of spoiled identity*. Englewood Cliffs, N.J.: Prentice-Hall.

Kandel, D. and Maloff, D. (1983). Commonalities in drug use: A sociological perspective. In *Commonalities in substance abuse and habitual behavior*, edited by P. Levinson, D. Gerstein, and D. Maloff. Lexington, Mass.: Lexington Books, 3–27.

Khantzian, E. (1981). Self-selection and progression of drug dependence. In *Classic contributions in the addictions*, edited by H. Shaffer and M. Burglass. New York: Brunner/Mazel, 154–160.

McClearn, G. E. (1983). Commonalities in substance abuse: A genetic perspective. In *Commonalities in substance abuse and habitual behavior*, edited by P. Levinson, D. Gerstein, and D. Maloff. Lexington, Mass.: Lexington Books, 323–341.

Milkman, H. and Frosch, W. (1977). The drug of choice. *Journal of Psychedelic Drugs* 9(1): 13–14.

Milkman, H. and Sunderwirth, S. (Oct. 1983). The chemistry of craving. *Psychology Today*, 36–44.

Schmeck, H. M. (Mar. 22, 1983). Drug abuse in America: Widening array brings new perils. *New York Times*, C1–C10.

Sunderwirth, S. (1985). Biological mechanisms: Neurotransmission and addiction. In *Addictions: Multidisciplinary perspectives and treatments*, edited by H. Milkman and H. Shaffer. Lexington, Mass.: Lexington Books, 11–19.

Sunderwirth, S. and Milkman, H. (Oct. 1991). Behavioral and neurochemical commonalities in addiction. In *Contemporary Family Therapy*, 421–433.

Wikler, A. (1973). Dynamics of drug dependence: Implications of a conditioning theory for research and treatment. *Archives of General Psychiatry* 28: 611–616.

Chapter 2

References

Bruch, H. (1961). Conceptual confusion in eating disorders. *Journal of Nervous and Mental Disease* 133: 46–54.

Bruch, H. and Touraine, G. (1940). Obesity in childhood, V: The family frame of obese children. *Psychosomatic Medicine* 2: 141–206.

Burns, M. (1980). Alcohol abuse among women as indirect self-destructive behavior. In *The many faces of suicide: Indirect self-destructive behavior*, edited by N. L. Farberow. New York: McGraw-Hill, 220–230.

Carnes, P. (1983). The sexual addiction. Minneapolis, Minn.: CompCare Publications.

Coleman, D. (Oct. 16, 1984). Some sexual behavior viewed as an addiction. *New York Times.*

Diaz del Castillo, B. (1963). *Conquest of New Spain.* New York: Penguin Books.

Freud, S. (1962). *Three essays on the theory of sexuality.* New York: Basic Books, 47.

Haley, J. (1973). The art of being schizophrenic. In *Exploring madness, experience, theory, and research,* edited by J. Fadiman and D. Kewman. Monterey, Calif.: Brooks/Cole.

Halmi, K. A., Falk, J. R., and Schwartz, E. (1981). Binge-eating and vomiting: A survey of a college population. *Psychological Medicine* 2(4): 697–706.

Hughes, J., Smith, T. W., Kosterlitz, H. W., Fothergill, L. A., Morgan, B. A., and Morris, H. R. (1975). Identification of two related pentapeptides from the brain with potent opiate agonist activity. *Nature* 258(5536): 577–579.

Jung, C. G., ed. (1964). *Man and his symbols.* New York: Dell.

Kagan, D. (May 1985). Mind nutrients. *Omni,* 36–40.

Khantzian, E. J. (1985). The self-medication hypothesis of addictive disorders: Focus on heroin and cocaine dependence. *American Journal of Psychiatry* 142(11): 1259–1264.

Klein, D. and Liebowitz, M. (Dec. 1979). Affective disorders: Special clinical forms. *Psychiatric Clinics of North America.*

Liebowitz, M. R. (1983). *The chemistry of love.* Boston: Little, Brown.

MacLennon, A., ed. (1976). *Women: Their use of alcohol and other legal drugs.* Toronto: Addiction Research Foundation of Ontario.

Mahoney, M. J. and Mahoney, K. (May 1976). Fight fat with behavior control. *Psychology Today,* 39–41.

Mahoney, M. J. and Mahoney, K. (1976). *Permanent weight control: A total solution to the dieter's dilemma.* New York: Norton.

Marlatt, G. A. and Gordon, J. R. (1979). Determinants of relapse: Implications for the maintenance of behavior change. In *Behavioral medicine: Changing health life-styles.* Edited by P. Davidson. New York: Brunner/Mazel, 410–452.

Masters, W. H. and Johnson, V. F. (1970). *Human sexual inadequacy.* Boston: Little, Brown.

Miller, P. (1985). *The change your metabolism diet.* London: Panther Books.

National Institute on Drug Abuse. (1979). *Psychological characteristics of drug-abusing women.* NIDA Research Monograph Series. DHEW Publication # (ADM)80.917. Washington, DC: U. S. Government Printing Office.

Obrien, W. B. and Biase, V. (1984). The therapeutic community: A current perspective. *The Journal of Psychoactive Drugs* 16(1): 9–23.

Peele, S. and Brodsky, A. (1975). Love and addiction. New York: Taplinger.

Peterson, K. S. (May 16, 1984). Can a little alcohol be good for you? *U.S.A. Today,* 3.

Rado, S. (1933). The psychoanalysis of pharmacothymia (drug addiction). *The Psychoanalytic Quarterly* 2: 1–23.

Ray, Oakley S. (1972). *Drugs, society and human behavior.* St. Louis: C. V. Mosby.

Rosenbaum, R. (1984). The chemistry of love. *Esquire* 100: 111.

Rowland, C. V. Jr. (1980). Hyperobesity as indirect self-destructive behavior. In *The many faces of suicide: Indirect self-destructive behavior,* edited by N. L. Farberow. New York: McGraw-Hill, 232–242.

Schachter, S. (1982). Recidivism and self-cure of smoking and obesity. *American Psychologist* 37: 436–444.
Schachter, S. and Gross, L. P. (1968). Manipulated time and eating behavior. *Journal of Personality and Social Psychology* 10: 98–106.
Shuckit, M. (1974). The alcoholic woman: A literature review. *Psychiatry in Medicine* 3(1); 37–43.
Stunkard, A. J. (1958). The management of obesity. *New York State Journal of Medicine* 58: 79–87.
Toufexis, A. (Jan. 20, 1986). Slimming down: What works, what won't, what's new. *Time*, 46–52.
Vaillant, G. (1983). Suggestions for would-be helpers. In *The natural history of alcoholism*. Cambridge, Mass.: Harvard University Press, 296–297.
Wood, H. P. and Duffy, E. L. (1966). Psychological factors in alcoholic women. *American Journal of Psychiatry* 123: 341–345.
Yankelovitch, Skelly, & White, Inc. (May 20, 1986). Poll of drinking patterns in America. *Time*, 56–61.

Notes

The SCIENCE method of weight control is adapted from Mahoney, M. J. and Mahoney, K. Fight fat with behavior control, *Psychology Today* (May 1976): 39–41.

Information for the case of Peter was adapted from "Free at Last," distributed by Sexaholics Anonymous, P.O. Box 300, Simi Valley, CA 93062.

An excellent review article by Ron Rosenbaum, "The Chemistry of Love," appeared in *Esquire* (June 1984): 100–110.

Research findings by psychopharmacologists Lewis Seiden and Charles Schuster of the University of Chicago and Ronald Siegel at UCLA on the toxicity of MDMA (Ecstasy) were cited by Marjory Roberts in "MDMA: Madness, not Ecstasy," *Psychology Today* (June 1986): 14–15.

The following information from the section, "Eating Yourself Sick," was adapted from "Slimming down: what works, what won't, what's new," cover story by Anastasis Toufexis, *Time* (Jan. 20, 1986): 46–52:

The studies by David Porte at the University of Washington and Martin Cohen at the National Institute on Mental Health, on the relationships between eating and endorphins.

Remarks by George Bray of the Los Angeles County University of California Medical Center.

Percentage of estimates of people in the United States who believe they are overweight.

Serotonin deficiency theory of obesity, studied by nutritional biochemist Judith Wurtman and neuroendocrinologist Richard Wurtman, both of MIT.

Studies of premenstrual gorging at the University of Toronto.

Studies of the relationship between child's body weight and biological versus adoptive parents, by Charles Bouchard, director of the Physical Activity Sciences Laboratory at Quebec's Laval University.

Prognosis for obese people by Amed Kissebah, Jules Hirsch, and John McCall.

Remarks by nutritionist Marion Nestle, of the Medical School at the University of California at San Francisco, on foods that predispose people to obesity.

Chapter 3

References

Blum, K. (1991). *Alcohol and the addictive brain: New hope for alcoholics from biogenic research.* New York: Macmillan.

Cleckley, H. (1964). *The mask of sanity.* St. Louis: Mosby.

Delk, J. L. (1980). High-risk sports as indirect self-destructive behavior. In *The many faces of suicide: Indirect self-destructive behavior*, edited by N. L. Farberow. New York: McGraw-Hill, 393–469.

Dietz, P. E. (1983). Recurrent discovery of autoerotic asphyxia. In *Autoerotic fatalities*, edited by R. R. Hazelwood, P. E. Dietz, and A. W. Burgess. Lexington, Mass.: Lexington Books, 13–44.

Farley, F. (May 1986). The thrill-seeking personality. *Psychology Today*, 44–52.

Glassman, A. (1984). Cited in Craving may be at the root of several drug addictions by B. Bower (1984). *Science News* 126: 310.

Goldstein A. and Goldstein D. B. (1968). Enzyme expansion theory of drug tolerance and physical dependence. *Association for Research in Nervous and Mental Disease* 46: 265–267.

Greengard, P. (1975). Cyclic nucleotides, protein phosporylation and neuronal function. In *Advances of Cyclic Nucleotide Research*, Vol. 5, edited by G. I. Drummond, P. Greengard, and G. Robinson. Proceedings of the 2nd International Conference on Cyclic AMP. New York: Raven Press, 585–601.

Litman, R. E. and Swearingen, C. (1972). Bondage and suicide. *Archives of General Psychiatry* 27: 80–85.

Lutfullah. (1857). Autobiography of Lutfullah, a Mohammedan gentleman. Cited in *Varieties of Religious Experience* by W. James (1958). Mentor Books, 138–139.

Lykken, D. T. (Sept. 1992). Fearlessness: Its carefree charm and deadly risks. *Psychology Today*, 20–28.

Mahler, M. (1967). *Journal of the American Psychoanalytic Association* 15: 740–760.

Milkman, H. and Frosch, W. (1977). The drug of choice. *Journal of Psychedelic Drugs* 9(1): 11–24.

Milkman, H. and Sunderwirth, S. (1982). Addictive processes. *Journal of Psychoactive Drugs* 14(3): 177–192.

Murphy, M. R., Bowie, D. L., and Pert, C. B. (1979). Copulation elevates plasma B-endorphin in the male hamster. *Society of Neurosciences, Alaska*, 470.

Reich, A. (1960). *Psychoanalytic study of the child* 15: 215–232.
Rosenblum, S. and Faber, M. M. (1979). The adolescent sexual asphyxia syndrome. *Journal of the American Academy of Child Psychiatry* 18: 456–558.
Rupp, J. C. (1980). Sex-related deaths. In *Modern legal medicine, psychiatry and forensic science*, edited by W. J. Curran, A. L. McGarry, and C. S. Petty. Philadelphia: F. A. Davis, 575–587.
Selye, H. (1969). Stress: It's a G.A.S. *Psychology Today* 3(4): 25–26, 56.
Solomon, R. L. and Corbit, J. D. (1974). An opponent-process theory of motivation, Part 1. Temporal dynamics of affect. *Psychological Review* 81(2): 119–145.
Tanda, G., Pontieri, F. E., and DiChiara, G. (1977). Cannabinoid and heroin activation of mesolimbic dopamine transmission by a common U_1 opioid receptor mechanism. *Science* 226: 2048.
Tyhurst, J. S. (1951). Individual reactions to community disaster. *American Journal of Psychiatry* 10: 746–769.
Volkow, N. D., Wang, G. J., Fischman, M. W., Foltin, R. W., Fowler, J. S., Abumrad, N. N., Vitkun, S., Logan, J., Gatley, S. J., Pappas, N., Hitzemann, R., and Shea, C. E. (1997). Relationship between subjective effects of cocaine and dopamine transporter occupancy. *Nature* 386: 327.
Wallis, C. (June 6, 1983). Stress: Can we cope? *Time*, 48–54.
Wolfe, T. (1980). *The right stuff*. New York: Bantam Books.
Zuckerman, M., ed. (1979). *Sensation seeking: Beyond the optimal level of arousal*. Hillsdale, N.J.: Lawrence Erlbaum.
Zuckerman, M., ed. (1983). *Biological bases of sensation seeking, impulsivity, and anxiety*. Hillsdale, N.J.: Lawrence Erlbaum, 229–232, 255.

Notes

For a general discussion of the dopamine theory of reward see *Time*, May 5, 1997.

Chapter 4

References

Bellack, L., ed. (1979). *Disorders of the schizophrenic syndrome*. New York: Basic Books.
Bettelheim, B. (1979). *The uses of enchantment: The meaning and importance of fairy tales*. New York: Knopf.
Bleuer, E. (1911). Dementia Praecox oder die Gruppe der Schizophrenien. In *Handbook der Psychiatrie*, edited by G. Aschaffenburg. Leipzig: Deuiticke.
Crick, F. and Mitchison, G. (July 14, 1983). The function of dream sleep. *Nature* 304: 111.
Eron, L. D. (1982). Parent-child interaction: Televised violence and aggression of children. *American Psychologist* 37(2): 197–211.
Fleming, C. B. (June 1983). Maidens of the sea can be alluring but sailor beware. *The Smithsonian*, 86–95.
Goldman-Rakic, P. (1982). Postnatal development of monoamine content and synthesis in the cerebral cortex of Rhesus monkeys. *Journal of Brain Research* 4(3): 339–349

Greenberg, H. R. (1975). *The movies on your mind: Film classics on the couch from Fellini to Frankenstein.* New York: E. P. Dutton, 3–4.

Gygax, G. E. (1978). *Official advanced dungeons & dragons players handbook.* Lake Geneva, Wis.: TSR Hobbies.

Hartman, E. (1973). *The functions of sleep.* New Haven, Conn.: Yale University Press.

Hebb, D. O. (1958). Brain cell assemblies. *Psychological Brain Abstracts.*

Humphrey, N. (1981). Four minutes to midnight. 3rd annual Jacob Bronowski Lecture. BBC Television, *BBC Radio Times.*

Jaffe, A. (1964). Symbolism in the visual arts. In *Man and his symbols,* edited by C. G. Jung. Garden City, N.Y.: Doubleday, 232–271.

Laing, R. D. (1960). *The divided self.* New York: Pantheon Books.

Lindner, R. (1955). *The jet-propelled couch, and other true psychoanalytic tales.* London: Secker and Warburg.

Lindsey, H. (1976). *The late great planet earth.* Grand Rapids, Mich.: Zondervan.

Mander, J. (1978). *Four arguments for the elimination of television.* New York: Morrow.

Marc, D. (Aug. 1984). Understanding television. *The Atlantic Monthly,* 33–44.

Meltzer, H. Y. (1979). Biochemical studies in schizophrenia. In *Disorders of the schizophrenic syndrome,* edited by L. Bellak. New York: Basic Books, 45–135.

Rado, S. (1981). The psychoanalysis of pharmacothymia. In *Classic contributions in the addictions,* edited by H. Shaffer and M. Burglass. New York: Brunner/Mazel, 77–94.

Rossel, R. D. (May 1983). Addictive video games. *Psychology Today,* 87.

Ryan, P. and Clifford, G. (Dec. 26, 1983–Jan. 2, 1984). Ronald Reagan: No way to make it easy. *People.*

Singer, J. L. (1981–82). Towards the scientific study of the imagination. *Imaginations, Cognition and Personality* 1(1): 5–28.

Szasz, T. S. (1961). *The myth of mental illness: Foundations of a theory of personal conduct.* New York: Hoeber-Harper.

Wanner, D. (Oct. 1982). The electronic bogeyman. *Psychology Today,* 8–11.

Zinberg, N. and Shaffer, H. (1985). The social psychology of intoxicant use. In *Addictions: Multidisciplinary perspectives and treatments,* edited by H. Milkman and H. Shaffer. Lexington, Mass.: Lexington Books, 57–74.

Chapter 5

References

Diagnostic and statistical manual of mental disorder. (1980). Washington, D.C.: American Psychiatric Association.

The drug crisis: crack and crime. (June 16, 1986). *Newsweek,* 16–22.

Jellinek, E. M. (1952). Phases of alcohol addiction. *Quarterly Journal of Studies of Alcohol* 13: 673–684.

Jellinek, E. M. (1960). *The disease concept of alcohol.* New Brunswick, N.J.: Hillhouse Press.

Kellerman, J. L. (1969). *Alcoholism: A merry-go-round named denial.* New York: Al-Anon Family Group Headquarters.

Lowe, C. (Oct. 26, 1985). *The parents movement.* Paper read at the National Anti-Drug Conference, Kuala Lumpur, Malaysia.

Marlatt, G. A. and Gordon, J. R. (1979). Determinants of relapse: Implications for the maintenance of behavior change. In *Behavioral medicine: Changing health life-styles.* Edited by P. Davidson. New York: Brunner/Mazel, 410–452.

Meichenbaum, D. and Turk, D. (1976). The cognitive-behavioral management of anxiety, anger and pain. In *The behavioral management of anxiety, depression and pain,* edited by P. O. Davidson. New York: Brunner/Mazel.

Milkman, H. (1979). Addictive processes: An introductory formulation. *Street Pharmacologist* 2(4): 1–5.

Shaffer, H., Beck, J., and Boothroyd, P. (1983). The primary prevention of smoking onset: An inoculation approach. *Journal of Psychoactive Drugs* 5: 177–184.

Smith, D., Milkman, H., and Sunderwirth S. (1985). Addictive disease: Concept and controversy. In *Addictions: Multidisciplinary perspectives and treatments,* edited by H. Milkman and H. Shaffer. Lexington, Mass.: Lexington Books, 144–159.

Vaillant, G. (1983). *The natural history of alcoholism.* Cambridge, Mass.: Harvard University Press, 44, 190.

Chapter 6

Notes

References for Chapter 6 are listed in the appendix, Suggested Reading and Information Resources.

The Counseling Interest Inventory was adapted from H. Milkman and N. Halliday, *Counseling: A self-instructional programmed course,* in the Idaho Instructional Programs, developed by Barbee Associates, 1976, under grant no. 750608, Western Area Alcohol Education and Training Program, the National Institute on Alcohol Abuse and Alcoholism and the National Institute on Drug Abuse, 5–9.

A review of drug and alcohol treatment facilities in the United States may be found in the article, Getting straight, *Newsweek* (June 4, 1984): 62–69.

An excellent selection of current literature of a multidisciplinary nature, relevant to all aspects of substances, their use and abuse, may be obtained through *The Journal of Psychoactive Drugs* (612 Clayton Street, San Francisco, CA 94117, 415–565–1904).

The authors wish to thank Eveline Yang of the Auraria Library, Denver, Colorado, for her referencing assistance.

Index

307 - 733 - 5564